A MAKER OF THE MODERN MIND

Mathematician, philosopher, mystic—Blaise Pascal is among those rare men whose thoughts have shaped the modern mind.

As Robert W. Gleason points out in his Introduction, Pascal is an enigma. To some, he is the skeptic, a piercing intellect ready to weigh any truth in the balance. To others, Pascal is the modern man of faith, a scientific inquirer who sustains his belief in delicate tension with his mathematical genius.

In this new translation, prepared especially for *The Essential Pascal,* the many facets of this 17th-century genius emerge with brilliant clarity.

The text includes, in addition to the Introduction and Commentary, a critical list of selected readings.

Other MENTOR-OMEGA Books of Special Interest to Catholics

THE ESSENTIAL AUGUSTINE, edited by Vernon J. Bourke

A wide selection of the writings of St. Augustine in a vibrant new translation. Includes a biography and introductory material. Mr. Bourke is Professor of Philosophy at St. Louis University. (MT601—75¢)

THE ESSENTIAL ERASMUS, edited with Introduction and Commentary by John P. Dolan

The first single volume in English to show the full range of thought of one of the great Catholic minds of the Renaissance. Selected and newly translated with Introduction and Commentary by John P. Dolan, Professor of European History at the University of Notre Dame. (MT571—75¢)

THE ESSENTIAL EUSEBIUS, edited and translated by Colm Luibheid

The story of the vital early centuries of the Christian Church, told by the first chronicler of Christianity. Introduction and Commentary by Colm Luibheid. (MT671—75¢)

THE ESSENTIAL NEWMAN, edited by Vincent Ferrer Blehl

The central writings of the master of English who infused new vigor into the nineteenth-century Catholic Church. Selected and edited by an eminent Newman scholar. Mr. Blehl is an Assistant Professor of English at Fordham University. (MT488—75¢)

Blaise Pascal, 1623-1662.

THE ESSENTIAL PASCAL

Selected and Edited,

with Introduction and Commentary, by

ROBERT W. GLEASON, S.J.

Newly translated

BY G. F. PULLEN.

A MENTOR-OMEGA BOOK

Published by The New American Library, New York and Toronto

The New English Library Limited, London

From twenty centuries of literature and scholarship, Mentor-Omega Books present a treasury of Catholic thought for the modern reader.

FIRST PRINTING, AUGUST, 1966

Library of Congress Catalog Card Number: 66-24515

MENTOR TRADEMARK REG. U.S. PAT. OFF. AND FOREIGN COUNTRIES
REGISTERED TRADEMARK—MARCA REGISTRADA
HECHO EN CHICAGO, U.S.A.

MENTOR-OMEGA BOOKS are published *in the United States* by
The New American Library, Inc.,
1301 Avenue of the Americas, New York, New York 10019,
in Canada by The New American Library of Canada Limited,
295 King Street East, Toronto 2, Ontario,
in the United Kingdom by The New English Library Limited,
Barnard's Inn, Holborn, London, E.C. 1, England

PRINTED IN THE UNITED STATES OF AMERICA

Nihil obstat: John A. Goodwine, J.C.D.

Censor Librorum

Imprimatur: ✠Terence J. Cooke, D.D., V.G.

New York, N. Y.
June 8, 1966

CONTENTS

INTRODUCTION

Pascal was an enigma in his own times, and today, three centuries later, the enigma remains, in large part, unsolved. Wc do not yet possess, and perhaps never will possess, a definitive edition of his great work, the *Pensées*. What is more, the most elementary notions of his aim, his method, and his inner spirit in this famous treatise on the Christian religion still remain a subject of dispute.

Despite the varying and often contradictory interpretations of his thought, Pascal has exercised and continues to exercise an undeviating attraction for the philosopher, the theologian, and the ordinary man. His sense of the concrete, his rapid, penetrating argumentation, his psychological finesse elude categories while surpassing them. His interests are close to the heart of man, his great preoccupations are as contemporary today as in his century and interest in his thought has never flagged. Today, he is celebrated as an existentialist. Actually, his thought is classically Augustinian, centered on concrete, historical man, on God, on mystery, on time and the eternal.

It is curious to note the diverging emphases that have been thrown into relief throughout history in this thelogian's thought. Was he actually, as Chateaubriand presented him, a romantic of the romantics? a man with such piercing irony, so distrustful of "systems," of a style so sober, chaste, suggestive? The sect of Port-Royal, determined to find in Pascal an orthodox Jansenist, did not hesitate to obscure his portrait by suppressing items in his writings which would reflect ill on his austerity, intransigence, and moral savagery. Yet did not Pascal, on his deathbed, renounce Jansenism and submit to the more humanist claims of the Roman Church? Or did he? We are not yet entirely certain that Pascal died an orthodox Catholic.

What shall we call him? Philosopher, theologian, *littérateur*, sceptic, believer, optimist, pessimist? For Voltaire, it was quite simple. Against this "fanatic"—the word occurs and reoccurs—the prophet of the Enlightenment feels obliged to take up the cudgels for humanism. Pascal to him was a "sublime misanthrope." As a matter of fact this strange opinion seemed to be the reigning hypothesis in the eighteenth century. Pascal passed for an ill man, whose poor health was reflected in the bitterness of his reflections on man as a whole. Many of these interpretations were backed up by legends. Pascal was thought to have suffered a permanent trauma of the "abyss" as a result of an accident on the Pont de Neuilly, where after the accident, his carriage hung halfway over the waters until rescued. It was from this experience, midway between sky and water, that Pascal would have derived his hallucination of life as poised between two abysses, the abyss of greatness and the abyss of wretchedness. From this could have dated his spiritual disquiet and his conversion from a worldly life to one of the spirit.

Was his dour view of man the result of his own reflections on experience, or superimposed on his character by Jansenism, with its dim view of man and his capacities? Was it a genuine *philosophical* pessimism, a real world view, or merely the mildly ironic result of a sensible man's dealings with other men? Vinet and Brunetière present Pascal as a convinced pessimist—though Vinet at least grants that from Pascal's realistic view of man and his intuitions, a clearer and even a joyous view of the universe can result.

It is a curious thing to find the author of an apology for the Christian religion accused of a radical skepticism. Did he believe in the Christian religion? Was his skepticism involuntary, the result of too close scrutiny, by too intelligent a man, of the claims of Christianity? Is the *Apology* actually the work of a man deeply troubled in his faith? Or is it rather the suggestive, intuitive argumentation of a man who did not challenge sufficiently the absurd convictions of a conventionally pious youth? Pascal seems at times so to depreciate the value of human reason that any attempt such as he made in his *Apology for the Christian Religion* is foredoomed. Or was he simply pointing out the limitations of rationalism and suggesting a more inductive "proof" of the Christian religion leaning heavily upon the convergence of probabilities?

Because of Pascal's curiously modern, fragmentary, direct approach to experience he was for a long time hardly taken seriously as a philosopher. Although Bergson remarked that Pascal and Descartes represent two classical forms of the modern philosophic mentality, for years Pascal was considered more a rhetorician, poet, or mystic than a philosopher. To some he seemed too subjective, too unsystematic in his analyses, too preoccupied with strictly theological themes to deserve the name of philosopher. Today, the tide of opinion has changed, as Bergson's remarks make clear. Pascal was certainly a philosopher, although no more systematic than Augustine or Newman. But he was also more than a philosopher. He was a scientist and a theologian.

Through all the different periods of his life Pascal retained his interest in mathematics. It is difficult for us to evaluate his genius here, but we must at least acknowledge the steps forward that he took in this area, as well as the philosophical and theological prolongations of his mathematical convictions. Pascal insisted, against Descartes, on the primacy of the evidence of facts of experience over reasonings. He was equally insistent that *religious* authority should not be substituted for the evidence of facts in questions of science—a bold opinion in his century. He drew from geometry reflections which bore on his theological interests—the calculus of probability, for example, convinced him that to spend years in Christian devotion with the hope of gaining an infinite reward in Heaven was a reasonable procedure. Pascal's devotion to Montaigne—the freethinker's breviary at the time—is well known. He admired Montaigne's skeptical exposé of the pretensions of rationalism and his nuanced analyses of the movements of the human heart. It seems that the very limitations of reason persuaded Pascal to seek in religion securities he could not obtain from philosophy, joining a moderate philosophical skepticism to a firm religious belief. The heart mysteriously recognizes the universal presence of God in mystery and obscurity. The heart for Pascal was not however a blind sentimentalism but a sort of knowledge by connaturality, an obscure intuition, a prephilosophic knowledge, but one bathed in the certainty that accompanies a direct experience of being.

To many of the above questions a definitive answer simply cannot be given today. Excerpts from his writings would support almost any of the hypotheses. But excerpts must be read in their remote and their proximate context. This is precisely what we cannot do with Pascal, because of the state of his work.

It may be helpful here to indicate briefly the main factors in Pascal's spiritual evolution. Pascal was born at Clermont-Ferrand, June 19, 1623. His father, Etienne Pascal, was a distinguished man of science. Of his two sisters, Gilberte was later to become Mme. Périer, a Port-Royalist and Jacqueline was to become a nun of Port Royal. Pascal's early education, undertaken by his father, was both classical and scientific. At the age of sixteen he had already composed a treatise on conic sections which gave considerable promise. At nineteen he was at work on a calculator. His scientific bent continued with experiments on the weight of air, etc. But at twenty-three he underwent his first religious conversion: to Jansenism, an austere form of Christianity. The young savant promptly set himself to convince his family that a Christian life must be lived solely for God. However, on the death of his father in 1651, Pascal interrupted his scientific and religious studies and entered upon a rather worldly phase of life. At this time he frequented the company of the Duc de Roannez and of de Méré and de Miton, entered a rather skeptical but not a dissolute milieu, and came strongly under the influence of Montaigne's writings. His health at this time was weak, and what energy he had left over from his worldly diversions he devoted more to mathematics than to religion. In 1654 he experienced his famous "second conversion." His distaste for the worldly amusements of the past few years became profound and on the evening of November 23, 1654, he underwent a mysterious religious experience which left so deep an impression on him that ever after he wore it recorded on a note sewed to his garments. In January of 1655 he left the world and retired to the Jansenist monastery of Port-Royal.

At the time when Pascal retired to Port-Royal this center of Jansenism was in serious difficulties. The Jansenists' particular brand of Christianity had aroused the ire of more orthodox Christians and many, the Jesuits in particular, were clamoring for their condemnation by the Church and the state. Wisely enough, the "gentlemen of Port-Royal" decided to appeal to public opinion and even more wisely they chose Blaise Pascal to defend them. Pascal then began to publish his celebrated *Provincial Letters*, one of the masterpieces of French irony. At this time his niece Marguerite was, apparently miraculously, cured at Port-Royal of an eye affliction, and Pascal took this as a sign of Heaven's blessing on his defense of the Jansenists against their adversaries. He then conceived also the idea of writing a defense of the Christian religion; his *Pensées* are the notes he gathered for this. In 1662 he died, renouncing Jansenism, it would appear, to rejoin the Catholic Church.

No introduction to Pascal's thought would be intelligible without reference to Jansenism—a theological position unfortunately not always accurately described. The spirit of Jansenism was one of rigorous austerity and it aimed at the reformation of Christian conduct and a return to a less worldly, less "accommodated" Christianity. Its doctrinal positions centered about grace and predestination. In both doctrinal theology and moral theology it opposed the Jesuits whose humanistic spirituality seemed to the Jansenists only too human.

The center of Jansenist studies and practice was the abbey of Port Royal des Champs, where Abbé Saint-Cyran and a group of solitaries had gathered together for prayer and penance and where Saint-Cyran acted as spiritual director to the nuns of the abbey. Among the devotees of the movement were Antoine Arnauld, who wrote numerous volumes denouncing both Protestants and Jesuits, Jacqueline Arnauld, Abbess of Port-Royal, and Pierre Nicole who assisted Pascal with his *Provincial Letters*. The influence of this group was enormous and long lasting, the spirit of their austere Christianity persevering long after the official condemnation of their doctrines by the Roman Church. Rome condemned the *Provincial Letters* almost immediately on their appearance, but the charm of Pascal's style, the wit, the irony, the skill in controversy, the eloquence, the passion, the impeccable clarity of his French, made them a lasting monument of French literature.

It is important to distinguish the three domains of Jansenistic thought—their conception of the Christian life as a whole, their doctrinal positions concerning grace, and their theological positions concerning Christian morals. The Jansenist concept of the Christian life heavily underscored the implacable and transcendent majesty of God, his "otherness," his infinite justice and grandeur. The movement wished to restore evangelical simplicity to the Christian life and to return to the biblical sources, free from medieval "accretions." Augustine was their hero and his doctrine of grace, as the Jansenists understood it, was the true Christian one. A rigid severity inculcated a spirit of fear of divine justice and urged a life of vigorous penitential discipline—including the suggestion that Christians return to the public penances of an earlier age. Frequent reception of the Eucharist was discouraged and the terror of the living God was instilled to such a point that even the devout might despair of salvation. One cannot doubt that this spiritual climate produced many noble and austere lives and effected no small purification of morals in its adherents. Its spirit however, was not the balanced spirit of the New Testament which insists on both filial fear and love of God.

The Jansenist positions on the theology of grace require more careful analysis. Roman Catholic theology teaches that man's salvation is dependent upon his free cooperation with God's freely given grace. How to reconcile the freedom of man and the divine dominion, how to explain the workings of grace and freedom is a theological problem which interested Christians from the beginning, which preoccupied Augustine, and which caused the celebrated disagreement between Jesuit and Dominican schools of theology. To Dominican theologians it seemed that the Jesuit explanation of how man cooperated with grace really did not preserve sufficiently the Catholic truth of God's sovereign dominion over all man's acts, even his free acts, and His infallible assurance that we will do His will. To the Jesuit theologians it seemed that the Dominican theory explained those points beautifully, but left us somewhat in doubt as to how man really was *free* under the influence of grace. Neither side of the controversy has offered a satisfactory explanation, and the mystery remains. But all Catholic schools of theology were in agreement about the basic facts: God is omnipotent and achieves His will even with His free creatures; man is genuinely free even under the influence of grace; God gives to all men sufficient grace to be saved; there are two different types of graces which are given by God to men, "efficacious" and "sufficient." An efficacious grace will, with absolute certainty, produce the good action for which it is given, since man will infallibly, but *freely*, accept it and cooperate with it. A sufficient grace is all the help, physical and moral, that man needs to produce the good action, but man may freely reject it. Where the two leading schools of theology differed was in their explanation of the difference between those two divine helps.

The Dominican school maintained an *intrinsic* difference between the two graces; Jesuits, or Molinists, a purely extrinsic difference. The Thomists maintained that an efficacious grace contained an impulse that led the will infallibly but freely to assent, whereas the sufficient grace lacked that impulse. In that case, replied their opponents, why call the sufficient grace "sufficient"? Especially since without that impulse the good action will not and *cannot* be performed? The Jesuit explanation maintained that the two graces really did not differ in their inner nature but rather the sufficient grace, differed from the efficacious in that God had foreseen that man might infallibly *but freely* reject it. How did God foresee that? The Jesuits explained this in their celebrated theory of *"scientia media"*; that is, God's awareness of what *would* happen in all conceivable circumstances with all conceivable graces. Against such a theory, the Dominicans launched a barrage of philosophical and theological arguments of no small moment. Both theories still enjoy a sort of peaceful coexistence in the Church.

In 1640 further controversy was aroused by the posthumous treatise of Jansenius, Bishop of Ypres, entitled *Augustinus*. Here, Jansenius claimed to present the authentic doctrine of Saint Augustine on grace (this was actually his own interpretation of Augustine, subsequently to be condemned by the Roman Church). According to Jansenius man has been so corrupted through the fall of Adam that he has lost free will and often sins. Grace can indeed assist man in his unfortunate state, but God does not always grant His grace. We have, it is true, a certain amount of freedom in the sense that the motives which necessitate our actions are motives interior to us and are not imposed from without. And, in fact, this small amount of freedom is enough for us to merit a reward or punishment from God. Jansenius added to this rather frightening doctrine the notion that Christ did not die for all men, nor does He send His graces to all. This doctrine, called Jansenism after its founder, was repudiated by the Roman Church in 1653, when the Church condemned five of the propositions drawn from the *Augustinus*. The Jansenists replied that the condemnation was just as regards the matter condemned but insisted that these propositions were not actually in the book. In 1656 the Pope intervened again, and insisted that the propositions *were* in the *Augustinus* and insisted that Catholics reject them and the book. Many of the followers of Port-Royal remained obdurate.

The echo of Jansenism's spirit, if not the actual condemned theses, can be discerned in Pascal's emphasis on man's fragility, and the weakness and powerlessness of the human will, as well as the disastrous consequences of original sin that we see portrayed in the *Apology*. In his *Provincial Letters,* Pascal dealt directly with many of these complicated and subtle questions and it must be confessed that he was in an area far beyond his theological competence.

Pascal himself may have realized this, for suddenly, in the fourth letter, he abandoned the dogmatic questions concerning grace and attacked his Jesuit adversaries directly concerning their "lax" moral theology. As the enormous success of the *Letters* proved, here he had material for an even more popular presentation of his theme. The Jesuits, he claims, have a moral theory easily adjustable to all their clients. In this fashion they disappoint none, and retain their great influence. For austere souls they propose rigorous maxims and for the less austere they have a store of gentler principles. With eloquence, passion, bitter irony, and profound conviction Pascal accuses the Jesuits of perverting evangelical morality and permitting almost anything to their penitents. His passionate attacks are directed especially at the theory of "probabilism" espoused by the Jesuits. According to this moral theory (still in practice in the Roman Church) a penitent is free to follow any solidly probable opinion of expert moral theologians, even if it be a less rigorous one. However, to be considered "probable" the opinion must be backed by solid, clear reasoning in its favor (even though the opposing opinion may have *more* probability to its arguments) or be backed by the authority of weighty experts in the disputed area. Thus obligations are not *imposed* upon a penitent unless the obligation is *certainly* there—the more perfect action may be counseled, but not imposed. Liberty of action is permitted if there is no certainty that liberty is morally wrong in a particular case. Where experts disagree one may follow the expert of one's choice, providing he actually *is* an expert in the area under discussion. In the *Provincial Letters,* from the fifth one on, Pascal attacks this policy as favoring laxism, and with wit and skill he selects some rather weird opinions from among the probabilists to prove his point: the Jesuits permit different moral opinions within their order so that, with Machiavellian skill, they may dominate the consciences of all comers and retain their great influence in the world.

As a matter of fact, Pascal and his collaborators collected a number of extravagant opinions, some of which were certainly lax. Laxism was, and is, always a real danger and Pascal did well to point out the excesses of probabilism and casuistry and to ridicule them. However, he enlarged the field of attack beyond the abuses to the whole of casuistry, which he mistakenly identified with one religious order—actually it has been common in the practice of the Church from then till now. Inexact citations of the authors he attacked occur occasionally, for Pascal's friends often did his research for him, although Pascal scrupulously tried to verify citations. Moreover his rapid style simply did not take into account all the distinctions made by his adversaries, so that often he lent them a meaning the author would never have accepted. His exaggerations, oversimplifications, and misunderstandings spoil the fun. However these errors were not due, as some have thought, to ill will or bad faith. Pascal was a noble soul and in his passion for Christian morals he erred more by his incompetence in a difficult terrain than through bad will.

The raillery, the comedy, the genuine eloquence of the *Provincial Letters* assure them a permanent place in the history of French letters. The style is everywhere wonderfully lucid even where it mounts to a furious violence. If the portrait Pascal draws of the Jesuit is a caricature, it is still a caricature worthy of a Molière.

Far more lasting, however, in its influence on man's heart is Pascal's *Apology for the Christian Religion.* Pascal had originally intended this as a demonstration of the divine foundation of the Christian religion, one which would both confound the Jesuits and win over the freethinkers. On his death he left a collection of fragments, some well developed, some mere notes, thoughts written on scraps of paper. Since Pascal did not live to order his thoughts as he would have wished to, the plan of the *Apology* has been and continues to be subject to controversy. Moreover, not all the fragments of his thoughts appear to have been destined for a place in the *Apology*. How much can one rely upon paleographic studies, upon internal evidence, on the testimony of those to whom Pascal spoke of his plan? Much remains uncertain. Modern scholars lay a heavy emphasis on the value of the First Copy (Bibliothèque Nationale No. 9203) which was almost certainly a partial classification by Pascal of the fragments. This copy indicates at least something of the order Pascal intended the *Pensées* to follow. It consists of twenty-seven separate bundles of papers, in their distribution agreeing with the outline he had himself noted in his talk to the Port-Royal community in 1658 and recorded by Filleau de la Chaise in his *Préface de Port-Royal.* None of the seven extant manuscripts of the *Pensées* are actually complete if we compare them with one another. Since 1670 editors of the *Pensées* have made attempt after attempt to produce an edition which would faithfully follow Pascal's plan and order. They still disagree however, since it remains to be determined how much weight we can give to Filleau de la Chaise's account of Pascal's plan, to internal evidence, etc. Moreover Pascal might have changed his plan many times before publication, even if Filleau's account was accurate with regard to Pascal's thought at that time. The Port-Royal edition of 1670 was the first edition of Pascal's *Pensées* and it did *not* follow his order but selected the more finished thoughts and published them grouped according to subject matter. The result is interesting but it is hardly Pascal's *Apology for the Christian Religion.* In 1776 Condorcet published a new edition which so arranges Pascal's text that Pascal appears antireligious! This subjective method continued for a century or so, editors arranging the *Pensées* according to their own religious convictions. In 1844 Faugère published an edition, based on the *Recueil Original* (Bibliothèque Nationale No. 9202), the original autograph manuscript left by Pascal. This edition divides the *Apology* into two parts; Part I concerns man's wretchedness without God, Part II, man's happiness with God in Christ the Redeemer. Michaut, in 1896, attempted a critical edition, publishing all the fragments, with no omissions, including variants. It also reproduced the disorder of the original. This very disorder stimulated new efforts to introduce order. Brunschvicg published a new edition in 1904 which returned to the order of Port-Royal one and attempted to give a logical continuity to the *Pensées*, but in fact succeeded in imposing a rather skeptical and fideistic order on them. This work is still of great importance for Pascal studies although recent scholars such as Lafuma and Tourneur insist more upon the First Copy than the *Recueil Original*. A later edition, Giraud's edition of 1907, presents us with a more religious, in fact a mystical Pascal. From 1923 until the present date Chevalier, Stewart, Strowski, Tourneur, and Lafuma have presented editions. Stewart, whose order we follow here, has the merit of presenting the *Pensées* according to the general order which Filleau de la Chaise stated Pascal explained to Port-Royal in 1658, and presents us with a Pascal who is at least a Christian. Lafuma's edition, following the First Copy for purposes of classification, has also received wide critical acclaim.

The mentality behind Pascal's *Apology* has been widely discussed. Voltaire sees only a sublime misanthropy as its fundamental philosophy. Claudel sees there the mentality of a sick man. The Romantics underscore Pascal's anguish, Modernists and liberal Protestants claim his thought as their own. His distrust of human reason has been exaggerated, his Jansenistic emphasis on the fall of man aligned with Lutheran positions. His "heart" has been compared to Newman's (who disapproved of him) illative sense, or to Bergson's intuition, or to Maine de Biran's *sens intime*. It appears to this author that he was an orthodox Christian, heavily influenced by Jansenism, but not to the point where he could be considered heterodox. He disturbed an earlier generation of Catholics by his insistence upon faith as a *sentiment*. But a more biblical understanding of his notions on faith might suggest that he was only underscoring the need of theoretical assent *and* a disposition to obey and submit in love to God. His depreciation of the rôle of reason in preparing an approach to faith seemed to some Catholics excessive but it is only an accentuation of a Catholic truth. His dislike of rational "demonstrations" of the existence of God upset others, but Pascal does not deny that we can come to know God with certainty through the use of reason.

He may not like certain deductive proofs, but he does not deny the validity of reason—he uses it to bring the free-thinker to acknowledge the living God. His reserves with regard to the power of human reason need not imply a radical skepticism. He certainly leans heavily on the doctrine of Original Sin and often his expressions of man's weakness, taken in isolation, are cause for unease. But they must be complemented by other expressions. We can admit that his Jansenism and his incomplete knowledge of theology have marred his work but it remains a masterpiece which will always intrigue and stimulate. Pascal has thrown into relief in a way most close to the human heart the need of a moral preparation to receive both insight and faith. He has described the anguish and wretchedness of man without God in terms perennially modern. His genius has illuminated the depths of man, both his greatness and weakness, in a fashion that is accurate, almost infallibly so.

This style, elevated, passionate, yet natural and poetic, is direct, clear, chaste. It speaks to the heart and appeals to the Pascalian "heart."

PASCAL'S INFLUENCE

It is always a delicate task to trace the influence of an author, but we can safely say that Pascal's influence in French thought has been extraordinary. It has also been startling at times. How many are aware, one wonders, that the great anti-Christian Voltaire began and ended his career, a fifty year span, with commentaries on Pascal? Or that most of the anti-Christian propagandists, the Stendhals, the Gibbons, the Bérangers, raided Pascal for their arms? Or that the arch-romantic Rousseau probably owes more to Pascal, the austerely classical, than to any other literary figure? With Rousseau and Chateaubriand, Pascal was one of the most formative influences on French literature. In a way it was inevitable; Pascal's genius is so typically French, with his love for irony, his cerebral poetry and lyricism, his exquisite clarity and objectivity. It has been said that in Pascal French classical literature received its final form, and this is especially true of the *Provincial Letters* where oratory and poetry are balanced with lucidity and wit.

Pascal's influence is generally admitted to have created the religious atmosphere of France in the second half of the seventeenth century. The great French dramatist Racine embodies Pascalian themes to such an extent that, as Brunetière remarked, if one wanted to disengage from Racine's works a general conception of life, one would only have to know his Pascal. The celebrated pulpit orators, Bossuet and Bourdaloue, stress the familiar Pascalian theme of man's wretchedness without grace and most of the seventeenth-century preachers orchestrate them. In the eighteenth century the Encyclopedists would have liked to bury Pascal, who stood antithetically opposed to most of their theses, but the nineteenth century shows him vigorously to the fore again. Chateaubriand's *Genius of Christianity* has the same method of appeal to the "heart," his general reasons for faith are those of Blaise Pascal. Through the channel of Chateaubriand many of Pascal's leading themes forced their way into the mainstream of French thought. Lamennais, Joseph de Maistre, Lacordaire owe much to him. Maine de Biran's journal notes the influence that Pascal exercised upon his philosophic evolution and the deists of the nineteenth century, the rationalists and sceptics claim him as their own, at least partially. In the last half of the nineteenth century, Pascal suffered a certain eclipse, leaving the field to Hegel, but the twentieth century has adopted him with enthusiasm.

Blondel shows signs of his influence in his search for an inner apologetic and the entire twentieth-century approach to faith in the Roman Church is much closer to Pascal than to the two preceding centuries. Their insistence that rationalistic "proofs" for the existence of God are insufficient to produce persuasion foreshadows the newer approaches in natural theology used by philosophers and theologians such as Sciacca, Maritain, and de Lubac.

Protestant thought has long admired Pascal and his direct, intuitive approach to religious problems. It is difficult to assay the influence that Pascal has on our contemporaries but the enormous number of sympathetic and profound studies on him that are appearing constantly indicate that there is indeed a "revival of Pascal." His insistence on lived sincerity, authentic existence, his evangelical seriousness cannot but appeal to a generation with existentialist background. His appeal for a deeply personal "engaged" spirituality, his sense of the abyss in man, his distaste for the reactionary, for the purely formal ethic mark him as one of our contemporaries. While it is not possible to trace his influence on all contemporaries it seems safe to say that at least as far as contemporary *French* thought is concerned, it would seem impossible that it could avoid the influence of Pascal. He is part of the living tradition of France, and it would be somewhat incredible if Pascal, whose preoccupations are so very close to modern man's, were not being studied. Some have seen his influence at work in the intuitionism of Bergson, in the "new" apologetic of Laberthonnière and Blondel, in the philosophy of action of Blondel, and the philosophy of Le Roy.

In the field of science also Pascal exerted considerable influence. It was he, with Fermat, who laid the basic foundations for the theory of probability in mathematics. His insistence on experimentation gave great impetus to the scientific method and was a healthy balance to the Cartesian rationalism. It is curious also to note that this highly speculative mind gave considerable encouragement to the development of applied sciences and the natural sciences. He might in some sense be said to be the forerunner of the positive scientist of today. And he might just as easily be called a father of ethical pragmatism with his "wager" argument for the existence of God. As poet, scientist, mystic, theologian, and philosopher, Pascal's thought continues to enrich contemporary existence.

THE TRANSLATION

The translations of Pascal in *The Essential Pascal* are entirely new. A number of English translations of the *Pensées* are already extant, but the other works of Pascal have received less attention from the English public. It is, in many cases, difficult or impossible to render into English the poetry and rhythm of Pascal's style with its precision, clarity, and brevity. The primary concern here has been to remain faithful to the nuances of Pascal's thought, even on the occasion when this required an ampler English version of the light French construction. The editor considers himself fortunate to have secured as translator Mr. G. F. Pullen, F.I.L., of Birmingham, England.

PENSÉES

PENSEES

1. The way of God, who orders all things with mildness, is to plant religion in the mind by persuasion, and in the heart by grace. But to desire to put it into either mind or heart by force or threat, is to introduce not religion, but fear—terror rather than religion.

2. For if men were to be filled with fear, and taught nothing, government would be seen to be unjust. Saint Augustine, Ep. 48 or 49: "Against lying, to Consentius."

3. *Order:* Men despise religion; they hate it, and fear to find that it may be true. We need to deal with this situation by showing that religion is certainly not contrary to reason, but deserving of reverence: we must inspire respect for it. Then we must make it attractive, so that men of goodwill may wish that it were true; and then demonstrate that it *is* true.

Deserving of reverence, because it well knows what is in man; attractive, because it offers him his truest good.

4. Begin by pitying unbelievers, who are made sufficiently wretched by their own condition. It is therefore unnecessary to reproach them, unless to do so would be for their benefit: as a rule, it would only antagonize them.

5. Pity those atheists who seek: are they not sufficiently unhappy? Reproach only those who plume themselves upon their unbelief.

6. There are but three classes of men: those who have found God, and serve Him; those that have not yet found Him, but seek Him earnestly; those who spend their lives

neither seeking nor finding. The first know where the true values lie, and they are happy; the last are stupid and unhappy; the class in the middle are unhappy, but they are rational.

7. In every dialogue and discourse we must be able to say to anyone who takes offense: "What are you complaining about?"

9. I blame equally those who make up their minds that humanity is worthy of praise, those who condemn the race out of hand, and those who make fun of mankind; I can commend only those who seek, groaning as they go.

10. The metaphysical proofs for God are so remote from man's ordinary processes of reasoning, and so involved, that they fail to catch his imagination; they may be useful to a few, but then only at the time when they see the point of this method of demonstration; an hour afterwards, they fear they may have been deceived. "What they came to know through curiosity they lost because of pride," Saint Augustine sermon: 110, 1.

This is one of the results of a knowledge of God which is gained apart from Jesus Christ; that is, they want to communicate, without a mediator, with a God whom they have known without a Mediator. Whereas those who have learned to know God through a Mediator are aware of the misery of their own condition.

11. How far apart are the knowledge of God and the love of Him!

12. They blaspheme against a thing of which they know nothing. The Christian religion contains two major dogmas; it is just as important that man should know them as it is dangerous that he should remain in ignorance of them. Moreover, it is part of the mercy of God that He has given man signs of both.

Yet these people reiterate that one of these dogmas has no real existence, and they argue to this conclusion from evidence which certainly supports the other dogma. The Patriarchs and Prophets who proclaimed one God were persecuted; the Jews were hated; Christians were hated even more. Both Jews and Christians saw, as by the light of nature, that if there be but one true religion upon earth, all things should tend toward it, as to their center.

The ordering of human affairs in general ought to have as its object the establishment of religion, and its greatness. Men should subordinate their personal judgments and conduct to the teachings of religion. In a word, religion ought to be so completely the object and center toward which all earthly activities are directed, that he who knows its principles should be well able to explain the condition of man in particular, and the best way of regulating the general affairs of the whole world.

Upon their own assumption, therefore [that one of the essential dogmas has no validity], these people make bold to blaspheme against the Christian religion, which clearly they do not fully understand. They devise for themselves a religion which consists in the adoration of a God who is great, Almighty, eternal; though this is, strictly speaking, Deism, and almost as far removed from Christianity as is atheism, its direct contrary. Whence they argue that such a religion cannot be true, for they do not perceive that all things work together to establish this one proposition: that God does not reveal Himself to mankind as convincingly as He might, with the whole of the evidence.

Let them apply this consideration as they please against the claims of the Deists—they will find it useless against Christianity, which is strictly the mystery of the Redeemer who, uniting in Himself the two natures, divine and human, has redeemed men from the corruption of sin in order to reconcile them to God in His own divine person.

Christianity then, instructs men on two truths; that there is a God whom they may know, and that there is in human nature something corrupted which renders men unworthy. These are the two dogmas which it is equally important that men should know; and it is as dangerous that they should know God, yet refuse to recognize their own misery, as it is, to be conscious of their misery without knowledge of the Redeemer, who can heal it. It is knowledge of one only of these dogmas which has been the cause, either of the pride of philosophers, who have acquired some knowledge of God, but not of their own wretchedness, or of the despair of atheists, who know their wretchedness, but not their Redeemer.

Thus, just as it is necessary that men should know these

two things, so it is fitting that God in His mercy should have revealed them to us. The Christian religion makes this revelation: it exists so that the revelation may be made.

Let them but examine the way the world is ordered in these matters, and they will see how all things contribute to establish the two cardinal tenets of the Christian religion: that Jesus Christ is the sole object of it, and that He is the central figure to whom all must come. He who understands this, knows the order and method of all things.

Those who go astray in this world only do so because they cannot see one or the other of these two things. We can indeed know God without realizing our condition of misery, and we can be aware of our wretched state although we have no knowledge of God. But once we come to the knowledge of Jesus Christ, we necessarily know both these truths: that God *is*, and that we without Him are wretched indeed.

This is why I shall here make no attempt to prove by ordinary reasoning either the existence of God, or of the Trinity, or the immortality of the soul, or anything of that kind. Not only because I am conscious that I have no sufficient knowledge to draw from Nature such arguments as would convince hardened atheists, but also because such knowledge would be useless and sterile without Jesus Christ. A man might firmly believe that numerical proportions are eternal, that they are immaterial truths, dependent upon a first principle in virtue of which they subsist, and that this first principle may be called God; but I should not think that such a belief had advanced him very far on his own way to salvation.

The God of Christians is not merely a divine author of geometrical truths and of the order of the elements: that is an idea fit only for pagan philosophers and the epicureans. Nor is He simply a God who bestows His providential care upon the earthly life and well-being of men, with happiness and length of days for those that worship Him; that was the inheritance expected by the Jews. But the God of Abraham, Isaac, and Jacob, the God of Christians, is a God of love and of consolation, a God who fills the souls and the hearts of those who are His, and who causes them to feel deeply within themselves their own misery and His infinite mercy; who unites Himself with them in the secret places of the heart, filling it with humility and joy, confidence and love, who renders them incapable of any object other than Himself.

They who seek God apart from Jesus Christ, either rest in Nature, where they find no light that satisfies them, or contrive a means of knowing and serving God without a Mediator. Thus they fall either into atheism or Deism—the two things which the Christian religion abominates above all others.

Without Jesus Christ the world could not continue in being. It would necessarily work its own destruction, or else it would become a kind of Hell.

If the world were being maintained in being, simply to teach men about God, His divinity would illuminate every part of it, and all things would speak plainly of Him; but it exists only through Jesus Christ and for Him, and to teach men that they were corrupt yet are redeemed. Therefore the proofs of these two truths are strikingly evident wherever we look.

The visible world provides neither argument that God is absent from His Creation, nor that He is manifestly present therein; it argues the presence of a hidden God. All things are marked by that presence.

Shall the lonely man who knows only Nature, know her only that he may be wretched? Shall he that knows only Nature be the only unhappy one?

It is not necessary that he should live as one blind, seeing nothing at all; nor is it necessary that he should see just so much as to believe that he sees it all; but he must see enough of the thing to realize what he has lost. For to know his loss, he must see, and yet not see, and that is precisely the state of him who knows only nature.

Whichever side he takes, I shall leave him no rest.

13. I will not allow him any rest, either in himself or in his substitutes, so that finding his spirit disordered and himself without a place of rest. . . .[1]

14. It is a remarkable fact that no canonical writer makes any appeal to Nature as proving God. They all aim at creating belief in Him. Nowhere did David, Solomon, etc.,

[1] Pascal the scientist would be conscious of the full significance of his terminology. The word used here, *assiette,* is still applied to a valve seat.

say, "There is no such thing as a vacuum, therefore there is a God." They were clearly much more astute than those much cleverer gentlemen who have come after them, all of whom have made use of the argument from Nature. The fact is worthy of note.

15. "What! Do not you Christians yourselves say that the heavens and the birds are proofs of God?" No. "And does not your religion say so?" No. For though it is in a sense true for a few souls whom God has enlightened on the subject, it is false for the majority.

16. If it is a mark of weakness to appeal to Nature as proof of God, do not therefore despise the Scriptures: if it be a mark of strength to have recognized these contradictions, praise the Scriptures for that.

17. Two things teach a man everything about his own nature: instinct and experience.

18. We are as a rule more easily persuaded by reasons we have discovered for ourselves than by those which have occurred to the minds of others.

19. All our reasoning is nothing but a surrender to feeling. But imagination is akin to feeling, though contrary to it, so that we cannot distinguish between these contraries. One man says that my feeling is fancy, another that his fancy is feeling. There ought to be a rule. Reason makes her claim, but reason may be made to give way in any direction. And so there is no rule.

20. There are two ways of persuading men as to the truths of our religion: one is by force of argument, the other is by the authority of the speaker. Most people will not be taught by the latter method, but only by the former. They do not say, "This is something we must believe, since it is taught by the Scriptures, and the Scriptures are divine"; but they say that such a thing must be believed for this or that "reason"—a weak argument, since reasons can be twisted to support any argument.

21. Those who are accustomed to judge according to

feeling understand nothing of reasoning processes. They want to see the whole of the subject at a single glance, and are not accustomed to look for the principles. Others, again, are well accustomed to an appeal to principles, but understand nothing of feeling, looking always for the principle and being incapable of insight.

23. First Part: The wretchedness of man without God.
Second Part: Man's happiness with God.
Alternatively:
First Part: That Nature has been corrupted, proved from Nature herself.
Second Part: That there is a Redeemer, proved from Scripture.

24. *Order:* Against the objection that there is nothing of order in the Scriptures. The heart has its order, so has the mind, and here the order depends on principle and demonstration. But the order of the heart is different. We do not prove that we ought to be loved by setting out in order the causes of love; that would be ridiculous.

Jesus Christ and Saint Paul have the order of charity, not of the mind, for they desired to warm the will, not to instruct. Saint Augustine does the same. This order mainly consists in suppleness on all points, provided the main purpose be achieved, and keeping that purpose always in view.

26. Nature keeps each one of her truths separate and distinct. Human art contrives to make one truth depend upon another, but that is not natural; each truth has its appropriate place.

27. *Skepticism:* I shall here write down my thoughts without arranging them in order, but not, perhaps, without a certain design in the confusion: this is the proper order, and the very confusion will define my objective. I should be doing the subject too much honor if I dealt with it in order, since I intend to show that it is not capable of orderly treatment.

28. Order: I might well have set out this discourse somewhat as follows. To show the vanity of all conditions of men, begin by showing the vanity of ordinary life, then the vanity

of life according to the philosophers, whether skeptics or Stoics; but this would not preserve the requisite order. I myself know something about that, but how few people really understand it. No activity of the human intellect has been able to adhere strictly to order: Saint Thomas himself was not able to do it. Mathematics indeed is based on order, but when mathematics begins to be abstruse it ceases to be useful.

33. If we know a man's ruling passion we have a sure way to please him. Yet every man has fancies which are contrary to his real good, when he forms his own idea of what is good. This is a curious fact which puts man in a class by himself.

34. How difficult it is to submit any question to the opinion of another without influencing his judgment by your manner of asking the question! If you say, "I think that's fine," or, "I find it obscure," or the like, you either predispose his imagination to accept your own opinion, or you provoke an immediate reaction in opposition to it. It would be better to say nothing. Then he can arrive at a judgment which is in conformity with his own opinion, that is to say, with his mind as it is at that moment, and with due allowance made by him for factors not under our control. But at least you will not have contributed anything to bias his opinion, unless indeed your very silence should have produced some effect, which depends upon the way he interprets it, or upon what he may conjecture (provided he is skilled in physiognomy[2]), from your gesture, the expression of your face, or the tone of your voice. It is indeed difficult to avoid biasing the judgment so that it is tipped out of its native seat[3]; or rather, how unstable, how insecure, the human judgment is!

36. A man must know himself. Though such knowledge may not help him to find the truth, at any rate it will help him to regulate his own life—and self-government, if en-

[2] Physiognomy was at that time, and for a century after, a science of some repute among European scholars. This fragment is a good example of Pascal's irony, which did not spare the mountebank.

[3] A reference to the geological phenomenon known as the Logan stone, of which some interesting examples had lately been discovered.

lightened by true self-knowledge, ought to be very strict.

37. If one knew oneself, God would heal and pardon. "Lest they . . . understand . . . and turn, and be healed," Isa. 6:10. "Lest they should . . . be forgiven," Mark 4:12.

39. *Preface to Part I.* Discuss those who have written of self-knowledge: of the divisions of Charron, which sadden and bore us; of the confusion in Montaigne; how well aware he was of his own lack of method, and how he tried to conceal the deficiency by skipping from topic to topic, which he thought was smart.

That foolish idea of his, that he would paint his own portrait! That was not a mere impulse, a thing against his own principles, a slip, such as happens to us all. It was done according to his own principles, for it was his primary purpose—it was basic to his plan. To say foolish things by accident or through weakness is an ordinary misfortune, but to say them deliberately is intolerable, and to say such things as . . .

42. I had spent much time in the study of the abstract sciences, and the limited extent to which I was able to share such studies with other persons disgusted me. When I turned to the study of man, I saw that those abstract studies were foreign to man, and that by engaging deeply in them, I was wandering farther from my normal condition than do others who know nothing about them. I therefore forgave them for knowing so little about the abstract sciences, but I certainly expected to find many who would associate themselves with me in the study of mankind, since that is a study proper to man. But I was mistaken: there are fewer students of mankind than there are of geometry. It is only because we do not know how to set about the study of mankind that we go looking for other things. But is it not true that those other things do not contain the knowledge that man needs, and ought to have? And that it is better he should remain in ignorance of himself, if he wants to be happy?

43. H. J. *Disproportion of man* (That is as far as our knowledge of nature takes us. If that knowledge is false, there is no truth in man, and if it is true, it provides good

reason for humility: thus in one way or another, humility is forced upon him. And since he cannot exist without some knowledge of Nature, I hope that before he embarks upon any deeper studies, he will consider her very seriously, and at leisure. Let him also consider his own capacity, and realize the disproportion. . . .)

Let man therefore contemplate the whole of Nature in her complete and lofty majesty; let him avert his eyes from the common objects that surround him. Let him look upon that dazzling light, hung aloft like an eternal lamp to give light to the universe. Let the earth appear to him a mere dot, compared with the vast orbit which our planet describes, and let him stand amazed as he considers that that mighty circuit is itself but a tiny point, when compared with that traced by some of the other stars as they revolve in the firmament.

But if our vision halts there, let imagination pass beyond. It will be more likely to weary of forming ideas, than will Nature of supplying the material for them. The whole of our visible world is no more than an imperceptible speck on the ample bosom of Nature. No idea that we can form will come anywhere near it. In vain we seek to extend our thought beyond imaginable space: in comparison with the reality, the human mind gives birth to mere atoms. Nature is an infinite sphere, whereof the center is everywhere, the circumference nowhere. When all is done, the imagination is brought to silence by this, the greatest accessible sign of the power of Almighty God.

And let man, when he recovers himself, consider what he is in comparison with Him who is. Let him regard himself as lost in this remote corner of Nature. And from the little cell that gives him lodging—the universe, that is—let him learn to estimate at their true value this earth and its kingdoms, its inhabited cities, and himself. What is a man, when faced with the infinite?

But let us then show him another marvel just as astonishing: let him seek out from among the things he knows, the tiniest of objects. Let him consider, for example, the tiny body of a mite with its parts, all smaller still: its tiny legs with their joints, the veins in the legs, blood in the veins, humors in the blood, drops in the humors, and vapors in the drops. Let him subdivide these things and exhaust his imagination upon them until his mind reels at such ideas, and let the final object of his quest be one with the subject of this present discussion. Now he may assume that this subject is the extremely small scale of most natural phenomena: but I intend to show him her infinite vastness. I want to make him see in her a new abyss. I will depict for him not only the visible universe, but also all the vastness of the natural system which the scientist can assume to be contained within this atomized atom. Let him see therein an infinity of universes, each with its firmament and its planets, and even its earth, all in the same proportion as in our visible world. In this earth there will be animals, down to the mites, in which he will find reproduced all the features that he has already seen in our own mites. In all of these he will find repeated the same features, the same unending and unresting purpose. Let him lose himself in these marvels, as wonderful in their minuteness as those others in their immensity. For a moment ago our human body was seen to be no more than an imperceptible speck in an insignificant planet of the universe: who then will not be amazed to see it become a colossus, a world, a vast whole, comparable even with that other vast nothingness into which we cannot penetrate?

Whoever considers himself in this way will be terrified of himself, and when he considers how he is upheld, in the substance that Nature has given him, between these two abysses of infinity and nothing, he will tremble at the sight of such marvels; and I think that as his curiosity changes into wonder, he will be more disposed to contemplate them in silence, than tempted to presumptuous investigation.

For what, after all, is man in Nature? A cipher, if you compare him with the infinite, a whole, as compared with the void, a middle term between the nothing and the all. Infinitely unable to grasp these extremes, the end of things and their beginning are impenetrably hidden from him in baffling mystery. He can see neither the nothingness from which he was drawn, nor the infinite in which he is swallowed up.

What then can he do, but glimpse the middle term, in an eternal despair of ever knowing either its origin or its end? All things emerge from the void, and are carried forward into the infinite. Who shall follow these astonishing preliminaries? The author of these marvels comprehends them. No one else can do so.

Because they have neglected the study of these two infinities, men have presumptuously set to work to investigate Nature, as though there were some degree of proportion between herself and them. Strange to say, they have attempted to grasp the origins of things, and have then proceeded to an explanation of the whole, with a presumptuousness as comprehensive as the subject. For it is not in doubt that so far-reaching a design could only originate in the mind of a man of limitless presumption—or of a capacity as infinite as that of Nature herself.

When we have learnt a little about it, we begin to understand that Nature has stamped upon all things her own image and that of her author, so that almost all things participate in her twofold infinity. For this reason, every branch of science is infinite as to the range of research required. Who can doubt, for example, that geometry has an infinity of infinities of problems still awaiting a solution? These problems are as infinite in the number as in the subtlety of their propositions. For who does not see that, when propositions represented as final are not self-evident, they rest upon other propositions, and these in turn upon others still, so that none of the terms can ever be called final?

But we tend to accept as final such conclusions as appeal to our reason, just as we do with material things: the point beyond the limit of visibility, where our senses can perceive nothing further, we term "invisible," though it is of its nature infinitely *di*visible.

Of these two scientific infinites, greatness is much more obvious and more easily measured. For this reason, a few people have ventured to claim that they knew everything. Democritus was one of the few: "I am going to speak of everything," he said.

But the infinitely small is much less perceptible. Philosophers have much more frequently claimed to have reached the limit of divisibility, the infinitely small, and here they all come to grief. Hence the frequent use of such commonplace titles as "first principles," "principles of philosophy," and so on, all equally pretentious in fact, though not in appearance, such as one that hits us in the eye: *De omni scibili* [Of all things knowable].

We naturally believe that we are much more capable of penetrating to the center of things than of encompassing the circumference within which they are contained, for the visible expanse of the world is visibly greater than we are ourselves; but since we surpass small things, we believe ourselves more capable of grasping them. Yet no less ability is demanded to attain to the nothing as to the all. An infinite capacity is required for both, and it seems to me that he who had grasped the final principles of being and existence could also attain to a knowledge of the infinite. The one depends upon the other, and the one leads to the other. These extremes meet and coalesce by virtue of having been separated: they meet again in God, and in Him alone.

Let us therefore know our limitations: we are something, but we are not everything. The conditions of our existence conceal from us the knowledge of first principles, which are born of Nothing, and the limitations of existence hide the Infinite from our sight.

In the order of intelligible things, our intelligence occupies the same position as does our body in the system of Nature. This middle state between two extremes is characteristic of all our faculties: we are hemmed in on every side, and every exercise of our powers does but hold the mean between two extremes which escape us entirely, for too much noise deafens us, too much light dazzles us; too great or too short a distance impedes our view; a speech may be obscure, whether long or short; too much truth baffles us (I know some people who can never understand that four from zero leaves nothing); first principles are too obvious; too much pleasure troubles us; too many concords in music are displeasing; too many benefits vex us, for a man likes to be able to repay kindnesses, "For services rendered are welcome, so long as it seems possible to repay them, but when they greatly exceed that point, they produce not gratitude, but hatred," Tacitus, *Annals,* IV, 18, quoted by Montaigne. We feel neither extreme heat nor extreme cold. Any excess of virtue is inimical to us and is not acceptable: we do not respond to it, but suffer it. Extremes of youth or age frustrate the mind, like too little or too much learning. In short, extremes have no existence for us, nor we for them. They escape us, or we them.

Such is our true condition, and our being in this state renders us incapable of either certain knowledge or absolute ignorance. We sail over a vast expanse, always uncertain, always drifting, carried by the winds. We seek an anchorage where we can rest and take stock of our position; it shifts, and we are adrift again. If we follow it, it eludes our grapple, slips away, and appears to evade us by eternal flight. Nothing stays for us. That is our condition, a normal one, yet most contrary to our inclinations. We are consumed with the desire to find a stable position, a solid foundation on which to build a tower which shall rise to infinity; but the entire foundation cracks, and the earth opens beneath us like a vast abyss. Let us not look therefore for any kind of security or stability. Our reason is always being cheated by deceitful appearances. Nothing can give stability to a finite poised between two infinites which always shut it in, and yet which it can never know.

Once this is clearly understood, I believe we may remain in a state of peace, each in that condition of life in which Nature has placed him. Since the middle state in which Nature has placed us is always far removed from either extreme, what can it matter if one man has a little more understanding of these things than another? If he has such deeper knowledge, it is simply that he has used his talents better, carried his investigation a little farther. He is still an infinite distance from the end; and if ten years be added to a human life, that life is still a long way from being eternal. When confronted with these infinites, all finite things are equal; and I do not see why I should allow my imagination to rest in the one rather than in the other. Merely to compare ourselves with finite things is painful.

Were a man to begin with self-examination, he would see how incapable he is of further advance. How can a part know the whole? But he may at least hope to know at least those parts to which he is proportioned. But all existing things are so intimately related, so linked together, that I believe it is impossible to know any one part in isolation, or to know such parts without acquiring some knowledge of the whole.

There is, for example, some relationship between a man and everything that he knows. He needs space to contain him, time in which to live and advance, movement, that he may survive, the chemical elements which make up his body, warmth and food to nourish him, air to breathe; he sees light, he feels material things, and in short, he has a relationship with everything. In order therefore to arrive at an understanding of man, we must also know why he needs air to breathe; and to have some knowledge of air, we have to understand why it should play the part it does in the life of man, etc. Flame cannot exist without air, therefore, if we are to understand the one, we must understand the other. Thus all things are cause and effect, dependent and sustaining, mediate and immediate, and all are held together by a natural but imperceptible bond which unites even the most distant and dissimilar things, so that in my view it is impossible to know the parts without knowing the whole, and equally impossible to know the whole without acquiring a knowledge of the parts in detail.

(The eternity of things, in itself or in God, must always be a cause for amazement in comparison with our brief human life. The fixed and unchanging immobility of nature, as compared with the changes constantly taking place in ourselves, ought to produce in us a similar wonder.)

And our incapacity to know things is crowned by the fact that things in themselves are simple, whereas we are composed of two natures opposite and different in kind, that is, of soul and body. For it is impossible that the reasoning part in us should be other than spiritual; and if it were alleged that we were mere bodies, that fact would exclude us even more effectively from the knowledge of things, since there is nothing so inconceivable as to say that matter knows itself. It is not possible for us to understand how matter could know itself.

And so, if we be composed of matter only, we can know nothing at all, and if we are composed of spirit and matter, we cannot know simple things perfectly, be they spiritual or material.

This is why nearly all the philosophers propound a confused doctrine of things, speaking of material things in abstract terms, and of spiritual things in terms of matter. For they boldly say that bodies fall, that they "tend toward" their center, that they "clash" with their environment, that they "abhor" a vacuum, that things "possess" inclinations, sympathies, antipathies: yet all of these attributes can belong only to minds. And when they speak of minds, they describe them as though they were localized, and endow them with the faculty of movement from place to place, but these are properties which belong only to bodies.

Thus we do not deal with pure ideas, but describe them in terms of our own attributes, and we impose the stamp of our own composite being upon all the simple things of which we have to take cognizance.

Who would not suppose, as he watched us endowing everything with mind and matter, that we should find such a mixture perfectly comprehensible? Yet it is the thing we comprehend least of all. Man himself is the most marvelous object in nature, for he cannot understand what body is, still less what mind is, and least of all how body and mind can be joined together. That is his supreme difficulty, and yet it is the essence of his being. "The manner in which the spirit is united to the body cannot be understood by man and yet it is his essential being," Saint Augustine: *De Civ. Dei,* 21, 10. Finally, to complete the proof of our weakness, I shall conclude by the two following considerations . . .

47. (Nature cannot . . . Nature has placed us so carefully in the middle, that if we alter one side of the balance, we must of necessity alter the other. [To say, for example:] *Je fesons, zôa trékei,* would obviously be impossible: the balance needs to be adjusted. This makes me think there are springs in our heads, so arranged that if you move one you also move its opposite.)

48. What a host of creatures have been discovered for us by the telescope, that were nonexistent for our philosophers of yesterday. They used to challenge the Scriptures on the multitude of stars, saying: "We know for a fact that there are no more than one thousand and twenty-two."

"There are plants on the earth: we can see them. From the moon we should not see them. And on these plants there are hairs, and little animals in the hairs; but after that, nothing." Presumptuous man! "Mineral ores are made up of elements; but what of the elements?" Presumptuous! Here is a subtle point: We must not say a thing exists which we do not see. We must, then, talk as others do, but not think as they do.

49. The last step to be taken by human reason is the recognition that there is an infinity of things lying beyond it. Reason is a poor thing, indeed, if it has not reached the point of knowing that.

Now, if natural things lie beyond it, what shall we say of the supernatural?

50. Description of man: dependence, desire of independence, need.

51. Man's condition: inconstancy, *ennui*, unrest.

52. What surprises me most of all is to observe that apparently nobody is astonished at his own weakness. Everybody goes about his business seriously, and each one follows his own way of life, not because it is in itself a good way of life and is recognized as such by social custom, but as though each person knew for himself and with certainty how reason and justice are to be served. They are always finding that they were in error on that point; but with a rather attractive humility they admit that they were wrong, and do not try to blame their error upon the philosophical system they have elected to live by. Of this they continue to be proud. All the same, it is a good thing that there are so many of this kind in the world—men who are not in fact skeptical upon literally everything. Thus the good name of the skeptic philosophy is saved—and man is seen to be capable of the most extravagant opinions, capable of believing that, so far from being in a state of natural and inescapable weakness, he is endowed with natural wisdom.

Nothing strengthens the skeptic position so much as the existence of so many "skeptics" who are not in the least skeptical. If skepticism were total and universal, it would be self-defeating.

53. *Weakness:* All the activities of men are undertaken that they may acquire wealth; and they could not produce any evidence that they possess it justly, for they have only the imaginative faculty of human beings; nor have they the strength which is essential to peaceful possession. So also with human knowledge, for a sickness can deprive us of it. We lack the capacity for the true and the good.

55. Man's inconstancy is due to his dissatisfaction with present pleasures, which he suspects are hollow: yet he does not know that the pleasures beyond his reach are [also] vain.

56. *Inconstancy:* In our dealings with man, we behave as though he were an old-fashioned positive organ. Man is in-

deed an organ, but he is odd, fickle, variable (and his pipes are not correctly ranked according to the stops). People who can only play on a reed organ will get no music out of this one: you have to know where the stops are.

57. *Inconstancy:* Things possess different qualities, and the soul has its passions; for nothing presented to the soul is simple, and the soul never approaches anything in complete simplicity. That is why we can both laugh and weep at one and the same thing.

58. *Inconstancy and eccentricity:* To live entirely upon one's own labor, and to rule over the mightiest of the kingdoms of this world, are very different things. They are combined in the person of the Grand Turk.

59. Such is the diversity [of Nature], that every tone of voice, every style of walking, every cough, the way a man blows his nose or sneezes [is different from everybody else's]. We distinguish grapes from other fruits and among the grapes we further distinguish the muscats, then for example, Condrieu, then Desargues, and then this cutting. Is that all? Did a vine ever produce two bunches exactly alike? And did a bunch ever produce two identical grapes? etc.

I have never judged a given thing twice running in precisely the same way. I cannot judge my own work while I am doing it: I have to do as painters do, and stand back—but not too far back. How far, then? Guess.

61. *Thoughts:* All is unity, all is diversity. How many natures in that of man! And how many employments! And what a matter of chance it all is! Each man tends to choose for himself the thing he has heard recommended. A well-turned heel.

63. The most important thing in the whole of life is the choice of a profession, yet it is decided by chance. Custom makes men masons, soldiers, roofers. "He's an excellent roofer," people say. And when they speak of soldiers, "They're a mad lot," they say. But others take a different view: "Nothing is great but war: the rest of mankind are knaves." It was because in our childhood we heard these callings praised, and all the others despised, that we made our choice. For

we naturally love the truth, and hate folly: the very words sway our judgment, and we only go wrong in the way we apply them. So powerful is the force of custom, that where Nature provides merely men, [society] is able to produce all kinds of men; for some districts are full of masons, and in others all the men are soldiers, etc. Nature is certainly not so consistent as that. It is custom that does that, bringing pressure to bear on Nature. And sometimes Nature hits back at custom, and contrives that a man shall follow his bent, whether good or bad.

64. *Callings:* The magic of "glory" is an attraction so powerful that we love everything to which it applies—even death.

66. *Martial's epigrams:* Men enjoy spitefulness, provided it is not directed against those blind in one eye, or otherwise unfortunate, but against the arrogance of lucky people. To act otherwise would be a great mistake.

For all our actions spring from concupiscence and from our human condition. We must please people of humane and tender feeling.

The epigram about the two one-eyed people is worthless: it gains a point for the author and adds to his renown as a wit, but it does nothing to comfort its victims. Anything of this kind, written for the benefit of the author only, is worthless. "The ambitious man abandons superfluous ornament," Horace: *Ars Poetica,* 447.

68. I wager that, if all men knew what other men were saying about them, there would not be four friends left in the world. This is evident from the quarrels sometimes caused by indiscreet repetition. Indeed, in my opinion all men would be . . .

69. Do you desire that men should think well of you? Say nothing about it.

70. A wit, but a bad character.

72. Tyranny is an inordinate desire to dominate other men.

There are various places of assembly where strong men, handsome men, intelligent men, and good men may upon occasion take the lead, though unable to do so anywhere else. And sometimes these men will engage in some foolish dispute, to see which shall be master, the strong or the handsome; for each seeks to exert his authority in a different way. They have nothing whatever in common, yet they make the mistake of wanting to lord it wherever they are. That is impossible, even when they are backed by force. Force is powerless in the realm of the intellect; force can only be master of external actions.

Tyranny is the desire to attain by one's own methods an objective which is in fact only attainable by some quite different means.

Homage is paid to merit in various ways; we pay tribute of love to what is pleasing, we are bound to fear him who can use force, we trust a man who knows.

Such homage is due and ought to be paid. It would be as unjust to refuse such tribute as it would be to demand it for the wrong reason. Thus the following claims would be unjust and therefore tyrannical: "I am handsome, therefore I should be feared"; "I am strong, and so I should be loved"; "I am . . . ," etc. It is equally unjust and tyrannical to say: "He is not strong, so I will not respect him"; "He is not clever, therefore I will not fear him."

73. *Order:* After "Corruption," say: "It is but just that all those who are in this state should be made aware of it; those who are pleased with the condition, and those who are not. But it is not right that all should see redemption."

74. Man is only a creature full of errors, which are natural and ineffaceable but for the action of grace. Nothing shows him the truth. Everything cheats him. These two sources of truth, reason and the senses, are not only both lacking in sincerity, but they also deceive one another. The senses delude reason by false appearances, and the same clever deception as the senses use to trick reason, is used by reason to confound the senses, so that reason has her revenge. The passions of the soul disturb the senses and distort the image.

But in addition to those images which are conveyed by accident and by lack of discrimination, by faculties which are in any case heterogeneous . . . (At this point we must begin the chapter on the deceiving powers.)

75. *Imagination:* It is the dominant faculty in man, and the mistress of error and falsehood; she is all the more treacherous because she does not always deceive, for she would be an infallible guide to the truth if she were an infallible rule in lying. But being mostly false, she gives no clue to her true character since she sets the same seal on true and false alike.

I am not speaking of fools, but of the wisest of men; for it is among these that imagination is most persuasive. Reason protests in vain, she is not given a chance to set a true value on things.

This proud power is the enemy of reason, and takes a delight in ruling and controlling her. To show what she is able to do wherever she pleases to intervene, imagination has given to man a second nature. She has her happy followers and her unfortunate, her healthy men and her sick, her rich and her poor. It is she who causes men to believe, to doubt, or to deny the things that reason proposes for their belief. She can suspend the operation of the senses, or she can sharpen them. She has her fools and her wise men, and nothing exasperates us more than to observe that she provides her victims with a satisfaction altogether different, fuller and more complete than anything that reason can give them. People gifted with a vivid imagination are far better pleased with themselves than prudent men would ever reasonably be: they treat other people with contempt; they dispute boldly, and with great confidence, whereas sensible men do so with modesty and self-distrust. The cheerful faces of imaginative persons often gain them an advantage with their hearers, for they make a good impression on critics of the same temperament. Imagination cannot make fools into wise men, but she can make them happy, and so she puts reason out of countenance: for reason can only make her friends wretched. Thus imagination covers her friends with glory, but reason covers hers with shame.

Who is it that hands out reputations? Who obtains respect and veneration for individuals, for creative work, for the laws, for men of rank and power, if not this imaginative faculty? All the wealth of the world would be insufficient without the help of the imagination.

Would you not say that this magistrate, whose venerable age commands the respect of the entire nation, controls his own public behavior according to the most detached and exalted principles of reason, that he judges things as they are, without taking account of mere trifles such as only touch the imaginations of the weak? But watch him as he comes in to hear a sermon, bringing to it a very devout zeal, his powerful mind warmed by his true charity. He comes prepared to listen with exemplary respect. Let the preacher appear, and let it be seen that nature has equipped him with a hoarse voice and a face exceedingly plain; let it be evident, too, that his barber has shaved that face very badly; and if, to crown all, it happens that he has thrown on his clothes in slovenly fashion—I will wager that, no matter what great truths he proceeds to expound, our magistrate's grave demeanor will disappear.

The greatest philosopher in the world may be standing upon a plank, much wider than is strictly necessary to support his weight: if a precipice were suddenly to open beneath that plank, his reason may well convince him that he is safe, but his imagination will intervene to govern his conduct. Some men could not bear even the thought of such a situation without turning pale and breaking into a sweat.

I have no desire to describe all the effects that can be wrought by the imagination. Who does not know that the sight of cats, or rats, or the crumbling of a lump of coal, etc., is enough to unhinge the reason? The tone of a speaker's voice can sway the judgment of the wisest and can alter the impact of a speech or a poem.

Love or hatred can alter the course of justice. Where an advocate has been well paid in advance, how much the more just will his client's cause appear! And how important to the judgment is his bold demeanor in court, making the case appear better than it is. How whimsical is reason, turned by a breath of air in any direction!

I could chronicle almost every human act, to show the extent to which impulses have to be provided by the imagination, before any serious social activity is undertaken; how reason has to yield, and the wisest take for their guidance principles boldly proposed and freely circulated by the human imagination.

Our magistrates are very well aware of the secret power of the imagination. Their red robes, the ermine in which they wrap themselves up like well-fed cats, the imposing courts in which they hold their assizes, the fleurs-de-lis, all that solemn paraphernalia was necessary to them; without their cassocks and their mules, their square caps and their gowns four times too big, the physicians and the divines would never have been able to deceive the world, which cannot resist a display which looks so authentic. If they really possessed the truth and the justice, if physicians truly knew the art of healing, there would be no need of square caps: the majesty of their respective sciences would be sufficient recommendation, without the trappings. But since their sciences are largely make-believe, they have to employ these vulgar ornaments to catch the imaginations of those with whom they are to have dealings. And it is precisely by this device that they acquire respect. Only soldiers on active service do not deck themselves out like that, because they are indeed engaged in matters of life or death. They have to gain their positions by force, not by making faces.

This is why our kings have not resorted to this kind of disguise. They do not dress up in extraordinary clothes to give themselves the royal air, but they have themselves escorted by guards of pikemen. The hands and strength of these armed rogues which will fight only for the king; the drums and trumpets which go before him, and the regiments marching before and behind, make the boldest men tremble. These have more than the uniform: they possess the power. We should need a very purified reason to regard the Grand Turk as a common man, when he sits amidst his forty thousand Janissaries in his magnificent seraglio.

The mere sight of counsel in cap and gown inspires great confidence in his ability.

Imagination governs all things: she creates beauty, does justice, bestows happiness, and these are the goods of mankind. I should very much like to see that Italian book, known to me only by its title (but the title alone is worth a whole library): *Della opinione regina del mondo*. I approve of what it says without having read it—evil apart, if there be any.

Such, broadly speaking, are the consequences of this deceitful faculty, which has apparently been bestowed upon us expressly to tempt us into necessary error. There are a good many other sources of such error.

Early impressions are not the only ones capable of deceiving us: the attractions of novelty have the same power. Hence arise all the quarrels of men, who blame themselves for being misled by the false impressions of childhood, or for recklessly running after novelties. Who is there that keeps the middle way? Let him come forward and prove it! There is no principle acquired during childhood or since, however natural it may appear, which cannot be represented as a false impression due to one's upbringing or to mere sense images.

"Simply because," someone says, "you have believed that a chest was empty when you saw nothing in it, you are willing to believe in the possibility of the vacuum. This is an illusion of the senses: habit has strengthened it, and science must correct it." And others say: "Because you were taught at school that there is no such thing as a vacuum, your common sense was corrupted, though before it received that misleading impression it understood the thing quite clearly; it needs to be corrected by a return to your unspoilt nature." Who, then, was the deceiver, your senses or your teachers?

We have yet another source of error, and this is sickness. It weakens our judgment and our senses; and if serious illnesses alter both to an appreciable extent, no doubt but slight ones produce comparable effects.

Self-interest is another marvelous instrument for closing our eyes to the facts in the pleasantest possible manner. It is not allowed that the most just of men should be judge in his own cause. I know some people who, to avoid this particular trap of self-love, have shown themselves capable of grave injustice out of mere reaction: the surest way of losing to them a perfectly straightforward case would be to introduce it to them through near relatives. Justice and truth are so delicate in form that our coarse grinding wheels are worn smooth upon them and cease to run true. Even when the wheels get close enough to the work to remove any material at all, there will be breaking or dislodgement of the abrasive grit, the wheel will be worn down instead of the work, and the result will be a ragged finish.[4]

76. We are not content with our personal, interior lives, but are always wanting to project upon the minds of others a fictitious notion of our own value: we actually drive

[4] This illustration, drawn from a scientist's observation of work done with a grinding wheel, is a striking application of the phenomena of chip flow in grinding operations to the interpretation of the law by a just and an unjust judge.

ourselves along so as to achieve this object. We labor ceaselessly at the cultivation and preservation of that image, and we neglect the reality that was already present. And if it happens that we do already possess such virtues as calm, or generosity, or fidelity, we eagerly proclaim them, so as to have these qualities also associated with that idealized being. Indeed, we would rather detach such virtues from ourselves, if we thought they would add anything to the image that we suppose other people to see. We would willingly be cowards, if we could thereby acquire a reputation for courage. A striking mark of the poverty of our human condition, that we are not satisfied with the one, the man as he is, unless we have also the other, the man we would like to be, and are so often ready to exchange the former for the latter! For a man who would not die to protect his honor would cover himself with shame.

77. Belief is natural to the mind, and it is natural for the will to love: so much so that if valid objects be lacking they will necessarily attach themselves to false ones.

78. How is it that a crippled man does not irritate us and a twisted mind does? Because the cripple is aware that we are walking upright, whereas the twisted mind declares that it is other men who are out of step. But for that, we should be sorry for him rather than irritated.

Epictetus, with considerably more force, inquires: "We are not displeased to be told we have a headache; why are we put out if someone says that our reasoning is faulty or our conclusion erroneous?" The reason is, that we can be quite certain we have no headache and are not lame; but we are not so certain that we are reaching a correct conclusion. Hence, our certitude is based only on what we can see for ourselves; so when someone else reaches a contrary conclusion from the same arguments, the fact disturbs and perplexes us; still more so, where a whole multitude derides our decision. For we are bound to prefer our own conclusion, though it is a bold and difficult thing to do. Our senses never experience any such contradiction in relation to a cripple.

80. Children are frightened by a face they themselves have blackened. They are children. But how is it that so weak a

creature as a child grows up to be a strong and vigorous man? All that changes in us is the imagery of the mind. All that progresses toward perfection is also destroyed by that very progress. That which once was weak can never attain to perfect strength. We say in vain: "How he has grown! How he has changed!"; he remains the same person.

82. Time heals our griefs and quarrels because we change; we are no longer the same person. Neither the offended party nor the offender is any longer the person he was. It is as with another nation with whom, two generations ago, we had a quarrel. They are still Frenchmen, but they are not the same Frenchmen.

83. He has ceased to love the woman he loved ten years ago. I can well believe it; she is not the same—nor he either. He was young, she also was young; she is now quite different. He might still love her, if she were still what she used to be.

84. Not only do we look at things from another angle, we see them with other eyes. We have no wish to find them the same.

85. The things to which we cling most obstinately, such as the desire to conceal our poverty, are very often of small consequence—a trifle which imagination magnifies into a mountain. A little more of imaginative effort would enable us to disclose it without difficulty.

87. The sensitivity of man to trifles, and his insensitivity to great things, shows a strange reversal of values.

88. Being insensitive to the point of despising things that are important, and becoming insensitive to that matter which is the most important one of all.

90. Men often mistake the imagination for the heart; and they believe themselves converted as soon as the idea of conversion comes into their heads.

91. *Vanity:* That a thing as evident as the vanity of the world should be so little known, and that it should be consid-

ered a strange and surprising thing to call it folly to seek greatness—these are wonderful things, indeed.

92. How many kingdoms remain in ignorance of us!

93. Anyone who wants to appreciate to the full the vanity of man needs only to reflect on the causes and effects of love. The cause is a *je ne sais quoi* (Corneille) and the effects are alarming. This *je ne sais quoi*, so tiny a thing that we cannot even identify it, rocks an entire country, sways princes, sets armies marching, convulses the world.

Cleopatra's nose: had it been shorter, the face of the whole earth would have been changed.

94. Anyone who does not perceive the vanity of this world must himself be exceedingly superficial. Indeed, who could fail to see it, apart from the young who are busy making a noise, absorbed in their amusements, or preparing for their future? But take away their amusements, and you will see them begin to wilt out of mere *ennui*. It is then that they feel their own inadequacy, without realizing what it is. For it is a most unfortunate situation for a man to find himself in—to find himself plunged into an unutterable sadness the moment he is reduced to thinking about himself. He does not find that subject amusing.

95. We are so unhappy that we can only take pleasure in doing a thing on the understanding that we may without blame be annoyed if it fails; which may and indeed does happen perpetually in a thousand instances. He who could discover the secret of how to be happy in the good, without being greatly displeased by the contrary evil, would have found the key to a great mystery. It is like perpetual motion.

96. Great and small are exposed to the same chances, the same vexations, the same passions; but one is at the top of the wheel, and the other near the hub, so that he is less disturbed by the same movements.

100. Those who continue to hope when their business affairs bring them disappointment, and rejoice when they turn out well, fall under suspicion (unless they appear equally distressed by reverses) of being pleased if they can show a

loss; and they are delighted to come across misleading grounds for hope, so that they can appear to take an interest and cover up with simulated joy their real satisfaction at seeing the venture lost.

101. Small things comfort us because little things afflict us.

102. The mind of this supreme judge of the world is not so independent that it can escape being upset by the slightest disturbance in its neighborhood. It does not require the report of a gun to break his train of thought: the creaking of a weathercock or a pulley is quite sufficient. Do not be surprised if he is unable to argue well just at this moment, for a fly is buzzing in his ears, and that is quite enough to render him incapable of sound judgment. If you want him to arrive at the truth, drive away this creature that holds his reason in check, and can trouble the powerful intellect that governs cities and kingdoms. An amusing sort of deity, this, indeed! O most ridiculous hero!

104. Men are necessarily mad, so that not to be mad would only be another form of madness.

105. My knowledge of the physical sciences will not console me in times of affliction for my ignorance of the moral law. But the moral law will always comfort me and make up what I lack in knowledge of the physical sciences.

107. Men are not taught the things that a cultivated man seems to know by intuition, though they are taught everything else. And they are not vexed about any other deficiency as they are about this one, that they are not taught formally any of the things that belong to a general culture. Their great and only desire is to know the one art they have no opportunity to learn.

110. When we do not know the truth about a thing, it is as well that there should be a common error to occupy men's minds: for example, we attribute the changes of the seasons, and the spread of epidemics, to the moon and so on. For the chief disorder from which men suffer is an anxious curiosity about things which he cannot know. This idle curiosity is a

worse condition for him to be in than is error itself.

But when I had thought it over a little more carefully, and had discovered the source of all our ills, I also wanted to know the reason for them. I then found that there is one very striking reason, namely, the natural evil in our weak human nature, which is so wretched that once we have begun to consider it carefully nothing can give us any comfort.

We may imagine ourselves placed in any state of life whatsoever, furnished with all the good things it is possible to possess, yet royalty is still the most advantageous of all conditions. Even so, we have but to imagine a king surrounded by everything that can give him satisfaction—if he lacks amusement, and is left to ponder what he is, and to reflect upon his condition, his affluence will not suffice to cheer his drooping spirits. He will of necessity brood over the constant threat from hostile interests, from the outbreak of revolt, from sickness and death, none of which things can be avoided. Thus, if he is without what we call "amusement," he will be unhappy, and more so than the least of his subjects, who are at least free to play games and find their own amusements.

Hence it is that gaming, female company, war, and positions of power in the state, are so much sought after. Not that these things give true contentment, nor that anyone really believes that true happiness comes from the possession of money won at cards, or from the successful coursing of a hare: we would not accept such things as gifts. We do not seek the soft and piping peace which would leave us free to brood upon our unhappy condition, nor do we desire for themselves the perils of war, nor the toilsome burden of high office; what we seek is the bustle and the noise to compel our thoughts away from our condition and from the need to think about it.

(Reasons why we prefer the hunt to the kill.)

This is why men are so fond of noise and agitation, why prison is so horrid a torment, why any delight in solitude is a thing not to be understood, and finally why the chief reason a king can have for being pleased with his position is that men endeavor to provide him with a round of amusements and to procure for him pleasures of every description.

111. *Ennui:* Nothing is so unbearable to a man as a condition of complete rest, without passions, without business,

without amusements, and without the need for application. It is then that he feels his own nothingness, his abandoned state, his insufficiency, his dependent condition, his powerlessness, the vacuum within. Forthwith there wells up from the depths of his soul, *ennui,* blackness, sadness, melancholy, disgust, despair.

112. Movement is essential to our human nature. Absolute rest is death.

113. *Agitation:* When a soldier complains of the hardness of his life, or a laborer, etc., try leaving him with nothing to do!

114. The boredom we feel if we lay aside the occupations to which we have become accustomed. A man lives pleasantly enough at home, but show him a charming woman, give him five or six days of happy play. He is wretched enough then, if he has to return to his former condition. Nothing is more familiar than that.

115. Without probing into the occupations of individuals, it is enough to group them under the heading of "distractions."

116. *Distractions:* When I set myself, as I sometimes do, to consider the various disturbances in men's lives, the perils and hardships to which they are exposed at Court and in war (both of them fertile fields for so many quarrels, so much violence, so many bold and often wicked enterprises), I have often remarked that all the unhappiness of man arises from one thing only, namely that he is incapable of abiding quietly in one room. A man who has enough to live on would never leave it to go to sea or to sit down before a fortress and besiege it, if only he knew how to stay happily at home. No man would pay so dear for his commission, but that he finds it unbearable never to leave town. And men only engage in conversation and the distractions of gaming because they are unable to remain happily at home.

(A king is surrounded by people whose sole preoccupation is his amusement, to prevent him from thinking about himself. For though he be a king, he is unhappy if he reflects upon the fact.)

That is all that men have been able to devise to make themselves happy. Those who make it an excuse to play the philosopher, and who think it unreasonable that men spend a whole day in hunting a hare which they would never have taken the trouble to buy, know very little about our human nature. The hare would not protect us against the spectacle of death or against the unhappiness we have yet to encounter before we meet it, whereas the hunt does provide us with necessary distraction, and therefore gives us a certain protection.

The advice given to Pyrrhus, to enjoy the rest he was so laboriously seeking, created a great many difficulties.

(To say to a man that he should live quietly, is as much as to say that he should live happily. It advises him to create for himself a condition altogether happy, in which he can reflect at his leisure without finding anything that need distress him. People who give such advice do not understand the laws of Nature.

And so men who are conscious of their condition avoid rest above all things: there is nothing they will not do to seek out trouble. They indeed have another secret instinct which teaches them that true happiness consists in . . . [vanity, the pleasure of showing off.]

Thus it is wrong to blame them; their fault is not that they seek bustle, provided that all they seek is some form of strenuous occupation. What is wrong is, that they seek it as though the mere possession of the things they seek could make them truly happy; and it is for this reason that we may rightly charge them with vanity. Thus the situation is completely misunderstood, and neither the persons blamed nor those who blame them have any understanding of the real nature of man.)

Thus, we might well reproach them with putting so much enthusiasm into a quest which cannot bring them the slightest satisfaction. They might reply—as they ought to do if they gave the matter any serious thought—that they were only engaging in a violent, impetuous activity which would serve to force their thoughts away from themselves, and that it was for this reason that they had chosen a pleasing object which drew them strongly toward it. This defense would leave their opponents speechless. But they do not make this answer because they do not know themselves. They do not realize that it is the chase they enjoy, rather than the capture.

(Dancing: We have to think carefully where we are going to put our feet. The country gentleman sincerely believes that hunting is a great and royal sport, but his beater is not of that opinion.)

They persuade themselves that if they had obtained the office they sought, they would then have been able to live both quietly and happily: they do not reckon with their own cupidity, nor realize how far-reaching it is. They claim that their search for a state of rest is sincere: whereas in reality what they seek is the excitement of a novel quest.

They have a secret instinct which drives them to look for diversion and occupation outside of themselves, and this urge originates in a consciousness of their own state of perpetual wretchedness; and another secret instinct they have, a relic of the high dignity of man's nature before his fall, which compels them to recognize that happiness is to be found only in a state of rest and not in turmoil. But of these two conflicting interests a confused project begins to take shape, though it remains hidden from their sight in the depths of the soul, which deludes them with the notion that they can attain a state of rest by plunging into activities; and they imagine that the contentment which they certainly do not now enjoy will be theirs when they have dealt with one or two foreseeable obstacles standing between themselves and the gateway to the state of rest.

Thus the whole of life slips away from them. They think to attain rest by eliminating one or two obstacles that stand in their path. And supposing they succeed in doing that, rest becomes intolerable to them because it turns into boredom. Then they have to seek escape from their rest, and run after excitement, for their thoughts are busy with present troubles, or with those that threaten them. And even if they could see that they were in fact adequately protected on every side, still it would not be long before boredom arose of its own accord in the depths of the heart, where it has its natural roots and filled the mind with its poison.

Thus the condition of man is so unhappy that he would still be bored, even where there is no cause for boredom. This is due to the complex nature of his being; and so frivolous is his mind that, though he had indeed a thousand perfectly valid reasons for despair, yet the most trifling thing, such as a billiard table and a ball to push about on it, is sufficient to distract him.

"But," you will ask, "what can be the object of such activity?" He wants to be able to boast to his friends tomorrow that he has played a better game than someone else. For the same reason, another man will sit sweating in his study, to prove to other scholars that he has solved a problem in algebra which no one before them had been able to solve. Others expose themselves to mortal danger, so that they can boast afterwards that they captured a strongpoint, and in my opinion this is just as stupid. Finally, yet other men wear themselves out with special studies, not that they may thereby become wiser, but only to display their knowledge. These are the most foolish of all, because their study and their display of it are deliberate; whereas we may suppose that the other types we have mentioned would abandon their respective follies once they were made aware of them.

A man in danger of boredom may pass a little of each day in gambling. Try giving him each morning the money he might expect to win during the day so that he need not gamble: you will make him anything but happy. It may be pleaded for him that what he seeks is the pleasure of play, and not the winnings. Well, then, make him play for nothing: he will get no excitement out of that at all and will merely be bored by the game. So it is not the mere pleasure of the game that attracts him: a mild pastime without a strong motive of excitement will merely bore him. He needs to get excited, and to delude himself with the thought that he may have the happiness of winning something (which he would not take if you offered it to him to stop him from gambling), so long as he can satisfy a craving for excitement, and stimulate his desire, his anger, his fear upon an illusory object which he has proposed to himself: just like those children who frighten themselves with a face they have themselves blackened.

How comes it that a man who, a few months ago, lost his only son, and who this very morning was deep in troubles, harrassed by lawsuits and disputes, no longer gives these things a thought? Do not be surprised. He is now completely absorbed in watching for the coming of the boar, which his hounds have been following closely for the last six hours. He needs nothing more. A man of sorrows he may be, but if you can induce him to take up some amusement, he will be happy while it lasts. And however happy a man may be, if he is not distracted and completely absorbed in some passion or pursuit which keeps away boredom, he will soon become morose and unhappy. Without amusement, there is no joy; with it, there is no sadness. This it is, also, which makes the happiness of persons of position who, having many people about them, are always provided with entertainment, and have the means to continue in that state.

But be careful: What does it mean to be a superintendent of finance, a chancellor, a judge, if not that the position of such men exposes them from morning till night to the importunities of a great many people who come from every quarter, and who leave them not an hour in the day when they can think about themselves? And when they fall into disgrace they are dismissed and banished to their estates, where they have no lack of material things, nor of servants to minister to every need; yet they are still wretched in the knowledge that they have been dropped, since they no longer have anyone to tear their thoughts away from themselves.

117. Men divert themselves by running after a ball or a hare; even for kings it is a diversion.

118. (How is it that this man, who is so afflicted by the death of his wife and his only son, and is also plagued by a great lawsuit, is not at this moment sad, and appears to be completely free from painful and disturbing thoughts? We need not wonder at this: he has just been served a ball and must return it to his partner; he is completely absorbed in the problem of how to counter his partner's ball by a stroke off the back penthouse, to win the set. How do you suppose he can spare a thought for serious business, with an important matter like this in hand? Here is a problem well adapted to the powers of a great soul, and calculated to blot out every other thought from his mind. Here is a man who was born to know the universe, to assess the values of all things, to govern a whole state; and behold him engaged to the limit of his considerable powers, in the business of catching a hare. And if he does not stoop so low, but wants to be always bolt-upright and full of his dignity, the more fool he, that he should want to raise himself above the common level. When all is said and done, he is but a man,

capable of little and much, of everything and nothing, neither angel nor beast, but simply man.)

119. Caesar was too old, it seems to me, to go wasting his time on world conquest. That kind of pastime was all right for Augustus or Alexander: they were young, and it is difficult to halt the young. But Caesar should have known better.

120. Despite all this misery, man desires to be happy, and desires only that; he cannot wish not to be happy. But how is he to set about it? To make a good job of it he would have to make himself immortal; but since he cannot do that, he has made up his mind to stop himself from thinking about it.

121. *Diversion:* Is not the dignity of a king sufficient in itself to make its possessor happy in the mere contemplation of what he is? Must he be diverted from thinking about himself, like common folk? I see clearly enough that one way of making a man happy is to tear his eyes away from the consideration of his private troubles, and make him concentrate all his powers on becoming a really good dancer. But is it the same with a king? Will he be the happier if he turns to such frivolous amusements as these, rather than to the contemplation of his own greatness? What more satisfying object than that could we present to his mind? Would it not spoil his pleasure, if he had to concentrate his thoughts on moving his feet according to the beats of a tune, or on the accurate throwing of a bar, instead of being left in the quiet enjoyment of the glory of majesty of which he is himself the center? Let someone put it to the test: Let a king be left all by himself, with nothing to gratify his senses, no care upon his mind, and no companion; let him thus be left to think at leisure about himself, and it will soon be seen that a king without diversions is a man full of wretchedness. For this reason, people are careful to see that it does not happen, and there is never any lack of persons about a king, whose job it is to see that amusement follows business, and who devote the whole of their leisure to devising entertainments and games for him, so as to leave no part of his time vacant. That is to say, a king is surrounded by people who take very good care

that he is not left alone, with nothing to do but think about himself; for they are well aware that, king though he be, he will only be miserable if he thinks about it.

In saying this, I am far from speaking of Christian kings as Christians, but only in so far as they are kings.

122. *Diversion:* Once they leave childhood behind, men are made responsible for the preservation of their own honor, their own goods, and their friendships, as well as with the safety of the goods and reputations of their friends. Society loads them with business, they begin to learn languages, they go in for bodily exercise, and they are made to understand that, unless their own health, wealth, and reputation and those of their friends also, are in good order, they cannot expect to be happy, and that if but one of these things be lacking it will be enough to make them miserable. Also they are given things to do, and business to keep them going from break of day.

That, you will say, is a strange way of making them happy! What, more than this, need be done, to render them miserable? Done, do you ask? You need only deprive them of all those responsibilities. For then they would have time to look at themselves, to reflect on what they are, and whence they came, and where they are going; and so one cannot do too much to keep them occupied, with their minds applied to their business. And that is why, having given them so much to do, we advise them to give any leisure they may have to wholehearted amusement and play, and to being fully occupied. ("For the heart of man is empty, and full of wickedness," Eccles. 24.)

123. *Thoughts:* "In all things I sought rest," Eccles. 24:7. If our condition were truly happy, we should not need to distract our thoughts from it so as to attain a little happiness.

125. *Wretchedness:* The only thing that consoles us in the midst of our wretchedness is diversion; and yet this is the greatest of our miseries, since it is mainly our diversions which frustrate self-examination, and so imperceptibly lead to our ruin. Without our diversions we should fall into a state of boredom, and this condition would drive us to seek

a more reliable way of escape. But our diversions entertain us and lead us imperceptibly toward death.

126. To fear death when out of danger, and not when in danger; for one must play the man.

127. Sudden death is the only thing that should be feared. That is why confessors dwell with the great.

128. The wretched conditions of human life have been the cause of our present situation. Having perceived this, men have taken to amusing themselves.

129. *Diversion:* Since they are unable to find a cure for death, misery, ignorance, men have decided that they can attain to happiness by not thinking about such things.

130. *Diversion:* If man were happy, he might be all the happier if he needed less amusement, like the saints and God. —Yes; but is not the capacity of being pleased by our amusements a happy state in itself? —No; because our amusements are derived from somewhere else, they are external to ourselves; so man is dependent, and liable to be disturbed by a thousand accidents which create for him inevitable troubles.

131. We are not bored by the necessity of eating and sleeping every day, for hunger returns, the need of sleep is felt again. If we lacked either of these needs, we might well be bored! Similarly, if we had no hunger for the things of the spirit, we should be bored by them. Hunger for justice: the eighth Beatitude.

132. Only the struggle pleases us, we are not concerned for victory. We enjoy watching a fight between animals, but not the spectacle of the winner mauling the victim; what else but the final victory should we wish to see? And by the time that comes, we have had enough. So with cards and with the search for truth. During a debate we enjoy following the collision of opinions; we are not so pleased with the truth which emerges from the debate. To get *that* accepted with approval, it has to be seen that it is fairly established by the debate. It is the same with the passions: there is

a pleasure gained from observing the clash of two opposed passions; but when one of these has prevailed, continuance of the strife is mere brutality. We never pursue things for themselves—it is the pursuit itself that we enjoy. At the theater, we care little for the tranquil scenes which lack the tension of terror; nor scenes of extreme and hopeless misery, of brutish love, or harsh cruelty.

133. All the popular amusements are a danger for the life of the Christian; but of all those pleasures which the world has invented, there is not one which is more to be feared than the theater. The representation of the passions is so subtle, so faithful to nature, that the same passions are awakened and strengthened in our own hearts; above all, the passion of love, especially when it is portrayed as very chaste and very proper. For the more innocent the appearance of love to simple minds, the more inclined they are to be attracted to it. Its impetuous violence pleases our own self-love, which instantly develops a desire to produce the same effects as we have seen so well represented. At the same time, we develop a conscience adapted to the well-regulated conduct we have been watching, which is very reassuring to ordinary souls who persuade themselves that where love is so obviously prudent, purity can suffer no harm.

We leave the theater with our hearts full of the beauty and tenderness of love, our hearts and minds convinced of its innocence, so that we are fully prepared for the reception of its first impressions, or rather, ready to seek out occasions for awakening love in the heart of someone else, so that we may ourselves experience the same pleasures and call for the same sacrifices as we have seen so well acted on the stage.

136. To speak with sympathy of the unfortunate is not opposed to concupiscence. On the contrary, we are well pleased to have an opportunity to give lip service to friendships, gain a reputation for benevolence, and still give nothing.

137. Vanity is so deeply rooted in the heart of man that a soldier, a camp follower, a cook, a common porter will brag to gain the admiration of the public. Even philosophers covet it, and critics, who adopt a hostile attitude to most writers, still desire the reputation of writing well themselves;

while those who read the critics hope to enhance their own reputation by such reading; and it may well be that I who write these words am moved by the same desire; and perhaps those who read them . . .

138. Good deeds are most praiseworthy if they be kept out of sight. Whenever I come across such actions in history they give me the greatest pleasure. All the same, these deeds have not been completely hidden, since the record is there, and although the doer may have done what he could to hide his action, the mere mention has kept the memory of it alive and so has spoilt everything, for the most appealing thing about it was the desire to hide it.

139. *On the desire to be thought well of by present company:* Pride keeps such a tight hold on us in the midst of our wretchedness, errors, etc. We would gladly lay down life itself, provided people would talk about it!

Vanity: gaming, hunting, paying visits, the theater, a bogus reputation.

141. *Pride:* Curiosity is nothing but vanity. Most men only want to know things so that they can talk about them. Otherwise, if there were no prospect of ever being able to tell people about it, nobody would ever go to sea merely for the pleasure of looking at it, and without the slightest hope of ever being able to communicate that pleasure.

142. *Glory:* Admiration ruins everything, from childhood onwards. "Oh, what a clever thing to say!" "He has done that very well!" "What a good child!" etc.

The children of Port-Royal are not spurred on in this way to emulation and glory, so *they* fall into listlessness.

143. *Contradiction:* Pride supplies a counterweight for every form of misery. Either a man will hide his wretchedness, or if he discloses it, he will be proud of the fact that he can face it and acknowledge it.

145. *Self-love:* It is the nature of self-love and of this human ego to love self alone and to think only of self. But what can a man do? He will not be able so to order things, as to

prevent this object of his love from being full of faults and wretchedness. He wants to be great, and finds that he is small; he wants to be happy, and finds himself unhappy; he wants to be perfect, and finds himself full of imperfections; he would like to be the object of the affection and esteem of men, yet he sees that his faults deserve nothing but their aversion and contempt. Thus he finds himself in a dilemma, and the situation creates in him the most unjust and wicked anger it is possible to imagine; for he conceives a deadly hatred for the truth itself, that truth which rebukes him and convinces him of his deficiencies. He would like to be able to annihilate it, but being unable to blot out the truth itself he destroys its power (so far as he can) over his own mind and the minds of other people; that is to say, he concentrates all his efforts on concealing his deficiencies not only from others but also from himself, and he cannot bear to have others point them out to him, or even that they should observe them.

No doubt it is a bad thing to be full of faults, but it is a greater evil to be full of them and yet to be unwilling to recognize them, since that is to add the further fault of self-delusion. We are watchful that other people do not fool us: we think it unjust that they should wish us to have a better opinion of them than they deserve. It is but justice therefore that we should not deceive them, nor desire that they should think better of us than we deserve.

When, therefore, people draw our attention only to such imperfections and vices as we do in fact possess, it is clear not only that they do us no wrong, since they in no way cause those faults, but that they actually do us a service, since they intervene to deliver us from a positive evil, which is our blindness to those imperfections. We ought not to be angry that they should know about them and despise us for them; for it is right that they should know us for what we are, and it is but just that they should despise us if we are despicable.

Such reflections would occur naturally to a heart that was full of equity and justice. What are we to say then of our own heart when we notice in it a completely opposite disposition? For is it not true that we hate the truth and those who tell us the truth, and that we are pleased that they should delude themselves, if it is to our own advantage?

And that we are willing to have them think of us as other than we really are?

Here is a proof of it which horrifies me. The Catholic religion does not compel us to disclose our sins indiscriminately to everybody; it allows us to remain hidden from all other men save one only, and to him we are commanded to reveal the depths of our hearts, and to show ourselves as we are. There is only this one man in the world, to whom at the command of the Church we must disclose everything; and upon him she imposes an inviolable secrecy, with the result that to all intents and purposes this knowledge he has acquired of us ceases to exist. Can anything more charitable or more tender be imagined? And yet the corruption of man is such, that he is always finding this law a hardship; and it is one of the chief reasons for the revolt of a great part of Europe against the Church.

How unjust and unreasonable is the heart of man, that he should feel it a hardship that he is made to do before one man what it would, in a way, be just that he should do in the presence of all. For would it be right that we should deceive all?

There are different degrees in this aversion to the truth, but it may be said to exist in all of us to some extent, because it is inseparable from self-love. It is this false sense of delicacy which impels those whose duty it is to administer rebuke, to take such devious ways, and use such carefully moderated phraseology in order to avoid giving offense. They feel they must diminish the gravity of our offenses, and even appear to make excuse for them; throw in a word of praise, and speak to us with zeal, with concern to protect our good repute.[5] But despite all this, the medicine is always bitter to self-love. We take as little of it as we can, and always with loathing, even a secret resentment, against those who administer it.

The consequence is that anyone who wants to retain our friendship will be careful not to render us a service of this kind, which they know would displease us: they treat us as we wish to be treated. We hate the truth, so they hide it

[5] The seventeenth-century connotations of the words used by Pascal in this passage bring out very clearly the delicacy and the accuracy of his thought on the subject of the sacrament of penance. Protestant writers tend to interpret him always as the writer of the *Provincial Letters.*

from us; we like to be flattered, so they flatter us; we enjoy being deceived, so they deceive us.

This is why each stroke of good fortune, while it raises us up in the world, also carries us farther away from the truth, because people are more afraid of upsetting those whose goodwill is likely to be useful, and to alienate whom might be dangerous. A prince may be a byword throughout Europe, and he himself be the only person who does not know it. I am not surprised: to tell the truth is useful to the man to whom it is told, but a handicap to those who tell it, because they make themselves unpopular. Now, those who live with princes prefer their own interest to that of the prince they serve, so they take great care not to do him the kind of good turn that will only bring harm to themselves.

No doubt this is a misfortune more common and more keenly felt in the members of the wealthier classes, but the simple are not exempt from it, because there is always something to be gained by making quite sure that people will like us. Thus life in society is nothing but a state of perpetual deceit, a round of mutual trickery and mutual flattery, and no man speaks of us in our presence as he speaks of us behind our backs. Such unity as is to be found among men is based upon no other principle but that of tacit hoodwinking, and few friendships would last if each of us knew what his friend was saying of him when out of his hearing, even though what was then said were a sincere and impartial opinion.

Man is then nothing but guile, dissimulation, and hypocrisy, self-deceived, and bluffing all with whom he has to do. He has no desire to be told the truth, and he avoids telling it to other people; and all these tendencies, so far removed from justice and from goodness, are rooted by his own nature in his own heart.

146. "The ego is hateful: you, Miton, cover it up, but that does not mean that you get rid of it. You are therefore always hateful." "Not at all; for by behaving as we do with civility toward all, nobody has any longer any reason to hate us." "That would be true enough, supposing that what people hated about our ego was the reaction of personal resentment it made them feel. But if I hate it because it is contrary to justice, because it makes itself the center of everything, I must of necessity always hate it."

In a word, the ego has two characteristics: it contains an element of injustice, because it makes itself the center of everything, and it is a nuisance to other people because it seeks to dominate and make use of them. For every ego is a foe to all men, and desires to tyrannize over them. You may lighten in various ways the burden imposed by tyranny, but you cannot remove the injustice of it, and so you cannot render it an object of love to those who hate it because it is unjust. You render it an object of love only to the unjust, who no longer find that the tyrant is their enemy; thus you remain unjust, and consequently you are acceptable only to them.

147. It is not true that we deserve the love of our neighbor, and it is contrary to justice for us to desire it. If we were born reasonable and impartial, knowing ourselves and knowing other men, we should never allow our will to entertain any such desire. However, it is born with us, so that we are born unjust—for every man seeks his own. This is contrary to order, for we ought to seek the common good, and the tendency to seek one's own is the fount of all disorder and disagreement, whether in military strategy, or in political and social policy, or in the management of the home, or even in the body of the individual. For the human will is depraved.

If the members of communities, whether of animals or human beings, were to seek the welfare of all, the communities themselves would necessarily tend to seek the good of the larger and wider organization of which they are members. To seek this common good is a natural tendency. That we do not do so is evidence that we are born in a state of injustice, and are depraved.

148. What a derangement of the judgment, that every individual should esteem himself above all other men, preferring his own good, that is, his own lasting happiness and length of life, to that of the rest of men!

149. Each man is to himself a complete being, for if he die, all things are dead to him. It is for this reason that each man comes to believe that he can himself be all things to all men. We must not measure nature by our human standards, but as she is in herself.

150. Self-will is never satisfied, even though all its desires be within its reach. But the moment we relinquish the desire, we find satisfaction. If we are without self-will, we cannot fall into discontent; and the gratifying of self-will cannot bestow happiness.

151. He who does not hate the self-love in himself and the impulse which drives him to make himself his own God, must be blind indeed. Can any man not see that nothing could be more contrary to justice and truth? For to claim that man merits such a position would be an error; and for any man to attain it would involve injustice and be impossible, since all men are claiming the same thing. It is clear that the claim springs from an impulse to injustice with which men are born; that they cannot themselves get rid of it, but that they must somehow get rid of it.

No [other] religion, however, has distinguished self-love as a sin, nor declared that men are born in sin, nor taught that we are obliged to resist sin, nor made provision of remedies for sin.

152. [Imagine] a man in a dungeon, not knowing whether sentence has been passed upon him, having but one hour in which to find out, and but one hour of grace in which to appeal, once the sentence has been pronounced. It would be contrary to nature if he spent that hour, not in finding out whether sentence had been pronounced, but in playing piquet. Thus it is by a dispensation of Providence, etc. It would be to make the hand of God too heavy.

Thus God is proved, not only by the zeal of those who seek Him, but also by the blindness of those who seek Him not.

153. In my opinion it is right not to investigate too closely the opinions of Copernicus: but this! . . . The whole course of life is decided by knowing whether the soul is mortal or immortal.

154. Let us imagine a number of men in fetters, and all condemned to death, some of whom are executed each day in the sight of the others, so that the survivors see their own state in that of their fellows and await their turn, looking at one another in sorrow and without hope. That is a picture of the human condition.

155. Man does not know where he belongs. He has obviously gone astray and has fallen from his proper place. He cannot find his way back to it, though he seeks it everywhere in great anxiety but without success, moving about in impenetrable darkness.

156. Our own temerity throws us over the edge of the precipice, although we had put something in front of us so that we should not see it.

157. *Thought:* It is thought that makes the greatness of man.

158. All the dignity of man lies in his power of thought. But how does he use this power of thought? Upon mere folly.

Thought, then, is of its nature marvelous and incomparable. It would need to undergo some very strange perversions before it became despicable, but it does in fact display aberrations of such a nature that nothing could be more ridiculous. How noble is the nature of thought! How debased by its aberrations!

159. Man is clearly made for thought: therein lies all his dignity and all his merit, and the whole of his duty is to think as he should. Now the order of thought is, to begin with oneself and to go on to one's Author and one's end. But what do people in fact think about? Never about *that,* but about dancing, playing the lute, singing, writing verses, tilting the ring, etc., fighting, making oneself a king—though with never a thought of what it means to be a king—or to be a man, for the matter of that.

160. *The thinking reed:* Man is but a reed, the weakest thing in nature; but he is a thinking reed. It is not necessary, in order to crush him, that the entire universe should take up arms: a mist, a drop of water, will suffice to kill him. But even if the universe were to crush him, man would still be nobler than his destroyer, because he would know himself to be dying, and he would know in what respect the universe is mightier than he; but of these things the universe knows nothing whatever.

All our dignity therefore lies in thought. It is by thought that man is exalted, and not by [his control of] space or time, which he can never fill. Let us therefore apply ourselves to right thinking: that is the starting point of morality.

161. *The thinking reed:* It is not from space that I must seek to obtain my dignity, but from the control of my thought. The possession of whole worlds would give me no more. The spaces of the universe enfold me and swallow me up like a speck; but I, by the power of thought, may comprehend the universe.

162. I can easily imagine a man without hands, feet, head (for it is only experience which teaches us that the head is more necessary than feet). But I cannot imagine a man lacking the power of thought: he would be but a stone or a brute.

163. The arithmetical machine achieves results which come nearer to thought than anything that animals can do; but it does nothing that would justify a claim that it possesses willpower, such as animals possess.

164. If an animal did by the power of thought what it does by instinct, and if it could communicate by the power of thought as it does by instinct when hunting, when it warns the rest of the pack that the quarry is found or lost, then surely it would also convey its thoughts about matters which affect it still more closely. For example, it would say: "Gnaw through this cord which is chafing me and which I can't reach."

165. Liancourt's story of the pike and the frog: the same unvarying activity, and never a trace of thought.

166. The parakeet forever wiping its beak, although it is perfectly clean.

167. *Pursuit of the true good:* Most men say that the true good lies in wealth, in material possessions, or at least in amusements. Philosophers have shown that such things are vain, and they look for their good where they can.

168. It is good to be weary and exhausted by the unrewarded search for the true good, so that we may stretch out our arms to the Redeemer.

169. The greatness of man is great in that he knows his own misery. A tree does not know its misery.

Therefore it is misery to know one's own misery; but that one knows oneself miserable is a mark of greatness.

170. The very multitude of his miseries is proof of his greatness. These are the miseries of a great lord, this is the wretchedness of a king deposed.

171. We are not wretched unless we feel it: a house in ruins is not wretched. Only man feels his wretchedness: "I am the man who has seen . . .," Jer. Lamentations 3:1.

172. *The greatness of man:* The greatness of man is so evident that it may be inferred even from his condition of wretchedness. For the condition which in animals is simply their state of nature, we describe as wretchedness when we speak of man; whereby we recognize that his nature today is on a level with that of animals, so that he must have fallen from a better nature that once was proper to him.

For what man was ever unhappy that he was not a king—except a king who has been deposed? Was Paulus Aemilius thought to be unhappy that he was no longer Consul? On the contrary: everyone acknowledged that he had once held the office and that each holder had to step down, and must not expect to occupy the position permanently. But it was recognized that Perseus was unhappy to be no longer king, since his tenure of the kingly office was supposed to be for life, and it seemed strange that he could endure life after being deprived of the royal dignity. Who is unhappy that he has but one mouth? And who will not be unhappy if he has but one eye? Probably nobody ever thought it worthwhile to fret because he had not three eyes; but a man who has none at all is inconsolable.

173. Despite the panorama of human sorrows, the woes that concern us directly and have us by the throat, there is in man an irrepressible instinct which lifts him up.

174. *Instinct. Reason:* Our inability to prove certain things renders us impervious to all forms of dogmatism. We have an idea of the truth which no skepticism is able to shake.

175. Reason governs men far more imperiously than any master: for if we disobey a master we may be unhappy, but if we disobey reason we show ourselves fools.

176. We desire the truth, and we find within ourselves only uncertainty. We seek happiness, and we find only misery and death. We cannot help desiring truth and happiness, yet we are incapable of either certainty or happiness. This desire persists in us, as much for our punishment as to make us realize the degree of perfection from which we have unhappily fallen.

177. *Man's greatness:* So high is our esteem of the reasoning power of man, that we cannot bear to be despised, or not to be esteemed, by reasonable men. And the measure of that esteem is our own estimate of the sum total of our happiness.

178. *Glory:* Animals do not admire one another. A horse does not admire another horse. It is not that they do not run to win when they are on the racecourse, but that confers no glory; for once they are back in the stable the ponderous, large-framed and heavy-headed horse does not give up his oats to the other, as men might wish to be treated. Their virtue is its own reward.

179. The most despicable feature of man is his desire for glory, and yet this very desire is also a mark of his excellence. For whatever worldly goods he may have, whatever health he may enjoy, or whatever material comforts, he is not satisfied unless he also have the esteem of other men. So important does it seem to him that he should stand well with them, that no matter what his own earthly advantage may be, he is not content unless he also have the deference of his neighbors. A high place in public opinion is the noblest situation in the world, and nothing can divert his attention

from it: this is the most enduring characteristic of the human heart.

And those who most despise humanity and reduce men to the level of animals, still desire to enjoy their goodwill and their confidence so that their own behavior gives the lie to the opinion they express; for their instinct is the strongest argument they acknowledge, and this has convinced them more effectively of man's greatness than their reasoning powers have persuaded them that the inferiority of man makes him of no account.

180. Admirable rules of civil government, morality, and justice have been founded upon, or derived from, concupiscence. But when we get down to rock bottom, that evil principle of corruption is only covered up, it is not taken away.

181. All men naturally hate one another. An appeal has been made to concupiscence, and every effort has been made to harness it for the public good; but this is only tactics, a feint, a bogus claim to a charity which is nonexistent, for in reality there is nothing but hatred.

182. A sneeze engages all the energies of man, in precisely the same way as the sexual act; but we do not derive from the sneeze the same arguments against the dignity of man, because his will is not involved. And even though we may ourselves provoke a sneeze, still it has to be caused, that is, it is exceptional and not normal; it is not provoked as an end in itself, but for a secondary purpose, and therefore it is not a sign of human weakness, nor does this act prove any kind of enslavement [as does the other].

It is not disgraceful that a man should sometimes give way when in pain, but it is shameful that he should become the victim of his pleasures. The reason for this is not that pain may come to us from some cause external to ourselves whereas we reach out after our pleasures. For we may deliberately invite pain and give way under it without being guilty of the degradation caused by surrender to certain pleasures. Why then is it a mark of nobility that reason should give way under the stress of pain, and shameful that it should yield to the enticements of pleasure? It is because it is not the pain that tempts and attracts us: it is we ourselves who freely accept it and allow it to have its way with us, so that we ourselves retain the mastery of the situation—this is a matter in which man consents to be mastered by his own weakness. But in pleasure, man is mastered by the pleasure. Now only mastery and control bestow glory; the condition of servitude is nothing but shame.

183. The example of Alexander's chastity has not made so many men continent as that of his drunkenness has made intemperate. There is no shame in not being as virtuous as he and it seems pardonable not to be more vicious. We delude ourselves that when we find ourselves indulging in the sins of the great, we are not really giving way to the vices of "the herd": we fail to perceive that in the matter of sin, the great reduce themselves to the common level of mankind. We touch the great at the very point at which they touch the people, for however high their position they are necessarily united with the least of men at some point or other: they are not suspended in mid-air, in some situation remote from our social system. No, no! If they are taller than we, it is because they hold their heads higher, but their feet, like our own, are planted on the ground. Thus so far as their feet are concerned they are all on the same level, supported by the same earth; at that lower extremity they stand as low as we, as the least of us, as our children and as animals.

184. *Contradictions:* Man is naturally credulous, skeptical, timid, and over-bold.

185. "A savage race, thinking that life without war is nothing worth," Livy XXXIV. 17. They prefer death to peace, whereas other men prefer death to war. Life may indeed be given for any opinion, and yet the love of life appears to be so strong and natural.

186. It is dangerous to show man too clearly that a large part of his nature is little superior to that of animals, unless we also make him aware of his own greatness. It is still more dangerous to allow him to form too clear a notion of his own greatness, without [a counterweight in the form of] an acknowledgment of his dependent conditon. It is most dangerous of all to leave him in ignorance of both. But it is very useful to draw his attention to both.

Man ought not to think that he is equal either to the animals or to angels. Nor should he remain in ignorance either of animals or angels; he should know something of both.

187. Man is neither angel nor beast, and unfortunately the man who tries to live as though he were an angel ends by sinking to the level of the beast.

188. Conferences on humility are a cause of pride to vain men, and of humility to the humble. And sermons on skepticism encourage those strong in the faith to speak dogmatically. Few people speak humbly of humility; few chastely, of chastity; few who discuss skepticism show the slightest hesitation. We are nothing but lies, duplicity, contradictions, and we conceal and disguise ourselves from ourselves.

189. *Greatness, misery:* The more light we enjoy, the more of greatness, and the more that is small and mean do we discover in man. There are ordinary men and those less ordinary: Philosophers astonish ordinary men—and Christains astonish philosophers.

Who then will be astonished to discover that religion does but instill a thorough knowledge of truths which become ever deeper and ever more acceptable as our understanding of them advances?

190. This religion imparts to little children truths which grown men, with all their greater enlightenment, have but imperfectly understood.

191. *Skepticism:* Too quick an intelligence, like the total lack of it, is generally held to be close to madness. Nothing is good but mediocrity. A majority vote has settled that, and the said majority will snap at anyone who detaches himself from the crowd, by whatever door he makes his escape. I make no difficulty about it and am perfectly content to sit in the middle; but I flatly refuse the lower end, not because it is low, but because it is "end"—and I would equally refuse if the end were at the top. If we leave the middle way, we part company with humanity. The greatness of the

human mind lies in knowing how to hold to that middle way. It is no sign of greatness that a man should separate himself from humanity: it is a more convincing sign of greatness if he does *not* part company with it.

192. The world is a good judge of things, for it is in a condition of natural ignorance, the true state of man. In all human knowledge there are two extremes which touch. The first is that of the pure natural ignorance into which all men are born. The other is that which is reached by great minds which, having traversed the entire range of human knowledge, find that they know nothing, but are back in the condition of natural ignorance from which they had set out; except that their ignorance is now instructed and aware of itself. Those between the two have left behind their natural ignorance but have failed to reach the enlightened kind; they have some tincture of pretentious learning and pose as learned men. They are a bugbear to everybody, and on the whole they are but very ill-informed. The people, and the men of practical ability, make up the real world. Those pretentious ones despise it—and are despised by it. They have a poor opinion of most things, and the world has an accurate opinion of them.

193. It is not a good thing to have too much freedom. It is not a good thing that all one's needs should be supplied.

194. Neither the very young nor the very old are of sound judgment. If you have not given sufficient thought to a subject (or if you have brooded on it too long), you become obstinate, you are infatuated with it. If you look at your work the moment it is done, you are predisposed to like it; if you leave it too long, you lose interest in it. Similarly with pictures, if they are viewed from too far or too near. There is one point, and one only, from which to look at a picture, and all other viewpoints are too close or too far away, too high or too low. In the art of painting, the viewpoint is settled by the rules of perspective. But who shall settle the viewpoint in truth and morals?

195. Those who live disorderly lives say of good-living people that it is they who have become estranged from nature, whereas the disorderly are nature's children: just as men on

board ship have an impression that the people on the shore are moving past them. Each proposition contains the same terms, and a fixed point is necessary before a judgment can be formed. The harbor is the fixed point for men on a ship at sea. But where shall we find our harbor in questions of morals?

197. *Skepticism:* Everything in the skeptic philosophy is part truth and part error. Truth itself is not like that—truth is all pure, all true. The skeptic mixture dishonors and destroys it: nothing is pure truth, and indeed, considered by the standard of pure truth, nothing can be true. You will say it is true that murder is an evil thing: that is so, because we are able to understand what is bad and false about it. But what can we mention that could be called good? Chastity? I say, no, for that would bring the world to an end. Marriage? No. Continence is better. Not to kill? No. The disorders would be fearful, and all the good would be murdered by the wicked. To kill? No, for that is to destroy nature. Our knowledge of the true and the good is but fragmentary, and it is mixed with evil and with error.

199. Disagreement with a truth proves that it is unpopular. Many things that are certain are nevertheless denied; much that is false is accepted without challenge. Denial of a truth is no evidence that it is false; nor does the absence of disagreement prove a thing to be true.

200. There is within a man a state of warfare between his reason and his passions.

If only he had his reasoning powers, and no passions. . . .

Or if he had only his passions, and no reason. . . .

But since he has both, he cannot be without this condition of warfare, for he cannot be at peace with the one unless he be at war with the other, so that he is always divided against himself.

201. This state of interior warfare between reason and the passions means that those who desire peace are divided into two parties. Some have wished to renounce the passions and to become gods. Others have wished to renounce reason and become brute beasts (Des Barreaux). But neither party has succeeded: reason remains, to denounce the baseness and

injustice of the passions, and to disturb the peace of mind of those who give way to them; and the passions are always alive in those who try to renounce them.

202. *At Port Royal. Greatness and misery:* Since misery may be inferred from greatness, and greatness from misery, some have tended to stress misery, as proving greatness; while others argue so much the more forcibly for greatness, because they can infer it from the existence of misery. Everything that one party can say in arguing for greatness merely supplies the other party with an argument for misery, since the higher the state from which we have fallen, the greater will be our condition of misery. The other side reverses the argument. They have been brought into collision by arguing in a circle, for it is certain that the perception of either greatness or misery in mankind is a matter of enlightenment. In a word, a man knows that he is miserable; he is wretched because he is miserable, but he is very great because he knows it.

203. This double nature in man is so obvious that some philosophers have thought that we have two souls. It seemed to them that a simple being would be incapable of such great and sudden leaps from boundless presumption to fearful depression.

204. Concupiscence has become natural to us, and a second nature. Thus there are two natures in us, one good, the other bad. Where is God? He is where you are not—and the Kingdom of God is within you.

204a. Instinct and reason, marks of the two natures.

205. Man is great, even in his concupiscence, since he has found a way of building it into a marvelous way of life, and making it look like a picture of chastity.

206. *Greatness:* The causes behind the effects are a sign of the greatness of man, since he has been able to construct, out of his very concupiscence, so noble an order.

207. *Contradictions. After having shown the baseness and greatness of man.* Let man now value himself at his proper

price. Let him love himself, for there is in him a nature that is capable of good. But let him not think that he is free to love the base things that are also there. Let him despise himself that his capacity is so unfruitful, yet let him not therefore despise that natural capacity. Let him hate himself and love himself. He has within himself the capacity to know the truth, and to be happy; but he has within himself no truth which is either enduring or satisfying.

I would therefore seek to instill in man the desire to find a measure of truth; to detach himself from his passions, that he may be the more ready to follow that truth wherever he may find it, well knowing that his understanding has been darkened by his passions. I would have him hate in himself that concupiscence which, without the aid of any other influence, is able to dominate him, so that it will not blind him when he comes to make his choice, nor bring him to a standstill when he has made it.

208. Miton is well aware that [human] nature is corrupted and that men are anything but virtuous; but he does not know why they cannot fly higher.

209. All these contradictions, which seemed likely to remove me far from any understanding of religion, have in fact led me soonest to the true religion.

210a. Before I go into the proofs of the Christian religion, I find it necessary to point out the injustice of men who live indifferent to the necessity of seeking the truth about a matter of so much importance to themselves, and touching them so closely.

Of all their aberrations, this is certainly the one which most clearly convicts them of folly and blindness, and in which it is easiest to reduce them to confusion quite offhand, by the application of common sense and an appeal to natural feeling.

For it is not to be doubted that this earthly life endures but for a moment; that the condition of death, whatever its nature, is eternal, and that all our thoughts and actions must therefore follow widely differing directions, according to whether eternal happiness may be hoped for or not. Therefore it should be impossible for us to take any step requiring prudence and judgment, without first considering that step from the standpoint of eternal life, which should be our final goal.

Nothing is more obvious than this, so that according to the principles of reasoning, men who follow any other course are behaving very foolishly.

We therefore know what to think of men who go through life without a thought of its final end; who allow themselves to be led by their inclinations and their pleasures, without reflection, without a moment of anxiety, as though they could abolish eternity simply by tearing their thoughts away from it, and whose only thought is to enjoy the present moment.

Eternal life, however, remains a fact, and death, which menaces them at every moment, will before long admit them to it. They will then be inescapably condemned to the prospect of annihilation or of eternal woe, and they will not know which of these two eternities awaits them.

This incertitude may involve them in fearful consequences. They are in danger of an eternity of misery. And in addition, as though their peril were not worth a thought, they take no step to inquire whether eternal life is not merely one of those beliefs that people swallow too easily and uncritically; or whether it is not one which, though in itself obscure, rests on a very solid though hidden foundation. Thus they do not know whether there is any truth or error in the idea, or whether the evidence for it is strong or weak. They have this evidence before their eyes, but they refuse to look at it, and in this attitude they deliberately do all that is necessary to merit the penalty which undoubtedly awaits them if the teaching be true, while they are content to wait for the moment of death to put it to the test. They are very satisfied with this attitude, professing it openly and even making a boast of it. Can we think seriously of the gravity of the issue in question, and not be shocked at the levity of such conduct?

To be at ease in this state of ignorance is a monstrous thing. The extravagance and stupidity of such sloth must be brought home to those who are spending their lives in this condition, by pointing it out to them, shaming them by the sight of their own folly. For this is how men will argue when they choose to live in ignorance of what they are, and decline to be enlightened: "I do not know," they say.

210b. Let them at least understand the nature of the religion they are attacking, before they begin the attack. If this religion prided itself that it had a clear vision of God, that it possessed Him openly and unveiled, then it would be a sufficiently damaging attack if they said they found no evidence on earth to justify such a claim. But since this religion says precisely the opposite, maintaining that men live in a darkness far removed from God, that God has hidden Himself from them, that this is the very name that He gives Himself in the Scriptures, *Deus absconditus,* "the hidden God," Isa. 14:15. And if, finally, this religion also strives to establish two things, that God has set visible signs in the Church, whereby He will be recognized by those who seek Him sincerely, but that He has nevertheless concealed those signs, so that He will only be seen by those who seek Him with their whole heart, what good does it do them to profess indifference to the search for truth, and yet to cry out that nothing reveals it to them? The very darkness in which they live, and which they use as an objection against the Church, does but prove one of the things the Church maintains, and that without reference to the other; so far from destroying anything, the existence of that darkness supports the Church's teaching.

If they want to attack religion, they would have to show convincingly that they have made strenuous efforts to find it everywhere, even in what the Church offers for their instruction, but without success. If they were to speak in these terms, they would indeed be attacking one of the claims of religion. But I hope to demonstrate that no reasonable person can say such a thing, and I will make bold to declare that no one has ever done so. We know well enough how people who hold such views behave. When they have spent an hour or two in reading some part of the Scriptures, or in questioning a priest about the truths of the faith, they think they have made great efforts to gain enlightenment, and boast that they have searched without success, in books and among men. But indeed I shall say again what I have often said, that such negligence is intolerable. This is not a case of a passing interest in some casual stranger, to be treated accordingly, and with suitable unconcern; this question touches ourselves—it is our all. The immortality of the soul is a matter which touches us so closely that a man must have lost all sensitivity of feeling if he does not want to know what it is all about. All our thoughts and actions must of necessity follow such very different courses, depending on whether or not we hope for eternal life, that it is impossible to take a single step with sense and judgment, unless we hold firmly to this hope, which ought to be our final aim.

Thus our primary interest and our first duty must be to get light on this matter, for upon it the whole of our conduct depends. And that is why, when I am dealing with those who are unconvinced, I draw an important distinction between those who are applying all their powers to learn the truth, and those who live without troubling themselves or giving any thought to it. I have nothing but compassion for those who are sincerely troubled by their doubt, who regard it as the greatest of misfortunes, who spare no pains to escape from it, making the search for truth their principal concern and their most serious occupation.

But I take a very different view of those who live through their days without giving a thought to their last end, and who, simply because they lack any interior enlightenment that would carry conviction, neglect to seek that enlightenment elsewhere. These men refuse to investigate carefully whether the belief in eternal life is merely one of those ideas which people accept uncritically, or whether it is not, rather, one which, though in itself obscure, has nevertheless a very firm and unshakable foundation. This negligence in a matter which concerns themselves, their eternal life, their all, causes me irritation rather than compassion; it astonishes and appalls me. There is in their attitude something monstrous. I do not say this out of any pious zeal that the negligent and the scoffer should turn to devotional practices. On the contrary, my meaning is that the scornful ought to be concerned for their own eternity according to the principle of human self-interest, even the interest of self-love. This is so obvious that it calls for nothing more than an ability to see what is clear to the least instructed.

No great elevation of soul is needed to realize that there is no true and solid satisfaction to be had in this world; that all our pleasures are but vanity, that our misfortunes are infinite, and that in the end death, which menaces every moment, must within a few years inevitably confront us with a dreadful necessity of eternal annihilation or everlasting wretchedness.

There is nothing more real than this final situation—nor more fearful. Let us put a bold face upon it if we will: that is what lies in store at the end of the most brilliant of human lives. Let the skeptic think it over and then say whether it is not beyond all question that the only good thing in this world is the hope of a better, that we are only happy in proportion to our readiness for that better state, and that, just as there shall be no more sorrow for those who put all their trust in eternal life, so also there can be no happiness for those who know nothing about it.

It is certainly a great evil therefore, to be in a state of doubt on this subject, but if we are so, it is our minimum duty, and an indispensable one, to seek an answer: for he who doubts, yet makes no effort to resolve his doubt, is both very unhappy and most unjust. That such a man should be calm and contented, that he should declare himself so, that he should even boast of it and be vain about it, and that he should regard this condition as a matter for joy, a reason for lighthearted pleasure—I can find no words to describe a person so misguided.

How far can we carry such ideas as these? If wretchedness beyond remedy is all they have in prospect, what grounds can such men have for their rejoicing? If they are to dwell in impenetrable shadow, is the outlook one to justify human vanity? And how is it possible that such methods of argument come to be used by reasonable beings? Or such as these:

"I know not who has placed me in this world, nor what the world is, nor what I am. My ignorance of all things is appalling. I know not what my body is nor what my senses are, nor what my soul is, nor even the part of me that thinks, and expresses what it thinks, which reflects upon all things as well as upon itself—and yet remains as ignorant of itself as it does of all things else.

"I look out upon those appalling spaces of the universe which confine me, and I find myself penned into one corner of that vast expanse, without my knowing why I am set in this one spot rather than in another; nor why the brief span of life granted to me has been allocated to this particular period rather than to any other in that eternity which went before me, or in the endless years that are to come. I see nothing but infinites on every side, and they shut me in, as though I were but an atom, or a shadow thrown for an instant. The instant passes, the shadow returns no more. All I know is, that I must shortly die; but what I know least of all about is this very death which I cannot escape.

"Just as I know not whence I came, neither do I know whither I am going. I only know that when I leave this world I shall fall forever, either into the void, or into the hands of a provoked and angry God, without knowing in advance which of the two states is to be my lot for eternity. Such is my state of mind, full of weakness and uncertainty. And the only conclusion I can draw from all this is that I had better spend the whole of my life without wasting a thought on what may become of me afterward. It may be that I can obtain some enlightenment as to my doubts, but I have no great wish to take any trouble about it, nor to take one step to look for it. And later on, while I shall be able to treat with scorn all such as have labored to discover the truth, I desire to be allowed to try the great venture, and to walk quietly toward death, without any forethought and without fear, totally uncertain as to whether or not my future state will endure for eternity."

Who would care to have as his friend a man who talks like that? Who would choose him for the discussion of any serious matter? Who would turn to him in affliction? In short, could such a man be of any practical use to anybody?

It is indeed one of the glories of religion that it has such unreasoning men for its enemies; and so far is their opposition from being dangerous that it serves, on the contrary, to establish the truths of religion. For the Christian faith may almost be said to have for its main object the establishment of two truths: the corruption of human nature, and its redemption through Jesus Christ. Now, I maintain that if these men do not exactly demonstrate the truth of the redemption by their holy living, at any rate their unnatural feelings prove most admirably that human nature is corrupt.

Nothing is so important to a man as the condition of his soul, nothing so much to be dreaded by him as the state in which he may expect to pass eternity; therefore it is not in the least natural that any man should be found indifferent to the loss of his own being, or to the prospect of an eternity of wretchedness. He behaves very differently with regard to everything else: the slightest trifle can alarm him, he anticipates it, he feels it. And this same man, who will spend so many nights and days in a state of rage and despair over the loss of some position, or some supposed affront to his honor, is also the man who knows, "without forethought and without fear," that at his death he is going to lose everything. It is a monstrous thing to see in one and the same heart this sensitivity to mere trifles and this strange lack of concern for matters of the very greatest moment. This is an incomprehensible spellbinding, a kind of preternatural torpor, which argues some very powerful influence as its cause.

There must have been some very strange subversive force at work in the heart of such a man, that he should find this state of mind (which it seems incredible that anyone could find even tolerable), a cause for satisfaction. But experience has brought so many of them to my notice that it would be surprising, did I not know that the majority of those who talk in this way are counterfeit coin and not at all what they pretend to be. They have heard it said that it is "good form," the way of the world, to win every argument by swaggering claims of this kind. They hear worldly people boasting that they have "shaken off the yoke," and they set out to imitate them; but it would not be difficult to show them how self-deluded they are when they seek by this means to make themselves popular. This is not the way to do it, even among men of the world, who are apt to be sound judges, and who know that the only way to a good reputation is to carry a conviction that one is honorable, loyal, judicious, and capable of being useful to a friend, because of course men only like people who can be useful to them. Now how useful can it be to anybody, to hear a man say that he has "shaken off the yoke," that he does not believe in any God who sees his every act, that as far as he is concerned, he is himself the sole judge of his own conduct, and that he has no intention of accounting for it to anyone but himself? Does he think that talk of that kind encourages us, from that moment forward, to place complete confidence in him, and to look to him for consolation, counsel, and help for all the needs of life? Does such a man think that he rejoices us greatly, when he informs us that in his belief the human soul is but a puff of wind or smoke, and when he does so, moreover, in a pleased, self-satisfied tone? Is that a thing to be said cheerfully? Should it not rather be announced mournfully, as the saddest thing in all the world?

If they gave it serious thought, they would see that such ideas create the worst possible impression, that they are so mistaken, so contrary to common sense, so opposed to what is expected of a gentleman, and so remote in every respect from that air of good breeding which they seek to acquire, that their general tendency would be to warn off, rather than corrupt, anyone who might have been inclined to follow them. And in fact, if you hold them to it, and compel them to explain their ideas, and the reasons they allege for doubting religion, they will use such weak and poor arguments that you will be more inclined to adopt the contrary opinion. That was said to them on one occasion by a certain person, and very much to the point, too: "If you go on holding forth like that," he said, "you will end by converting me." And he was quite right, too; for would not anyone be horrified to discover that if he were to adopt to such ways of thinking, he would find himself in the company of such contemptible fellows?

Thus those who hesitate, who suspend judgment, would be very ill-advised if they were to do violence to their ordinary good sense, for if they began to think along those lines they would show themselves the most light-minded of men. If in their heart of hearts they are inclined to be ashamed of their lack of sympathy for such notions, they need not conceal the fact: such an admission would not be in the least shameful. It is only shameful to have no shame. Nothing indicates more plainly a weakness of understanding than the failure to realize that to be deprived of God is to have suffered calamity, nothing is so plain a mark of an evil disposition as the refusal to hope in the eternal truth of the promises of God, and nothing can be so unmanly as an act of bravado with respect to God. Let them then leave such impiety to such as are so lowborn as to be naturally capable of it. If they cannot be Christians, at least let them behave like men; and finally, let them realize that there are only two classes of men who can be called rational: those who serve God with all their heart, because they know Him, and those who seek Him with all their heart, because as yet they know Him not.

But as for those who live without knowing Him and without seeking Him, they judge themselves: they are so lacking in true self-respect that they forfeit the respect of others.

It needs all the charity of the religion they despise not to despise them so utterly as to abandon them to their folly. But since this religion obliges us always to look upon them, so long as they are in this life, as capable of receiving illuminating grace, and also to believe that within a brief space of time they could be more richly endowed with faith than we ourselves, while we on the other hand are capable of falling into their state of blindness, we must do for them what we would wish them to do for us were we in their place: we must entreat them to take pity on themselves and to go forward at least a step or two in quest of enlightenment. Let them spend some few of the hours they might waste in other ways in the reading of these words. Whatever distaste they may bring to it, they may find something useful, and in any event their loss will be small. But I hope that they who bring to the search a perfect sincerity and a genuine desire to find the truth, will be satisfied, and be convinced by the proofs of the divine religion, which I have here collected, and which I propose to discuss in more or less the following order....

210f. Your "gentleman," your man of good breeding, cares not a rap whether he pleases other people, but the truly good man tries to give happiness to those about him.

211. Incomprehensible that God should exist, and incomprehensible that he should not exist, that the soul should be one with the body, or that we should have no soul, that the world should have been created, or that it should not have been created, etc., that there should be such a thing as Original Sin, or that there should be no such thing.

212. "Do you think it impossible that God should be infinite and without parts?"—"Yes."—"Well, then I would like to show you something that is infinite and indivisible: a point, moving in every direction and at infinite speed, one wherever it is, and the whole of it present, wherever it may be."

This is a natural phenomenon, and until at this moment you hear it mentioned as a fact, you would have said it was an impossibility. Consider it, and maybe it will bring you to realize that there may be other facts which as yet you do not know. Do not assume that you learned everything during your apprenticeship, and that nothing remains for you to learn. But believe that you still have an infinite amount to learn.

213. Infinite movement, the point filling all things, the movement of rest; infinity without quantity, indivisible and infinite.

214. The ungodly, who claim that they follow reason, ought to be uncommonly well equipped for argument. Now, what do they say?

"Now, do we not see," they say, "that animals live and die, just as do men? Turks also, just like Christians, live and die. They, too have their ceremonies, their prophets, their doctors, their saints, their separated religious orders, like ourselves, etc." (Is this contrary to Scripture? Does not Scripture say all this?)

If you can scarcely take the trouble to learn the truth, that will be enough to keep you quiet. But if you desire with all your heart to know the truth, what we have said will by no means satisfy you. Consider the matter therefore, in more detail. . . . If it were merely some problem in philosophy, we should have said enough; but here, where it is a question of all—or nothing. And yet, after bestowing on this vital question a merely perfunctory thought, we can still go off and amuse ourselves, etc. We ought to inform ourselves about this religion, even if it does not fully explain all the obscurities; perhaps it will teach you something.

216. Suppose an heir were to find the title deeds to his own house. Would he say, "They may be forgeries," and not take the trouble to examine them?

217. The arguments used by atheists ought to be perfectly clear; but it is very far from being perfectly clear that the soul is material.

218. *Atheists:* What grounds have they for saying that there cannot be any resurrection? Which is more difficult, to be born or to rise from the dead? That a thing that has never happened should come to pass, or that something which has happened once should happen again? Is it more difficult to come into being than to return to existence? Custom makes

he one seem easy for us; that it is not the custom, makes he other impossible. Such is popular reasoning.

Why cannot a virgin bear a child? Does not a hen lay ggs without a cock? What distinguishes these outwardly rom other similar examples? And how do we know that the en cannot form the germ as well as the cock?

219. The atheist's plea: "But we have no light."

220. What objection can they have to the Resurrection or o the Virgin Birth? Which is the more difficult—to create a nan or an animal, or to reproduce them? And if they had never seen a given species of animal, would they be able to guess whether such species had been produced without nating?

221. Atheism is an indication of a powerful mind, but only up to a certain point.

222. How I hate that nonsense about not believing in the Eucharist, etc.! If the Gospel is true, if Jesus Christ is God, where is the difficulty?

223. *Infinity—Nothing:* The soul is cast into the body, where it becomes subject to time, and finds number and dinensions. About these things it reasons, calling them nature, or necessity, and it cannot believe in anything else.

A unit added to infinity does not increase it, any more than he addition of a foot adds anything to an infinite dimension. n the presence of the infinite, the finite is annihilated—it becomes mere nothing. Similarly with the human mind and God, and with the disparity between our human justice and he divine justice. The measure of disproportion between hunan justice and the justice of God is even greater than that between unity and the infinite. Now, the fact that His justice should be exercised upon the reprobate is less disconcerting, and ought to amaze us less, than that He should have mercy on the elect.

We know that there is an infinite, but we are ignorant of ts nature. Since we know it to be false that numbers are finite, it follows that there is such a thing as numerical infinity, though we do not know what it is. It is untrue to say that it is odd. For the addition of a unit does not alter its nature, yet it remains a number, and every number is either odd or even (it is true that this applies to all finite numbers). Thus it is quite possible to know that there is a God, yet not to know what He is.

Is there not one substantial truth, seeing that there are so many true things that are not the whole of truth?

We know, therefore, the existence and the nature of the finite, because we ourselves are also finite and have extension in space. We know the existence of the infinite, but we do not know its nature because, although like ourselves it has extension, unlike ourselves it has no limits.

We cannot know who God is, or what His nature is, because He has neither extension nor limits.

But we know by faith that He exists, and in the glorified life we shall know His nature. Now I have already shown that we may know the existence of a thing, and yet we may not be acquainted with its nature.

Let us now speak according to such light as we may obtain from the phenomena of Nature.

If there be a God, He is of necessity infinitely incomprehensible, since He has neither parts nor limits and therefore has no relation with us. We are therefore incapable of knowing either what He is or whether He is. This being so, who will dare to undertake the solution of the problem? Not we poor men, who have no relation with Him.

Who then will blame Christians for their inability to give reasons for their belief, and who profess a religion which they cannot explain in rational terms. When they expound their religion to the world, they actually call it *stultitiam*, foolishness—and then you complain because they do not prove it! If they proved it they would be contradicting their own statement, whereas by doing without the proofs they show that they are not without judgment.

"Yes, but while that argument would excuse those who expound their reasons for belief in such a way, and if it exonerates them from blame when they declare their belief, but do not support it with arguments, it does not excuse those who accept it on such terms."

Well, let us take your point, and let us begin by saying: "Either God is, or He is not." But which way shall we lean? Here, reason can decide nothing. A vast gulf separates us, and across this infinite void a game is being played that depends upon the toss of a coin. What is your wager, heads or fails? According to reason, you cannot bet on either, because (also strictly in conformity with reason) neither probability can be ruled out.

But do not charge with error such as have made their choice, since you know nothing about it.

"No, I won't. But I'll attack them, not for making a particular choice, but for making any choice at all. For it remains true that both he who calls 'Heads!' and his opponent are both in error, both wrong. The prudent thing is not to wager."

Certainly. But in this case you *must* wager: you have no option, you have embarked upon it (and you cannot now withdraw from the game). Which will you take, then? Come! Since you must choose, let us see what cards you might throw away. You have two things you stand to lose, the true and the good and two things that you stake, your reason and your will—your understanding, that is, and your final Beatitude. And you have a natural horror of error and of misery. Your reason will not be outraged by your choice of the one rather than the other, since choose you must, so that disposes of one card. But what of your Beatitude? Let us estimate the gain and the loss if we call, "Heads!" and wager "That God is." Compare the two chances: if you win, you win everything; if you lose, you lose nothing. Don't hesitate, then. Make a bet that God exists.

"Fine! Yes, I must certainly make a bet. . . . but perhaps I am staking too much?"

We shall see. The chance of winning or losing is fifty-fifty. Therefore, suppose the stake to be your own life, with the chance of winning only two lives for your one, you could still safely bet. But suppose there were three lives to be won (and still you are obliged to remain in the game), it would be foolish not to play and to hazard your one life for the three you stand to gain by calling "Heads!", since the chances of losing or winning are equal. But now—suppose the prize to be eternal life, eternal happiness, and suppose that the odds lengthen, and that, of an infinite number of chances, only one is for you; you would still be right to risk your one life to win two, and since you cannot avoid playing, you would be very ill-advised to refuse to stake one life for three, in a game where although the number of chances is infinite, one is certainly for you, and the prize is an eternal life of perfect happiness. But here is a game in which the prize actually is eternal life and eternal happiness, with one chance of winning against a finite number of chances of losing, and your stake is also finite. That removes the element of chance, and settles the matter: wherever there is an infinite opportunity, and where there is no infinity of chances of losing against the one chance of winning, there is no need for hesitation. You can and you must stake all. And thus, where you are forced to play, you must renounce reason and save your life, rather than risk your life for the infinite gain, where the chance of winning is as likely as losing—and remember that we said the loss was nothing.

For it is useless to say that winning is doubtful and that it is certain that we are running a risk, that an infinite distance separates the *certainty* of what we stake and the *uncertainty* of what we may win, and that this infinite distance is equal to the finite good which we must certainly stake against the uncertain infinite: this is not the case. Every gambler risks something certain in the hope of winning something uncertain: he risks a finite certainty to win a finite uncertainty—yet he does not thereby commit any sin against reason. There is in his case no infinite distance between the certainty of his risk and the uncertainty of his win: to say that, is quite wrong. There is, it is true, an infinite distance between the certainty of winning and the certainty of losing. But the uncertainty of winning bears a proportion to the certainty of the amount we stake, according to the proportion between the chances of winning and losing. Thus, if there are as many chances on the one side as on the other, the odds are even, and the certainty of the stake is equal to the uncertainty of the prize: so far is it from being true that they are separated by an infinite distance. Therefore our argument is of overwhelming force where the stake is finite, the chances of winning or losing are equal, and the prize is infinite. This can be demonstrated; and if any truth is within the grasp of human intelligence, this truth, certainly, is within man's comprehension.

"I confess it, I admit it. But, still, is there never any opportunity of seeing the cards?" Yes: Scripture, and so on. . .

"Yes, but my hands are tied, and my mouth is gagged. I am obliged to play, so I am not free. People will not let go of me, and I am so made that I find belief impossible. What then do you expect me to do?"

True. But you will have to recognize, at any rate, that

although the natural tendency of your human reason is to believe, you are unable to believe—to make any act of faith. You must accept the fact that this inability lies in the will: it comes from your passions. Your problem therefore will not be to attain certitude by multiplying the proofs of the existence of God, but by bringing your passions under control. You have a desire to find a state of rest, but you do not know the way? You want to cure yourself of unbelief, and you ask for the remedy? Learn of those who have been fettered like yourself, but who have now staked all that they possess. These are the people who know the road that you would like to follow, who have been cured of that same disorder of which you desire to be cured. Follow the method by which they began, which was, to behave as though they believed, by taking holy water, having Masses said, etc. This will lead you naturally toward belief and will calm you . . . drive the beast out of you.

"But that's just what I'm afraid of."

But why? What have you to lose? And to prove to you that it works—you will find that it will reduce the power of your passions, which are for you the great stumbling block.

The end of this discourse: Now, what harm can come to you if you take this road? You will be faithful, honest, humble, grateful, kindly, a true and dependable friend. Indeed, you will never be entangled in corrupt pleasures, in the desire for glory or luxury, but will you not have pleasures of another kind? I tell you that you will gain even in this life, and that at every step you take along this road you will see such certainty of winning, and perceive so clearly the worthlessness of what you risk, that you will end by realizing that you have after all gambled on something that was certain and of infinite value, and that it has cost you nothing.

"Oh, these words delight me, quite carry me away," etc.

If the argument appeals to you, and seems to carry weight, you must know that it is the work of a man who has thrown himself on his knees both before and after, to pray to that infinite and indivisible Being, to whom he submits his own soul, that He would subdue yours also, for your own good and for His glory, so that His strength might be granted to aid your weakness.

224. If it were an accepted rule of human life that noth-

ing should ever be done except on a certainty, then nothing would ever be done for religion's sake, since religion is not a certainty. And yet—how many things are done of which the outcome is uncertain, such as going on sea voyages, or into battle! I say, then, that if we never worked for an uncertainty, we should do nothing at all, for nothing is certain; and that there is more certitude in religion, than there is that we shall live to see tomorrow. For it is by no means certain that we shall see tomorrow, whereas it is certainly possible that we shall not see it. This cannot be said of religion. It is not certain that religion is true, but who will dare to say that it is certainly possible that religion is not true? Now, if we work for tomorrow and for what is uncertain, we act reasonably, for we ought to labor for the uncertain, as we have already demonstrated in our discussion of the wager and the laws of chance.

Saint Augustine saw that men labor for what is uncertain, as for example, at sea, or in a battle, etc., but he failed to perceive the part played by the laws of chance, which demonstrate that we ought so to labor. Montaigne saw that the healthy human mind is offended by the necessity to associate with meaner intellects, and that custom, the normal, is willingly followed, because it is in fact so powerful. But he did not perceive the cause of this effect.

Both these men could see the effects, but they failed to identify the causes, and compared with those who have discovered the causes, they are like people of whom the best we can say is that they have eyes, compared with men of mind, of intelligence; since effects may be said to be tangible, whereas their causes are perceptible only to the intellect. And although we may say that effects may be *perceived* by the mind, it remains true that such a mind, as compared with one that perceives the causes of the effects, is as coarse as are the physical senses of man in their object and their range, as compared with the powers and range of his intellect.

224a. "They see the thing, they do not see its cause," Saint Augustine, *contra Pelag. IV*. 60.

225. *The rules of the game:* The way we order our lives in this world will necessarily vary according to the following assumptions: 1. That we may be here forever. 2. That it

; certain that we shall not be here for long, and uncertain ʼhether we shall be here one hour. This last assumption is ı fact our state.

:25a. According to the terms of our wager, you owe it to ʼourself to take some trouble to seek out the truth, for if you hould die without worshiping the truth, you are lost. "But," ʼou will say, "if He had desired that I should worship Him, Ɨe would have left me some signs of His will." He *has* lone so—but you neglect them. Seek them, then: it will be vorth your while.

:26. What do you promise me then (for the agreed term of en years) if not ten years of self-love, spent in trying hard to ›lease, but never succeeding; with the certainty in addition ›f a great many difficulties.

:27. *Objection:* Those who hope for salvation are happy ›n that score; but the hope is counterbalanced by the fear of Ɨell.

:28. *Answer:* Who has more reason to fear Hell, the man vho professes not to know whether Hell exists, but is cer- ain of damnation if it does, or he who is inclined to believe hat it exists, but hopes to be saved if it does?

The Christian hope of possessing an infinite good is tinged vith a deep joy and also with fear, for Christians are not ike people who look forward to a kingdom in which, since hey are subjects, they will have no position; their hope is ʼor holiness, and for an end of injustice, and of these things hey already have a foretaste.

:29. "I should very soon have given up pleasures," they ay, "if I had had faith." But I tell you, you would soon have ıad the faith had you but given up the pleasures. Now it is ıp to you to make a beginning. I would give you faith if I :ould. Since I cannot, I cannot test the truth of your asser- ion. You, however, are well able to leave your pleasures and est the truth of what I say.

:30. Are you any less a slave because you are loved and :aressed by your master? You are in luck, slave. Your master s flattering you now, but soon he will beat you.

231. *Order:* I ought to be more afraid that I might be mistaken, and of having to discover that the Christian religion is true, than of not being mistaken in the belief that it is true.

232. *Superstition and concupiscence. Scruples—Evil desires:* The wrong kind of fear: not the fear of the man who believes in God, but the fear of the doubter, who does not know whether He exists or not. The right kind of fear springs from faith, the wrong kind, from doubt. The right kind of fear is mingled with hope because it is born of faith, and because we hope in the God in whom we believe. The bad kind of fear is close to despair, because we fear a God in whom we have no faith. Some fear to lose Him—others dread that they may find Him.

233. Faith tells us things that our senses cannot communicate, but it does not go counter to what the senses would register if they were able to do so. Faith is of a higher order than the senses, but is not in conflict with them.

234. *Order:* After the letter, "That we ought to seek God," write the letter "On removing obstacles," which is the discourse on "the machine," running-in the machine, seeking by the use of our reason.

235. *Order:* A letter of exhortation to a friend, urging him to seek. He will reply: "What should I gain by such a search? Nothing becomes any plainer." We answer: "Do not give up hope." And he replies that he would be happy to find some light, but that according to the teaching of this same religion, even if he adopted the beliefs they would not help him in the least, so that he would rather not seek. To this argument the answer is, the "machine."

236. *A letter showing the usefulness of proofs from the "machine" argument:* Faith is a different thing from the arguments that justify faith. The one is human, but the other is the gift of God: "As it is written, He who through faith is righteous shall live," Rom. 1:17b. He shall live by this faith which God Himself plants in the heart, and which He strengthens by trials. "Faith comes from what is heard,"

Rom. 10: 17, but this kind of faith is in our hearts, and it makes us say, not, "I know," but "I believe."

237. It would be superstitious to base your hope upon ceremonies, but it would be pride to refuse to make use of them.

238. If God is to hear our petition, the outward man and the interior man must both be in subjection; that is to say, we must go down on our knees, pray with our lips, etc., so that presumptuous man, unwilling to humble himself before God, should now show his obedience even in his bodily posture. To expect to receive the help we ask merely by adopting a certain external attitude would be superstition, but to refuse to show our inner obedience by a submissive demeanor would be a sign of pride.

239. *External works:* There can be nothing so perilous as an act calculated to please both God and man; for a condition pleasing to both God and man must contain an element pleasing to God, and another element pleasing to man. We may instance the greatness of Saint Teresa: What pleases God is the profound humility of her revelations, but men are pleased with her visions. And so many people wear themselves out with copying her mode of speech, thinking that thus they reproduce her mature holiness, and giving never a thought to loving those that are dear to God, or of themselves advancing in virtue, so that God will also love them.

It is better not to fast and to be ashamed of the fact, than to fast and to be self-satisfied. The Pharisee and the publican.

What will it benefit me to remember my good works, which may in fact either harm or help me, seeing that their value depends on whether they have the blessing of God? This blessing He bestows only upon works done for Him, according to His will and His ways; the manner and motive being as important as the thing done, and perhaps more so, since God is able to bring good out of evil, and since without [the grace of] God, men are apt to turn good things to evil uses.

240. Other religions, such as paganism, are more widely popular because they are essentially concerned with exter-

nals, but this is because they are not intended for men of ability. A purely intellectual religion would be better suited to very learned people—but this, again, would have nothing to say to the great majority of mankind. Christianity alone, with its spirituality and its use of externals, is suitable for everybody. It satisfies the spiritual needs of the humble, and compels the more privileged to stand before God with humility. Without both of these elements it would not be perfect, for the people must be able to understand the spirit of the Christian message, and the learned also must be willing to submit to that spirit.

241. For we must not misunderstand ourselves: we are as much machine as mind, and hence the means by which men are effectively persuaded include other methods besides demonstration. How few things there are which can be demonstrated! Proofs only convince the mind. The strongest and the most widely accepted proofs are provided by habit. Habit inclines the machine, and the machine carries the mind with it even before the mind can consent. Who has ever been able to prove that tomorrow will come, or that we shall die? Yet what is more generally believed? It is habit, therefore, that persuades us of both facts; it is habit [in the more general sense of custom] that makes men Turks and pagans, traders and soldiers, etc. (The one advantage that Christians have over Turks is the faith they receive in baptism.) And once the mind has perceived where the truth lies, it is upon the gift of faith that we must rely for the refreshment of our spirits and the strengthening of belief—for it would be burdensome to be forever returning to first principles. We need to develop a simple faith which becomes a habit and which leads us to believe things, and inclines all our faculties in favor of belief, so that without violence, without tricks, without argument, our soul absorbs it naturally. It is not sufficient to believe only through the force of strong convictions, while the machine in us tends still to respond as though we believed the contrary. Both parts of our nature must be made to act according to belief: the mind must be persuaded by reasons, which it is sufficient to have seen once in a lifetime, and the machine must be run in by forming it to habit, and by not allowing it to go into reverse. "Incline my heart, O God," Ps. 118:36.

243. There are three modes of belief: by reason, by habit, and by grace. Christianity is the only religion that bases its appeal to mankind upon reason, and it does not regard as her true children those who claim that they are able to believe without the aid of sanctifying grace. It is not that Christianity excludes reason and habit—quite the contrary; but we must be ready to approach the evidences for the Christian faith with an open mind. We must confirm ourselves in the supernatural virtues by the formation of habits, and we must at all times offer ourselves with perfect humility to the promptings of grace, which alone can work in us any true and lasting effect: "Lest the Cross of Christ be emptied of its power," I. Cor. 1:17.

244. This religion, so rich in miracles and in saints, in men of goodwill and of blameless life; in men eminent for their learning; in witnesses and in martyrs; in kings, governing without challenge, safe on their thrones (David); Isaiah, a prince of the blood; so eminent for her knowledge—she lays out and shows us all her miracles and all her wisdom, and then casts it all away, declaring that she has neither wisdom nor great works, but only the Cross, and foolishness.

For those who by these miracles and this wisdom have merited your confidence and proved to you their character, declare to you that nothing of all this can either change us or make us capable of knowing and loving God, but only that power of the Cross which was foolishness to the Greeks, because the Cross was to them bereft of wisdom and because it produced to them no miracle: and no miracle can be worked without that power. Thus our religion is foolishness as to its active cause, the Cross, and wise because it looks to the divine wisdom, which provided such a religion for the saving of men.

245. Our religion is wisdom and foolishness: wisdom, because it is richest in understanding, richest also and strongest in its wealth of miracles, prophecies etc.; foolishness because it is not for any of these things that we are members of it. Her wisdom and her foolishness alike are a condemnation of those who willfully remain outside her, but they are not the reasons for the belief of those who are her members. The one ground of the Christian belief is the cross, "lest the cross be emptied of its power," I. Cor.1:17. So it is that Saint

Paul, though indeed he came with both wisdom and miracles, could say that he came with neither miracles nor wisdom but only to convert. But those who come only to convince may say that they come with wisdom and signs.

246. *Preface to Part II:* To speak of those who have dealt with this subject: I marvel at the boldness with which these people undertake to speak of God. When they are shaping their argument for unbelievers, their first chapter sets out to prove the deity from the works of Nature. This hardihood would not dumbfound me, if their argument were designed for the faithful, since it is certain that those with a living faith in their hearts are able to see at once that all that is, is the handiwork of the God they worship. But those in whom this light has been extinguished, and in whom it is our object to revive it, are men destitute of faith and grace; but they *are* seeking out, with all the intellectual power they have, everything in Nature which may lead them to this knowledge, and yet they find nothing but perplexity and darkness. Now to say to *these* men that they have only to look at the least of the things about them, to see God made manifest; and to offer them, as sole proof of this great and important doctrine, the revolutions of the moon and the planets; to claim, moreover, that such an argument, and such a discourse, offer complete and sufficient proof of God, would be enough to make them think that the proofs of our religion are weak indeed. And reason and experience alike have taught me that nothing is more likely to arouse their contempt for religion.

It is not in this way that Scripture speaks—and the Scriptures are much better acquainted with the things of God. Scripture says quite the contrary: that God is a hidden God, and that ever since Nature was corrupted, He has left mankind in a blindness from which they are unable to escape except by Jesus Christ, without whom all communication with God is cut off. "No one knows the Father except the Son, and any to whom the Son chooses to reveal Him," Matt. 11:27.

This is what the Scriptures affirm when they say in so many places that those who seek God shall find Him. It is not in such terms as these that we speak of a light "like the noonday sun." We do not say of those who look for the sun at noon, or for water in the sea, that they shall find it.

Therefore the evidences for God cannot possibly be drawn from this kind of natural phenomenon. Moreover, Scripture says in another passage: "Truly, Thou art a God who hidest Thyself," Isa. 45:15.

247. *That God has willed to hide Himself:* If there were only one religion, God would be unmistakably revealed therein. Similarly, if our religion were the only one to produce martyrs.

Since God is, therefore, hidden, it follows that any religion which does not declare that He is hidden, is not true, and any religion which fails to declare the reasons for His hiddenness, fails to teach. Our religion does all this: "Truly, Thou art a God who hidest Thyself," Isa. 45:15.

248. If there were no obscurity, man would not be conscious of his corruption. If there were no light, man would not hope for relief. Thus it is not only right but also useful to mankind that God should be partly hidden and partly revealed, since it is equally perilous for man to know God without also being conscious of his own wretchedness; and to know his own wretchedness without knowing God.

249. *A*[*t*] *P*[*ort*] *R*[*oyal*]. *The beginning, after explaining incomprehensibility:*

The greatness and the wretchedness of man are both so evident, that the true religion must of necessity inform us about two things: that there is in man a certain deeply rooted principle of greatness, and also a nostalgia, or root of misery, lying equally deep in his being. It must also offer us some explanation of this astounding contradiction.

If she is to make man happy, religion must show him that there is a God, that man is bound to love Him, that our true happiness consists in being united to Him, and our only evil, in being separated from Him. Religion must also recognize that the soul of man is in fact full of darkness, which hinders him from knowing and loving God. Thus, while our human condition [makes us debtors to God, and our indebtedness] obliges us to love Him, our appetites draw us away from Him [our debt of love is not paid], and so we remain in a condition of injustice. Thus religion must be able to account to us for this opposition to God and to our own good: it must teach us what are the remedies for our infirmities, and how we may obtain them. Let us then examine, on the basis of this test alone, all the religions of the world, and see whether there be any, other than Christianity, which satisfies these conditions.

Shall we go to the philosophers, who offer us as the sole and sufficient good, those elements of good which are within ourselves? Does the true good consist of those elements? And have the philosophers found therein the remedy for human ills? Does it cure the arrogance of man to set him on a level with God? Or have those who have reduced us to the levels of animals, or Mahometans—who offer us earthly pleasures as the supreme good, even for eternity—provided a remedy for our sensual appetite? In a word, what religion is there that will teach us how to cure our pride and lust? What religion is there, in fact, that will teach us the nature of good and of our duty, and point out the weaknesses which turn us away from them; that shows us the cause of the weaknesses, the remedies that will cure them, and the means of obtaining those remedies?

All the other religions have failed. Let us see what the wisdom of God will do.

This wisdom tells us: "Do not expect either truth or consolation from men. It is I who created you, and who alone can teach you what you are. But you are no longer in the state in which I created you. I made man holy, innocent, and perfect; I filled him with light and intelligence; I made known to him my glories and my wonders. In that day, the eyes of man saw the majesty of God. He was not then in the darkness which now blinds him, nor subject to death, nor burdened with the miseries which now afflict him. But he was unable to bear so much glory, and he fell into presumption. He wanted to become his own center, and to be independent of my aid. He withdrew himself from my rule; and when, in his desire to find his own happiness in himself, he sought to be my equal, I abandoned him to himself. I raised in revolt the living things that had been made subject to him, so that they became his enemies. Today, therefore man has become like the beasts, and is so far removed from me that there scarcely remains to him so much as a confused vision of his author, so entirely is all his knowledge of me extinguished or dimmed. His senses made themselves independent of his reason, and were very often its masters, and they have swept him along in the pursuit of pleasures.

All creatures either distress or tempt him, and they rule over him, either subduing him by strength or charming him by sweetness, and this is a much more terrible and injurious form of tyranny.

"Such is the state in which men are today. They are left with a dim memory of their primal nature, and they lie entangled in the miseries of their blindness and desire—a condition which has become their second nature.

"By applying this principle which I now disclose to you, you may recognize the cause of all the contradictions, which have bewildered mankind, and divided it into so many parties. Observe now all the tendencies toward greatness and glory, which is not stifled, even by the experience of so many misfortunes, and inquire whether the origin of these good tendencies does not lie in another nature."

A[*t*] *P*[*ort*] *R*[*oyal*]. *For tomorrow. A declamation:*

"It is in vain, O men, that you seek within yourselves the cure for your miseries. All that your intelligence can teach you is, that within yourselves you will find neither the true nor the good. The philosophers promised you success in your search: they could not guarantee that success. They do not know what your true good is, nor what is your true state. How should they provide you with remedies for ills which they simply have not understood? Your chief disorders are pride, which alienates you from God, and desire, which binds you to the earth; and the most they have done for you is to inflame at least one of these disorders. If they have indeed proposed God as your goal, this was done only to swell your pride: they led you to think that you were like Him and partook of His nature. Those, on the other hand, who saw the absurdity of this claim have cast you over another precipice, by making you believe that your nature was no better than that of animals, and inviting you to find good in satisfying those appetities which, certainly, you have in common with animals. That is not the medicine that will cure the human condition of injustice—a malady that those sages could never have recognized. Only I can teach you what you are." A[dam] . . .

Adam. Jesus Christ: If you are one with God, it is by grace, and not by nature. If you are brought low, it is by penitence, and not by nature.

Thus there is a dual capacity. . . .

You are not in the state in which you were created.

These two states once made known to you, you cannot fail to recognize them. Follow your own movements, observe yourself, and see if you do not find in yourself the living characteristics of both these conditions. Would so many contradictions be found in a simple subject?

Incomprehensible: The incomprehensible does not cease to be. Infinite number. An infinite space equal to a finite.

Incredible that God should unite Himself with us? This objection is drawn solely from a realization of the lowness of all creatures in relation to God. But if you have a clear and balanced view of this relation, press the thought home (as I have done), and confess that the low condition of humanity is such that we cannot of ourselves even know with certainty that His mercy is able to make us capable of knowing Him. For I would like to know: Whence does this creature, man, who knows himself to be so weak, derive any right whatsoever to measure God's mercy, and to set such limits for it as his imagination may suggest? So little, indeed, does man understand the nature of God, that he still does not know what he himself is; and being alarmed (and not without reason) at what he sees of his own condition, he dares to assert that God cannot render him fit for communication with Himself.

But, I would like to ask him, does God require anything else of man, except that he should love Him and know Him? And why does he believe that God is unable to make Himself known to man—since man is by nature capable of loving and knowing? The least of men entertains no doubt of his own existence, nor of the existence of some things that he can love. Hence if he can see anything at all in the darkness in which he lives, if he finds anything at all that he can love among the things of this earth, and if God has given him a glimpse of the divine nature—why should man *not* be capable, in his degree, of knowing and loving Him, after the manner in which it pleases God to communicate Himself to us? It cannot be doubted, therefore, that an intolerable presumption underlies this argument (that it is incredible that God should unite Himself with us), even though the objection seems to be founded on humility. But such "humility" is neither real nor reasonable, if it does not lead us to admit that we do not know ourselves as we really are, and can only be taught it by God.

[The wisdom of God speaks:] "I do not require that you make an act of faith in me without the consent of your reason. Nor do I claim any tyrannical right to subject you to myself by the exercise of my greater power. Neither, may I say, do I concede your claim that I should provide you with reasons for my actions. And, to reconcile these contradictions, I intend to show you plainly, by incontestable proofs, certain signs of my Divine Nature, which will convince you of what I am. By miracles and other demonstrations which your reason will not be able to reject, I will invest myself with authority. And I intend that, these things once done, you shall accept my teaching, since your only reason for rejecting it would be your own inability to know for yourselves whether it be true or not."

It was God's will to redeem man, and to open the way to salvation for those who seek it; but men have made themselves so little worthy of it, that because of the hardness of their hearts, God rightly refuses to some of them what He grants to others out of a compassion which is by no means a debt to them. Had it been His will to compel the submission of the most hardened, He might have done so, by a manifestation of Himself so overwhelming as to leave them in no doubt of the fact of His being—that form in which He will appear on the Last Day in a blaze of lightning and overthrow of Nature, when He shall be seen by the risen dead, and by the blindest of the blind.

It was not in the midst of such convulsions as these that He chose to appear when He began His reign of mildness. Since so many had rendered themselves unworthy of His clemency, it was His will that they suffer privation of the good they did not desire to accept. It would therefore not have been according to justice, if He had appeared in a form manifestly divine and obviously of a nature to convince every beholder; but neither would it have been just for Him to appear in a disguise so effective as to conceal Him completely from those also who were sincerely seeking Him. It was His will that to these He should be perfectly recognizable. Therefore, willing to appear undisguised to those who sought Him with their whole hearts, and concealed from those who with an equal repulsion flee from Him, He has left in His Church signs of Himself, visible to those that seek, yet invisible to those who do not. There is light enough for those whose only desire is to see, and sufficient shadow to hide those of a contrary disposition.

250. *Part II. That without faith, man cannot know either the true good or justice.*

All men seek happiness, without exception. However different the means they use, they all aim at this objective. What causes some men to go to the wars and others not, is this same desire, which is common to both of them, but judged from different standpoints. The will never makes the least movement that is not toward this goal. Happiness is the motive of every action of all men, even of him who is just about to hang himself.

And yet, throughout the centuries, no man ever attained that objective, the one aim common to all men, unless he had faith. All men complain of their condition: prince and subject; noble and commoner; old and young; strong and weak; the learned and the ignorant; the healthy and the sick; men of every country, in every age, and of all conditions.

An effort so protracted, so unremitting, so determined, ought certainly to have convinced men of their inability to attain the good life by their own efforts. Few people, however, learn anything from example, for no two instances are ever so closely alike that there is not some very slight difference. This is why we are always hoping that we shall not be disappointed this time as we were before. And so the present never satisfies us, and experience lures us from one disaster to another until our cup overflows in the final calamity of death.

What is it, then, that our desires and our weakness cry aloud to us? Do they not declare that there was formerly in man a true happiness, of which there now remains only a vague impression, an empty outline which he vainly tries to fill from the things that surround him, seeking from things absent the help he demands in vain from things present, and that these are powerless to help him, since an infinite abyss can only be filled by a boundless and changeless object, that is to say, by God Himself?

God alone is man's true good, and ever since the time

when man departed from that good there is, strange to say, nothing in Nature that has not at some time served to take its place: the stars and the heavens; the earth and the elements; plants, cabbages, leeks; animals, insects, calves, and serpents; fever and the plague, war and famine; vice, adultery, incest. And since he lost that true good, all things else can appear equally good to him—even to his own destruction, though that is so contrary to God, to reason, and to the whole course of nature.

Some seek their good in authority, others in scientific research or in sensual delight. Others again, and these indeed come closer to the truth, have held that this universal good, which all men indeed desire, is not to be found in particular objects, since these can only be possessed by single persons, and which, once they are divided, cause their owner more distress by reason of the part that is not his, than pleasure in the enjoyment of the part he has gained. They have understood that the true good must be such that all may possess it at one and the same time, without diminution and without envy, and that no one could suffer the loss of it without an act of the will. And they argue that this desire [for the good] is natural to man, and is of necessity held by all, wherefore, since he cannot be without it . . .

251. There is nothing upon earth which does not demonstrate either the misery of man or the mercy of God; either the powerlessness of man without God—or his power in union with God.

252. A letter, inviting men to seek God. And then to have them seek Him among the philosophers, the freethinkers and the dogmatists, who disquiet anyone who inquires of them.

253. *Against the skeptics:* (It is, then, a strange thing that we cannot define these things without obscuring them, for we are talking about them all the time.) We assume that everybody regards them in the same way, but this assumption is gratuitous, for we have no evidence whatsoever to support it. I notice, of course, that the same words are used on the same occasions, and that whenever two men see a body change its position, they both express what they see, which is one and the same object, by the same word: they

both say that the object has moved. From this conformity of application we derive a well-founded conjecture that their ideas are the same. This is not, however, absolutely and finally convincing (though there might be very good reason for wagering that it is correct), because we know that the same conclusions are often drawn from different premisses.

This is quite enough at any rate to introduce confusion, although it does not finally extinguish the natural light that assures us of these things. The academicians would have wagered on it, but the light is dimmed thereby, and the dogmatists are perplexed, to the advantage of the skeptical clique. Those people glory in making ambiguity still more ambiguous, and they live in a certain dubious obscurity, from which our doubts cannot quite remove all clarity, nor our natural lights expel all the darkness.

254. The nature of man may be considered from two points of view: one, according to his end, and then he is great, incomparable; the other, as he is in a crowd; just as we judge the points of a horse or a dog as they compare with the standard, observing the way they run, and the spirit they show when they run; from this point of view, man is abject and his behavior is bad. These two ways of studying man have led to conflicting opinions concerning him, and they have caused many a dispute among philosophers.

For one denies the premisses of the other. One says, "He is not born for this end, for all his actions are in conflict with it." The other says, "He is not in conformity with his end when he does such mean things."

255. *Concupiscence of the flesh, concupiscence of the eyes, pride, etc.:* There are three orders of things: the flesh, the mind, the will. The carnal are the rich men, the kings: their object is the body. The investigator and the scholar: their object is the mind. The wise: their object is justice.

God must reign over all things, and all things must tend toward Him. In things of the flesh, concupiscence is the real master; in the investigator, the spirit of inquiry is master. Not that a man may not be generally respected for his possessions or his knowledge, but these things are not a proper basis for personal pride; for while we may grant that a man is learned, we shall not fail to point out to him that it is a mistake to be vain about it. A proper cause of pride might be wisdom, for it would scarcely be possible to acknowledge that a man has acquired wisdom, and yet to affirm that to be pleased with the attainment is a mistake. Such satisfaction might in justice be allowed him. Moreover, since it is God alone who bestows wisdom, we may truly say: "Let him that boasts, boast of the Lord," I. Cor. 1:31.

256. The three concupiscences (1 John 2:16) have given rise to three sects; philosophers have simply fallen into one of the three delusions of self-love.

257. *Reasons for effects:* Concupiscence and power provide the motives for all our actions: concupiscence of the voluntary, power of the involuntary.

258. The most formidable attack of the skeptics—for I need not consider the minor objections—are, *firstly,* that apart from faith and revelation we have no certitude of the truth of these principles except in so far as we feel them naturally within ourselves. Now, this natural feeling is by no means a convincing proof of the truth of these principles, since apart from faith we have no certitude whatever as to the creation of man, whether by a good God, by an evil demon or by chance. So that it is doubtful whether, according to our supposed origin, these principles are true, because revealed by God, or false, because suggested by the devil, or incapable of demonstration, because they are the fortuitous results of custom or habit. *Secondly,* they assert that no one, apart from faith, can have any assurance that at a given time he is either awake or asleep, since during sleep we are as firmly convinced that we are wide awake as we are certain of it at this moment. We believe that we see objects of various shapes and sizes, [6] and people moving about, we are conscious of the passage of time, and we even measure time, so that in short we behave in exactly the same way as if we were awake. As half our life, upon our own admission, is spent in sleep, and as whatever images may be presented to the mind during sleep, we are unable to judge of them, since all our judgments during that time are illusory—who can tell whether

[6] Reading *espèces* for *espaces.* See Malebranche, *La Recherche de la Vérité.* 1674–1675, and Jungo, *Le vocabulaire de Pascal,* 1950, on his orthography and probable pronunciation.

that other half of life wherein we suppose ourselves to be awake is not another sleep, only a little different from the other, from which we awake when we compose ourselves for sleep?

(And who can doubt that, if I dreamed in company with others, and our dreams happened to agree (which is common enough), and I were the only one to stay awake—should I not believe things to be the other way round? In short, we often dream that we are dreaming, piling dream upon dream, and it may very well be that this life is itself no more than a dream upon which those other dreams are grafted, a dream from which we shall awake at death, and that during this dream of life we have as little perception of the principles of the true and the good as we have during natural sleep. The different thoughts that trouble us here being perhaps no more than illusions, like the consciousness of the passage of time, and the illusion of objects seen, and people moving about, which are the familiar features of our dreams.)

Such are the principal arguments they use, and we may hear them anywhere.

I need not discuss the feeble kind of excuse, such as the skeptic outcry about the influence of habit, upbringing, manners, the custom of the country, and the like; we know that such arguments appeal to simple folk, who do not dogmatize at all except on such fragile pleas, which are easily disposed of by arguments drawn from the skeptics themselves. You have only to look at their books if you do not believe it: you soon will be convinced of it, and perhaps even too strongly.

I pause therefore, to deal only with their one strong argument, [and I say that] if we are speaking in good faith and in sincerity, no one can have any doubt that there are such things as natural principles. But against this, the skeptics allege one objection only: the uncertainty of human origins, including that of our nature—and the dogmatists are still looking for the answer to that one, as they have been, since the world began.

So there is a state of open warfare between men, in which we have no option but to take sides, either with the dogmatists or the skeptics. Anyone who imagines that upon this one issue he can remain neutral would indeed be the greatest skeptic of them all; for neutrality is the basic notion of the sect, and whoever is not against them is put in the front

ank of their supporters. This appears to give them an ad-
antage. They are not even for themselves; they are simply
ieutral, indifferent, in a state of suspended judgment about
everything, including themselves.

What then should a man do in such circumstances? Shall
ie doubt everything? Shall he doubt whether he is awake, or
f someone pinches him—if they burn him? Will he doubt
vhether he doubts, or whether he *is*? Nobody can go that
far, and indeed I would wager that there has never been a
perfectly consistent, total unbeliever. Nature lends her support to tottering reason, and intervenes to prevent it from
going so far astray as that.

Will he then say, on the contrary, that he is in possession
of truth, and certain truth at that—this man who, if you
press him ever so gently, can appeal to no authority for his
"truth," and has to let go of it, as being no truth at all?

What a chimera then is man! A strange freak, and how
monstrous! A chaos, a contradiction, a prodigy. Judge of
all things, yet a poor worm of the earth; the repository of
truth, and yet a very cesspool of incertitude and error, the
glory and the garbage can of all the universe!

Who shall unravel such a tangled skein? Nature herself
confounds the skeptic, but the dogmatist is defeated by the
incapacity of his own reason. What then is to become of
you, O men, if you persist in the endeavor to search out
and know your true condition, by your mere natural reason?
You cannot avoid a choice. You cannot avoid deciding upon
one or other of these three sects, and yet you cannot live
with any one of them.

Know then, proud man, how great a paradox you are to
yourself. Bow down, proud reason! Silence, slow-witted fellow! Learn that man is infinitely beyond the comprehension
of man, and understand, by listening to your master, your
true condition—which as yet you do not know. Listen to
God.

For, in a word, if man had never been corrupted, he would
in his state of innocence be confidently enjoying both truth
and happiness; and if he had never been other than corrupt, he would have no notion of truth, nor of a condition
of blessedness. But, wretches as we are, and the more so
because there is in our condition an element of greatness,
we have a notion of happiness, yet we cannot attain it.
We perceive an image of the truth, but we possess only the

deceptive shadow; incapable alike of total ignorance and of certain knowledge, so manifest is it that we at one time lived in a high state of perfection, from which we have unhappily fallen.

The marvel is, however, that the mystery which is farthest removed from our knowledge, namely the transmission of sin, should be something without which we can have no knowledge of ourselves. For certainly nothing gives our reason a greater shock than to hear that the sin of the first man has transmitted guilt to others, and that those others are so far distant from it as to seem incapable of participating in that sin. This transmission seems to us not only impossible but most unjust. For what could be more contrary to the rules of [even] our wretched justice, than to damn eternally an infant as yet incapable of an act of the will, for a sin in which he had apparently so small a share, that it was committed six thousand years before he came into existence? Indeed, nothing shocks us more rudely than this doctrine, and yet without this mystery, the least comprehensible of them all, we are incomprehensible to ourselves. The knot of our condition acquired its twists and turns in that abyss, so that we can no more conceive of man without this mystery, than man can conceive such a state for himself.

(Whence it appears that God, willing to render the problem of our being unintelligible to us, has hidden the knot so high, or rather so deep, that we are quite incapable of reaching it; so that it is not through the arrogant exertion of our reason, but by the humble submission of our reason, that we truly come to know ourselves.

These foundations firmly established on the inviolable authority of religion, teach us that there are two truths of the faith of equal permanence: the first, that man at his creation, in the state of grace, was raised above the whole of Nature and was made like unto God, participating in His divinity; the second, that man has fallen from this state into a condition of corruption and sin, and has become like the animals.

These two propositions are equally sound and certain. Scripture declares this plainly, when it says in various places: "I delighted in the sons of men," Prov. 8:31; "I will pour out my spirit on all flesh," Joel 2:28; "All flesh is grass," Isa. 40:6; "Man is like the beasts that perish," Ps. 49:20; and "I said in my heart with regard to the sons of men, that God is testing them, to show them that they are but beasts," Eccles. 3:18.

Whence it appears clearly, that by grace man is made like to God and a sharer in His divinity, and that lacking grace, he resembles the beasts of the field.)

260. This sect draws more strength from its enemies than from its friends, for man's weakness is far more evident in those who do not recognize it, than in those who do.

261. No other [religion] has understood that man is the most excellent of creatures. Some religions have indeed fully acknowledged his dignity, and have regarded as cowardice or ingratitude the modest opinions which a man would normally hold concerning himself. Others have been somewhat too well aware of the existence of real grounds for humility, and have treated with arrogant scorn that sense of his own greatness which is just as natural to man.

"Lift up your eyes," says the first of these, "to God, and look upon Him in whose likeness you were made, and who created you that you might worship Him. You can make yourself like Him: wisdom will make you equal to Him, if you choose to follow her." "Lift up your heads, for you are free men," said Epictetus. But the others say to him: "Look upon the ground, miserable worm that you are, and look upon the animals about you, fit companions for so poor a creature."

What then will become of man? Shall he be as God, or shall he be no better than animals? What a terrifying distance separates the two! What then shall become of us? Who does not perceive from all this that man has gonc astray, that he has fallen from his proper place, that he is anxiously seeking the way back to it, that he can no longer find it? And who is there who any longer desires to help him? The greatest men have failed to do so.

262. The standard of conduct set up by the Stoics is difficult of attainment and unrealistic. They say: "All who do not live according to a high degree of wisdom are as stupid and vicious as those who drown themselves in two inches of water."

264. *Stoics:* They believe that what can be done once

can be done always, and that since the desire for fame inspires the ambitious to do something well, others ought to be able to emulate the achievement. But activities under the spur of ambition are no better than feverish impulses—and ordinary good health could not imitate them.

Epictetus infers, from the fact that some Christians persevere, that all Christians are perfectly capable of perseverance.

265. These great spiritual heights are occasionally reached by the soul, but she cannot remain there: she can at times take a leap forward, not as one ascending a throne where she is to sit as queen, but for a moment only.

266. A man's achievement should be measured, not by his special efforts, but by his average performance.

267. I am no admirer of an excess of virtue—valor, for example—unless I can see at the same time an excess of the opposed virtue, as one does in Epaminondas who displayed extreme valor with extreme humanity. For otherwise it is not an ascent but a fall. Greatness is not demonstrated by adopting extreme positions, but rather by touching both extremes at once and filling all the space between. "But perhaps this is only a sudden leap of the soul from one extreme to the other, the soul remaining steadily fixed at one point, as when you whirl a burning stick." Maybe, but at any rate this indicates that even where there is no great intellectual range, there is at least agility.

268. We cannot visualize Plato and Aristotle, except in the gown of the scholar. They were good-mannered men, and enjoyed a laugh with their friends as much as the rest of us do. When they relaxed a little, and sat down to write their *Laws* and their *Politics,* they looked upon it as a joke. That was the least philosophical and least serious part of their lives: The true philosophy was to live plainly and quietly. If they wrote about politics, it was as though they were drawing up a set of rules for running a madhouse. And if they made pretense of writing on grave matters, this was only because they knew that the crazy folk to whom they were speaking fancied themselves to be kings and emperors.

They entered into the spirit of the game, to keep folly within bounds and do as little harm as possible.

269. It is not in man's nature always to go forward: sometimes he advances, but sometimes he falls back.

Fever has its shivering fits and its heats; the shivering fits are as sure an indication of high fever as is the high temperature.

Man is constantly inventing and discovering, from one century to another. Similarly with the malice and goodwill to be found in the world at large: "Changes are welcome principally to the great," Horace, *Odes III*. xxix. 13.

270. There are certain failings which cling to us because of other failings [which we have not eradicated]. But if you cut through the trunk of the tree, the branches will necessarily fall with it.

271. Nature works progressively, *itus et reditus,* going and coming, forward and backward; she advances, and then retires, then goes forward again, a little farther this time; then two more advances, but not so far; then forward again, and farther than ever, and so on. This is the action of the tide, and also the sun.[7]

272. When we are making a serious effort to practice the virtues, aiming at all the perfection possible to us,[8] we notice that temptations are presented to us, so small at first as to be trivial, but gaining in strength if we should yield to them in the slightest. At the same time, our imperfections appear to multiply and crowd upon us, so that we seem to be in danger of being overwhelmed by faults and losing our hold on the virtues. It is at this stage that we have to hold on to our resolution to achieve perfection.[9]

[7] The manuscript of this fragment is illustrated by a diagram drawn in the margin by Pascal, which provides a remarkably interesting illustration of the rhythmic movement of nature. It is particularly applicable to the sun's ecliptic and the phenomena of the equinox.

[8] *De part et d'autre:* here, "come what may," since it is impossible to practice a virtue in a negative or retrograde sense.

[9] Reading *s'y prendre.*

273. We do not grow in virtue by our own power, but by the balancing of two opposed imperfections; just as we are kept on our feet by two crosswinds. Cure one of the faults, and you will fall into the other.

274. *The soul immaterial*: The philosophers who have mastered their passions . . . would matter be able to do that?

275. *Philosophers*: We are full of things which dissipate our attention. Instinct inclines us to seek our happiness in external things; and our inclinations also urge us upon the outward object—even where no temptation is actually present to excite them. External objects tempt us and offer their attraction, even though we were not thinking about them. It is all very well, then, for philosophers to say, "Retire into yourselves. That is where you will find your true good." We simply don't believe them—and those who do, are the most futile and foolish of all.

276. The Stoics say: "Withdraw within yourselves: it is there you will find peace," and it is not true.

Others say: "Go out of yourselves. Seek happiness in distractions," and that is not true, either. Illnesses come.

Happiness is neither within nor without: happiness is in God—both within and without.

277. Even if Epictetus had seen the way perfectly clearly, he would still have said to men: "You are on the wrong road." He asserts that there is another way, but he does not show us what it is. It is to will what God wills, and Jesus Christ alone can lead us to it: *Via, veritas* (*I* am the way, the truth . . .)

The very vices of Zeno.

278. *The reasons for effects:* Epictetus. When people say, "you have a headache," it is not quite the same thing. We can be quite certain about the state of our own health, but not about questions of justice. And in fact the ideas of Epictetus about justice were merely silly.

And yet he thought he had made his doctrine of justice unanswerable when he said, "Either it is within our power or it is not." But he did not see that it is not in our power to control the heart, and he was quite wrong in concluding that we could, from the fact that some people were Christians.

279. All the premisses of skeptics, Stoics, atheists, and so on, are correct, but they draw the wrong conclusions; for the contrary premisses are also correct.

280. *Philosophers:* A fine thing, to tell a man who does not even know himself, that he should come to God of his own accord! Not much use saying that to a man who does know himself!

281. *Against those philosophers who have God without Jesus Christ. Philosophers:* They believe that God alone is worthy to be loved and held in awe, yet they themselves desire the love and admiration of men, and they do not acknowledge their own corruption. Now, if they should be filled with the spirit of devotion, so that they love God and adore Him, finding in Him all their joy, and thanking God that He has been good to them—what of it? Is this more than Christians do? But if devotion and gratitude are in fact irksome to them, and their only motive is to be esteemed of men, if their idea of the good life is that they themselves should bask in the secure enjoyment of public approval (and that, mark you, without resort to any special pressure), then I say that "the good life" so interpreted can only repel. What! Have they indeed known God? How then can they be moved by any other desire than this one only, that all men should love Him? And how should it be thinkable that men should stop short of God, and be content with loving—a philosopher! They have desired that they themselves should be "final" causes, that men should find happiness in according recognition to—philosophers.

282. Philosophers have been careful not to lay down rules which would divide a man against himself.

They have exalted man, by suggesting a greatness of nature which is certainly not his condition.

Or they have degraded him, but imputing to him every conceivable perversion of heart and will, and neither is that his true condition.

Humility has to arise from a known need: it is not natural

to man, but grows with penitence. Nor should a man remain in low condition, he must rise from his knees and go forward. He needs to realize his own dignity, which is not of his own merits but of the grace of God: and that realization comes *after* penitence.

283. How dishonest are those philosophers who will not discuss the immortality of the soul. The consequences of such dishonesty are clearly perceptible in Montaigne.

284. It is not to be doubted that the mortality or immortality of the soul must of necessity make all the difference to the moral life. Yet there are philosophers who have constructed whole systems of morality without reference to the dogma. They only talk to pass the time.

Plato is a good preparation for Christianity.

285. I cannot forgive Descartes. He would have been glad to leave God out of his philosophy altogether. But he could not avoid bringing God in, for He had to give the world one flip to set it in motion; after that, he had no more use for God.

287. (But it may be that this topic is beyond the reach of reason, and so we will examine her findings as to ideas that are within her range. If there be any topic to which mere self-interest would have bid her apply herself most earnestly, it would surely be that of the sovereign good. Let us see then, where these powerful and penetrating minds locate it, and whether they are in agreement.

One philosopher says that the sovereign good resides in virtue, another finds it in pleasure, another in understanding the works of Nature, and yet another, in truth: "Happy is he who can discover the causes of things," Virgil, *Georgics* II, 490. One man will find it in total oblivion, another in indolence, others in a fine disregard for probability, others again, in finding nothing to admire. "To be surprised at nothing is probably the only thing that can make and keep any man happy," Horace, *Epistles* I, vi, 1. And then we have these worthy Pyrrhonians, with their ataraxy, doubt, and perpetual suspension of judgment. And there are others—and these perhaps the wisest—who say it cannot be found, even in thought and desire. But what a conclusion!

But we certainly must inquire whether these fine philosophers have gained nothing at all by all this long and concentrated study: At any rate, the soul may have achieved some understanding of itself. Let us listen to the world's teachers on this theme. What, do they think, is the substance of the soul? Have they given it location—a happier one? And what have they discovered about its origin, its length of life, and its departure?

Can it be that the soul is still too noble a subject for their poor intellects? Let us then bring the inquiry down to matter, and see whether the soul knows what that body, to which it gives life, is made of, and those other bodies also, which it can contemplate, and which it can move as it will. What have they discovered about the soul, these great dogmatists to whom nothing remains unknown? "Of these opinions, [which is the true one? Only a God could decide.]," Cicero, *Tusculan Disputations,* I. ii.

This would suffice, no doubt, if reason were reasonable. She is quite reasonable enough to admit that she has so far found no firm footing, but she does not yet despair of finding an answer. On the contrary, she is as eager in the pursuit as ever, and confident that she has in herself sufficient resources to carry it through to the end. Let us then finish the inquiry, and having measured the power of reason by her achievements, let us proceed to study those achievements in detail. Let us see whether she has any measure of strength, and the grasp [of principles] necessary for comprehension of the truth.)

Jesus Christ

Heathens Mahomet

Ignorance of God

290. *On the objection that Christianity is not unique:* So far from this objection showing that Christianity is not the true religion, it proves on the contrary that it *is.*

291. The errors of other religions. They have no witnesses: ours has them. God challenges other religions to produce such signs as ours: Isa. 43:7; 44:8.

292. In matters of religion men must be sincere: true pagans, true Jews, true Christians.

293. The faith is a gift of God: do not believe that I ever called it a gift of reason. Other religions make no such claim for their beliefs: they allege that reasoning leads to their beliefs—but it does not do so, all the same.

296. *History of China*: I believe only those histories whose witnesses are ready to face death.[10]

(Which of the two is the more credible, Moses or China?)

It is not sufficient to be given an overall view. I tell you there is something here to delude us, and also something to enlighten.

By this one word only I can ruin all your arguments. You say: "But [the quarrel about] China has confused all the issues." I answer: "Certainly the Chinese dispute is confusing; but enlightenment can still be found. Look for it."

Thus everything you say tends to support one of those methods [of apostolic missionary work], without prejudice to the other. So either method will serve, and no harm will be done.

We need more detailed information, with documents for study and factual evidence.

297. *Against the* History of China: The historians of *Mexico of the Five Suns* (and the newest of them only eight centuries old.)[11] The difference between a book that is accepted by a people, and one that serves to educate a people.

298. *Mahomet without authority*: His reasons must then have been very convincing, since they had no authority but their own force.

What does he say, then? That we have to believe in *him!*

299. The Psalms, that are sung throughout the world.

[10] *History of China.* This was the *Sinaicae historiae decas prima,* by Père Martini, S.J., which had appeared in 1656. The reference is evidence of the vigilance with which Pascal was following current controversy in the Church.

[11] *Mexico of the Five Suns.* The histories that were being written by missionaries and soldiers of the affairs of "New Spain," had been read by the intellectual class throughout Europe. The piety and independence of the Church in the Indies provided Pascal with a two-edged weapon.

Who bears witness to Mahomet? He himself. Jesus
Christ desired that His own testimony should be rejected
John 5:31: "If I bear witness of myself . . .") The distinguishing feature of witnesses is that they are always and everywhere present. Mahomet, poor wretch, stands alone.

300. *Against Mahomet*: The Koran is no more by Mahomet
than the First Gospel is by Saint Matthew, which is quoted
by various authors from century to century: even its enemies,
Celsus and Porphyry, never rejected Saint Matthew.

Now, the Koran says that Saint Matthew was a trustworthy
man. Therefore Mahomet was a false prophet, either because
he called honest men wicked, or because he ceased to hold
the doctrine they had taught concerning Jesus Christ.

301. The obscurities in Mahomet might well be interpreted in a mystical sense. It is not by these that I would
have him judged, but by what is clear in him—by his para-
dise, and so on; and here he is ridiculous. This is why it is
not right to regard his obscurities as mystic passages, seeing
that when he does write clearly he is absurd.

It is not the same with Scripture. I concede that it contains
passages as obscure as anything in Mahomet; but there are
also passages of a marvelous clarity, and many Scripture
prophecies have plainly been fulfilled. The odds therefore
are not even. We must not confuse, or treat as equal, things
which certainly have in common the feature of obscurity,
but which by no means share that quality of clarity, in virtue
of which the Scriptures compel veneration for those passages
that are obscure.

302. *Difference between Jesus Christ and Mahomet*: Mahomet was not foretold. Jesus Christ was foretold.

Mahomet came as a slayer; Jesus Christ caused His
followers to be slain.

Mahomet forebade reading; the Apostles ordered reading
(I. Tim. 4:13).

In short, they are so opposed that if Mahomet may be
said to have chosen the path of earthly success, Jesus Christ
apparently, in the eyes of men, chose the way of death;
and instead of concluding that since Mahomet succeeded,
Jesus Christ might well have succeeded, we have to say that
since Mahomet succeeded, Jesus Christ was bound to die.

303. What Mahomet did, any man may do. He did no miracles, he was not foretold. No man may do the things that Jesus Christ did.

304. Paganism has no foundation today. They say that it once had a basis in the responses of the Oracle. But what are the books that assure us of this? Are they trustworthy because of the authority of their authors? Have they been so carefully preserved that we can be certain the text has not been corrupted?

Mahometanism has as its foundation the Koran and the prophets. But this prophet, who was to be the last hope of the world—were there any prophecies concerning him? What mark has he that is not possessed by any man who chooses to call himself a prophet? What miracles does he himself claim to have wrought? What mysteries did he teach, even according to the tradition of the religion he founded? What moral system? And what ideal of happiness?

The Jewish religion should be examined from two different standpoints: from the tradition in their sacred books, and from the [oral] traditions of the people. The morality and the ideal of happiness found in the popular tradition are absurd; but in the tradition preserved in the sacred books they are admirable. (All religions are the same: for Christianity wears one aspect in its sacred books, but quite another in the Casuists.) The foundation of Christianity is admirable: it is based on the oldest book in the world, and the best authenticated; and whereas Mahomet sought to ensure the permanence of his own book by forbidding the reading of it, Moses perpetuated his own book by ordering that all should read it.

Our religion is so divine, that another religion, also divine, possesses no more than a similar foundation—[it is "the religion of a book"].

305. No other religion teaches that man is born in sin No philosophical system says so, so that none of them teaches truth.

No other sect or religion but Christianity has been in existence upon earth from the beginning.

306. This is what I see and what disturbs me: I look around me in all directions, and I see nothing but darkness every-

where; Nature offers me nothing that is not casue for doubt and disquiet. If I saw no sign in Nature of any divinity, I should deny the existence of a God; if I saw signs of the Creator everywhere, I should believe and be at peace. But I see too much to doubt Him, too little to comfort me, I am in a pitiable state. A hundred times have I wished that if Nature be indeed maintained in being by a God she would unequivocally declare it, and that if the signs she gives of Him are deceptive, she would suppress them altogether. Let her say all or nothing, that I may see which side I ought to take. Whereas now, in my present state, I do not know what I am nor what I ought to do. My heart is wholly bent on understanding where the true good lies, so that I may follow it. No price would be too high, so I might be sure of eternal life.

"I envy those whom I see, living in the faith with so lukewarm a love of it, and making such poor use of a gift that I believe I should use very differently."

307. *Conversation*: Big words against religion. I don't believe it. Skepticism is useful to religion.

309. I reflect that, since my ego consists in my thinking, I might never have come into existence. Therefore I, the thinking being, would never have been, if my mother had been killed before the breath of life had been breathed into me. I am not, therefore, a necessary being, nor am I either eternal or infinite. But I can see clearly that there is in Nature one necessary Being, eternal and infinite.

310. Between ourselves and Hell (or Heaven) there is but this one life—and that is the most fragile thing in the world.

311. When I behold the blindness and misery of man, when I survey the vast, dumb universe, and man without light, left to himself and gone astray in this corner of it, without knowing who has put him there, nor what he has to do, nor what will become of him when he dies, and incapable of knowledge of any kind, then I am seized with terror. I am like a man who has been carried off in his sleep to some fearful desert island, and who wakes up not knowing where he is, and with no means of getting away from this savage

solitude. And then I wonder that the wretchedness of our condition does not reduce us to utter despair. I see other people about me, all in the same state of perplexity as myself. I ask them if they are any better informed than myself, and they say, "No." And thereupon these wretched wandering beings look around them, and catching sight of some pleasing objects, have embraced them and attached themselves to them. But for my part I could never form such attachments; but reflecting on the strong probability that there is something else beyond the limit of human vision, I set out to discover whether this God may not have left us some sign of Himself.

I see several religions, all in conflict with one another, and therefore all false but one. Each of these religions demands belief upon its own authority, and utters threats against the unbeliever—two circumstances which make me skeptical about their assertions. Anybody could make such claims, anyone may call himself a prophet. But I see the Christian religion—and there the prophecies are fulfilled. That is something that none of those other religions can do.

312. When I consider the short duration of my life, swallowed up in the eternity that went before me and the eternity that comes after, the small extent of space I fill, the narrow limits of my field of view, swallowed up as I am in the infinite immensities of space, which I do not know, and which know not me, I am terrified and astonished to find myself here rather than there. For there is no reason whatever why I should be here rather than there, why now rather than then. Who put me here? By whose order and direction have this place and this time been assigned to me? "The memory of a guest that tarrieth for a day," Wisd. 5:15.

313. The eternal silence of those infinite spaces fills me with fear.

314. Why is my knowledge limited? And my stature? Why my life, to a hundred years rather than a thousand? What reason had Nature for ordering it so, and for choosing that one number rather than any other in the infinite series, since there was no reason to choose one rather than another, since no one number offers advantages over another?

315. It is a thing to wonder at, that we are content merely to relax in the company of our fellow men: they are as wretched as we, powerless, like ourselves, and therefore cannot help us. Each one of us must die alone. We must therefore act as though we were indeed alone; and in that case, should we build splendid houses, etc.? We ought to seek the truth without faltering; and if we refuse to do so, it shows that we value the esteem of men more than the search for the truth.

316. It is a dreadful thing to feel that all one possesses is slipping away.

317. The last act is bloody, however entertaining the rest of the play; and then—a handful of dust thrown on the head, and all is over.

318. *Order*: To see what is clear and indisputable as to the Jews and their destiny.

319. These are the undisputed facts. When all the philosophies were splitting up into different sects, there was to be found in one corner of the world a people already ancient, declaring that the rest of mankind was in error, that God had revealed the truth to themselves, and that they, His people, should be established on earth forever. And in fact, while all those other sects have disappeared, this one still endures, and has done, this four thousand years.

They declare that their fathers have told them how man fell from communion with God and is altogether estranged from Him; and how He promised to redeem them; that this doctrine will endure upon earth; that their law has a double meaning; that throughout a period of one thousand and six hundred years they had men they believed to be prophets, who foretold the time and manner [of redemption]; that four hundred years later they were scattered everywhere, because Jesus Christ must be proclaimed everywhere; that Jesus Christ came, in the manner and at the time foretold; that since that time, the Jews have been scattered everywhere, a people accursed, but none the less surviving.

320. I see the Christian religion, founded upon a previous religion, and here is the evidence I find. I say nothing here

of the miracles of Moses, of Jesus Christ, of the Apostles, because these are not the things that most persuade us, and I mean to put in evidence only those unchallengeable foundations of this our Christian religion which are not in doubt, which cannot therefore be called in question by any person whatsoever. It is certain that in a number of places upon earth we see a peculiar people, separated out from all other peoples, and they are called the Jews.

I see then an abundance of religions in many parts of the world and in all ages, but they have neither a moral system that satisfies me, nor evidences that convince me. Therefore I should have to reject not only the religions of Mahomet and of China, but also those of ancient Rome and Egypt, for the sole reason that as no one of them possesses more marks of truth than another, nor anything to compel my belief, reason cannot incline me to one rather than to another.

But as I thus consider the strange and every-changing variety of religious beliefs and systems of morals which have existed at different periods, I find in one corner of the world a peculiar people, separated from all other peoples and the most ancient of them all, whose chronicles antedate, by several hundred years, the oldest known to Europe.

I find then this great and numerous people descended from one man, worshiping one God, and governed by one Law which they claim to have received from His hands. They maintain that they themselves are the only people in the world to whom God has revealed His mysteries; that all other men are corrupt and have become estranged from God; that they are altogether abandoned to sensual pleasures and are at the mercy of their imagination, whence arise the strange errors and the restless changes in religion and morals that take place among them. The Jews claim that they have adhered unshakeably to their way of life. They say that God will not, however, leave the other nations forever in darkness; that a deliverer will come who shall redeem all men; and that the Jews are in the world for the express purpose of proclaiming his coming to men, to be the heralds and forerunners of his great advent, and to call upon all peoples to join with them in watchful waiting for this Redeemer.

My encounter with this people has astounded me: it seems to me they are worthy of study. I consider the Law which, as they boast, they were given by God, and I find it admirable. It is the oldest of all laws, and of such a character that the Jews had received and observed it without a break for nearly a thousand years, long before so much as the word "law" was in use among the Greeks. It seems strange that the oldest law in the world should also, on examination, be found the most perfect, so that the greatest of legislators have borrowed from it for their own systems, as appears from the Athenian "Law of the Twelve Tables," which was afterwards adopted by the Romans. It would be easy enough to prove this, if Josephus (*Contra Apion* II, 16) and other writers had not already dealt adequately with the matter.

321. *Advantages of the Jewish People*: At the very beginning of my inquiry, the Jewish people at once attracted my attention by a number of remarkable and singular features which this people displays.

First. I note that this is a people consisting entirely of brothers, and that, while other peoples are composed of a vast number of families, the Jews, though strikingly prolific, are all descended from a single man. Thus they are all of one flesh and members one of another, and they constitute a powerful state consisting of a single family. This is unique.

This family or people is the most ancient known to man; a fact which (or so it seems to me) entitles it to special veneration, particularly in connection with our present inquiry; because if God has at all times communicated with men, it is to those men that we must turn for knowledge of the tradition.

This people is not only of very great antiquity, it is even more remarkable for the manner in which it has survived, preserving a continuous life from its beginnings to the present day. For the peoples of Greece and Italy, of Sparta, Athens, Rome, and others who came much later, all perished long ago. But this people still survives, despite the endeavors of many powerful kings, who again and again have tried to destroy them, as their own historians testify, and as might have been readily conjectured from the ordinary course of things. The Jews have nevertheless been preserved through many centuries—and that preservation also was foretold. Their history stretches from the earliest to the most recent times, and encloses within its span all our much shorter stories.

The Law by which the Jewish people are governed is at once the most ancient in the world, the most perfect, and the only one which has been observed without interruption in any State. This is admirably shown by Josephus, in his *Contra Apion,* II, 29, and by Philo Judaeus in many places, which prove that the Law of the Jews is so ancient, that the very term, "law," was unknown to other ancient peoples, until more than a thousand years later. Thus Homer, who described the history of so many nations, never used it. We have only to read that Law to judge of its perfection, for it will be seen that it provides for every situation with such wisdom, such equity, and judgment, that the earliest of the Greek and Roman legislators, having acquired some knowledge of it, borrowed from it their principal laws. This is clear from a study of the "Law of the Twelve Tables," and other sources cited by Josephus. But in all that relates to their religious worship, this Law is at the same time the most severe, the most rigorous, of them all: in order to keep this people to their duty, it prescribes a thousand special and onerous observances, under penalty of death. This fact makes it truly astonishing that this Law should have been observed unchanged through so many centuries, by a rebellious and impatient people like the Jews, while other nations were changing their law codes from time to time, although their legal systems were already far more lenient.

The book containing this Law, the earliest of all, is itself the oldest book in the world, those of Homer, Hesiod and the rest coming six or seven hundred years later.

322. After the Creation and the Flood, when God was no longer determined to make an end of the earth, nor to create it anew, nor to show forth His power by mighty works, He began to establish on earth a people formed to fulfill His purpose, a people that should endure until the rise of that other people that should consent to be fashioned by the spirit of the Messiah.

323. *Types:* It was the purpose of God to raise up for Himself a holy people, whom He would separate from all other nations of the earth, whom he would deliver from their enemies and set in a place of rest. He both promised to do

so, and foretold by His prophets the time and manner of His coming. And yet, to confirm His elect in hope, He showed them His promises as it were in types, from one generation to another, and He never left them without these assurances of His power, and of His will to save them. For at the Creation of man, Adam was witness and recipient of a promise (of the Saviour to be born of a woman) at a time when men were still so close in time to the Creation, that they could not yet have forgotten their creation and their fall. When those who had known Adam were no longer living, God sent Noah, and saved him when He drowned the whole earth. By this miracle He sufficiently showed His power to save the world and His will to do so, and to raise up from the seed of a woman Him whom He had promised. This miracle was sufficient to confirm the hope of mankind. While the memory of the Flood was still fresh in the minds of men, and while Noah was still alive, God made His promises to Abraham, and in the lifetime of Sem, God sent Moses, etc. . . .

324. *The sincerity of the Jews:* After Prophecy had ceased came the Maccabees; after Jesus Christ, the Masorah.

"This book will serve as testimony on your behalf." [12]

The defective and final letters.

Completely honest, although it was against their own interest, and ready to die for it. This is without example in human history, and has no root in nature.

325. *Sincerity of the Jews:* Lovingly and faithfully they preserve the book in which they are told by Moses that they have been ungrateful to God throughout their lives, and that he knows they will be even more so after his death; that he calls upon heaven and earth to witness against them; and that he has taught them enough.

[12] The Jews preserved their holy books, copying them with the greatest fidelity. When the line of Prophets, inspired authors writing in Hebrew, had come to an end, the Maccabees continued the work of preservation. After the time of Christ, the Greek translators of the Hebrew Scriptures followed the Hebrew text known as the Masorah, modifying only a few details such as the "defective and final letters" mentioned by Pascal. The Masoretic text, upon which our own Bible directly depends, is commented by every Rabbi, down to our own day. Hence Pascal's remarks in this fragment, suggesting that "the Jewish Doctors continue to bear witness for Christianity and against themselves."

He declares that God will at last be angry with them, and scatter them abroad among all the nations of the earth; and that, as they have angered Him by worshiping gods who were not their God, so He in turn will provoke them by calling a people who are not His people. Moses also declares the will of God, that all His words be preserved forever, and that His book be put in the Ark of the Covenant, to serve as a witness against them. Deut. 31:26. Isaiah says the same thing (Isa. 30:8).

326. The zeal of the Jews for their Law and their temple (Josephus and Philo Judaeus, ad Caium). What other people ever had such zeal? It was the destiny of the Jews.

Jesus Christ was foretold, both as to the time of His appearance and the condition of the world into which He was to be born: The ruler taken from the thigh, and the fourth monarchy (Dan. 2:44). What a blessing, to have this light in this darkness!

How wonderful it is, to see by the eye of faith, Darius and Cyrus, Alexander, the Romans, Pompey and Herod, all working for the glory of the Gospel, and yet without any knowledge of the Gospel!

326a. It is a wonderful thing that we can read the history of Herod or of Caesar with the eyes of faith.

327. The zeal of the Jewish people for their Law, especially since the line of Prophets came to an end.

328. The devil disturbed the zeal of the Jews before the coming of Jesus Christ, because He might have been their Redeemer (Luke 24:21), but not afterwards.

The Jewish people, scorned by the Gentiles; and Christians persecuted.

329. While the Prophets were among them to maintain the Law, the people were neglectful; but since the line of the Prophets ceased, zeal has supplied for them.

330. When the memory of the Creation began to fade, God raised up a unique contemporary historian, and entrusted a whole people with the preservation of his book, so that His record might be the best authenticated in the

world, that all men might learn from it what it was so necessary for them to know, and that this necessary knowledge might only be acquired from this one source.

331. The Jews are clearly a people formed expressly to witness to the Messiah (Isa. 43:9, 44:8); they preserve the books, and they love them, but they do not understand them. All this is foretold: that the judgments of God are entrusted to them, but as the words of a book that is sealed (Isa. 29:11).

332. Why should Moses have made the lives of men so long and their generations so few?

Because it is not length of years but the number of generations that causes obscurity. For truth alters only as men change. Yet Moses brings together two events, and those the most memorable that any man could imagine, namely the Creation and the Flood, setting the two narratives in such close succession that they almost touch.

333. Shem, who saw Lamech, who saw Adam, also saw Jacob, and Jacob saw those who saw Moses. Therefore the Flood and the Creation are true. This argument, for those who understand it correctly, is conclusive.

334. The longevity of the Patriarchs did not cause the remembrance of things past to be lost: on the contrary, it tended to preserve traditions. For if we are not always well informed about the lives of our own ancestors, that is because we did not live very long with them, for very often they have died before we ourselves reached the age of reason. Now in the days of the Patriarchs, when men lived so long, children also lived many years with their parents, and could have lengthy conversations with them. And what should they talk about, if not the tradition of their elders, since this was literally the marrow, the subject matter, of history? In those days they had as yet none of the learning, the arts, the sciences, which nowadays feature so largely in our ordinary conversation. Moreover, we can see that in those days people took particular care to preserve their genealogies.

335. *Antiquity of the Jews:* What a difference there is between one book and another! I am not astonished that

the Greeks made the *Iliad,* nor that the Egyptians and the Chinese compiled their annals.

We have only to see how this came about. These chroniclers of fable were not contemporary with the events they profess to describe. Homer composed a tale which was recited and accepted as such: nobody supposed Troy and Agamemnon had ever really existed, any more than they believed the tale of the golden apple. Neither had he any intention of writing serious history, for his only purpose was to entertain. He was the only writer of his time, and the beauty of his work caused it to survive: everybody learnt it and talked about it; indeed a knowledge of it was a social necessity, and everybody knew it by heart. But four hundred years pass, and the witnesses of such things are no longer alive. Nobody any longer knows at first hand whether the events of the *Iliad* were fact or fiction. One simply received it from one's ancestors, and it could be accepted as true.

Any history that is not a contemporary record is suspect. Thus the Sybilline books, Trismegistus, and so many others which formerly the world accepted, are false, and with the passage of time are seen to be so. But it is quite otherwise with contemporary authors.

There is a great deal of difference between a book written by a known author and released to the public, and a book upon which rested the way of life of an entire nation. One cannot doubt that such a book would be as ancient as that people.

339. *The Canon of Scripture:* In the early days of the Church, the writings of heretics served to consolidate the Canon of the Scriptures.

340. Miton is well aware that [human] nature is corrupt, and that men are opposed to morality; but he does not know why they cannot rise to a higher level.

341. If man is not made for God, why is he not happy except in God? If man is made for God, why is he so opposed to Him?

342. Christianity is a strange religion. It bids man recognize that he is low, and even an abomination; and also plants in him the desire to be like God. Without such a

counterpoise, the promotion to a higher dignity would make man vain; or the humbling of his pride would crush his spirit altogether.

343. All the objections raised by the various sects of opponents, tell only against themselves, and not at all against religion. What unbelievers assert . . .

344. Man does not know his rightful place in the natural order. It is clear that he has gone astray, fallen from his true position, which he cannot find again. He seeks it everywhere, in a state of anxiety and in vain, and in impenetrable darkness.

345. Man's true nature having been lost, all sorts of [alien tendencies] find their way into his character; just as his true good has been lost, so that all things become the true good for him.

346. The true nature of man, his true happiness, real powers, and capacity for religion, are matters which have to be learned simultaneously.

347. For myself, I admit that as soon as Christianity reveals the principle that human nature is corrupt and has fallen away from God, my eyes are opened, and I see indications of this truth wherever I look. For Nature is such that she testifies everywhere to a God who has been lost, both within man and about him—to a Nature who has herself suffered corruption.

348. In the time of man's innocence, his dignity lay in the power conferred upon him, to have dominion over the animal creation, and to have it for food; but today, man's dignity lies in his separateness from animals and his subordination to them.

349. Man is not worthy of God, but he is not incapable of being made worthy of Him.

It is unworthy of God to unite Himself to man in his condition of misery; but it is not unworthy of God to deliver man from his misery.

350. You must be a very clever fellow to have arrived at the opinion that man is too small to merit communion with God.

351. It is true then that all created things instruct man as to his condition—but we must be clear that we understand what is being taught. For it is not true that all things reveal God, nor is it true that all things hide Him. But it is true that He conceals Himself from those who provoke Him, and also that He discovers Himself to those who seek Him: because men are capable of attaining knowledge of Him, just as they are unworthy to do so—unworthy because corrupt, capable by reason of their original nature.

353. What shall we gather from all our darkness, if not a conviction of our unworthiness?

354. If there had never been any revelation of God, it would have been very difficult to prove that man had suffered eternal loss, and any such loss might have referred as much to the nonexistence of a Divinity, as to any unworthiness in man to have knowledge of Him. But the fact that He has shown Himself to men occasionally, though not in every age, disposes of this difficulty. If He appears but once, He endures forever. We can only conclude therefore that there is indeed a God, and that men are unworthy of Him.

355. There are perfections in Nature which demonstrate that she is the image of God, and imperfections, to assure us that she is no more than His image.

356. God desires rather to bend the will than to subdue the intellect. Perfect enlightenment would assist the mind but would be harmful to the will. To humble the proud.

357. Solomon and Job best knew the wretchedness of man, and have spoken of it better than any. One was the most fortunate, the other the unhappiest, of mankind. One knew from experience the vanity of pleasure; the other, the reality of misfortune.

358. The Preacher proclaims that man without God is in

a condition of general ignorance and inevitable misery; for to desire and yet to lack the power to satisfy the desire is misery. Now man desires happiness, and he also desires knowledge of a certain truth. Yet he cannot have that knowledge, nor can he rid himself of the desire for it. He is not satisfied with doubt.

359. *After reaching an understanding of the whole nature of man:* If a religion is to be accepted as true, it must display some knowledge of our nature. It must have perceived its greatness and its pettiness, and understood the reasons for both. What religion other than Christianity has done that?

360. If there is a single source of all things, there must also be a single end: all through Him, all for Him. The true religion therefore is the one which teaches us to worship and love Him alone. But as we find ourselves powerless to worship what we know not, or to love anything but ourselves, any religion which teaches us the duty of worship, must also instruct us as to our lack of power, and teach us the remedy for it. Christianity teaches us that through one man all was lost, so that the bond between God and ourselves was broken; she also teaches us that by one Man that relationship was restored.

We are born with such an aversion to the love of God, and that love is so necessary to us, that we must surely have been born in a condition of guilt: otherwise there would be injustice in God.

361. The word of God is the truth: it cannot lie. Therefore when what is said is false in a literal sense, it is true in a spiritual sense: "Sit at my right hand," Ps. 110:1, is clearly false in a literal sense, but is therefore true in the spiritual sense.

In such expressions as these, God is spoken of in human terms, and this particular passage simply means that the intention of God is the same as that of men, when they invite someone to take a seat on their right hand. The passage therefore indicates God's intention, but not the manner in which He will carry it out.

Thus, when Scripture says, "God has accepted the smell of your incense, and He will give you in recompense a fat land," the words express the same intention in God as a man would have who accepted your incense and bestowed "a fat land" in recompense.

Similarly, "His anger is not turned away," He is "a jealous God," Is. 5:25, Ex. 20:5; for since the things of God are inexpressible, they cannot be spoken of in any other way. The Church still makes use of such expressions: "For He strengthens the bars of your gates," Ps. 147:13, etc.

It is not permissible to assign to Scripture meanings which are not matter of revelation. Thus it has not been revealed that the closed *mem* of Isaiah means six hundred, nor that the final *tsade* or the *defective He* [13] signify mysteries reserved to initiates. It is therefore not permissible to say that they do, still less to say that we have in these letters a formula for the philosopher's stone. But we do say that the literal sense is not the true one, because the Prophets have said so themselves.

361a. I do not say that the *mem* has any occult meaning.

362. In order that the Messiah should be recognizable by the good, and rejected by the bad, God provided that His coming should be foretold in this manner. If the manner of the coming of the Messiah had been clearly foretold, there would have been no obscurity about it, even for the wicked. If the time of His coming had been foretold, though only in obscure terms, even the good would have found the prediction obscure: for in the simplicity of their hearts, they would not have understood, for example, that the closed *mem* signifies six hundred years. But the time of His coming had been precisely foretold, and the manner of it also had been expressed in symbols.

Because of this device the wicked went astray, assuming that the promised benefits consisted of material riches; and they did so, despite the fact that the time of His coming had been clearly foretold. But the good were not deceived. For the manner of understanding the promised benefits depends upon the heart, which describes as "good" the thing it loves. But the manner of understanding the time of His coming does not depend upon the heart. And so the prophecy, explicit as to the time of His coming, but obscure as to the

[13] Letters of the Hebrew alphabet.

promised benefits, deceived the wicked, and them alone.

362a. We must put into the chapter on fundamentals, the substance of the one on types, concerning the reasons for the use of types.[14] Why the first coming of Jesus Christ was foretold, and why the manner of that coming was prophesied in terms that were obscure.

363. The God of Christians is a God who makes the soul feel that He is her only good; that her rest is to be found in Him alone; that all her peace lies in Him; that she can find no joy save in the love of Him who makes her hate whatever holds her back, whatever hinders her from loving Him with all her strength. The self-love and sensual pleasure which stop her progress are intolerable to her. Thus God makes her aware of a root of self-love which is luring her away, and also of the truth] that He alone can cure it.

364. *Types:* The Jews had grown old in certain worldly thoughts: that God loved their father Abraham, his flesh and his progeny; that because of this love He had caused the Jews to multiply, and had set them apart from all other peoples, with whom He would not allow them to mix; that when they were languishing in Egypt, He brought them out, with many mighty wonders worked for their assistance; that He fed them with manna in the wilderness, and led them into a very fertile country; that He gave them kings, and a well-built temple wherein to offer sacrifice, that by the shedding of that blood they might be cleansed; and that His purposes concerning them would be consummated by the sending of a Messiah, who would make them masters of the whole world; and that the time of His coming had been foretold.

When the world had grown old in these carnal errors, Jesus Christ came at the appointed time, but not in the blaze of glory the Jews expected, so that they did not believe that this was He. After His death came Saint Paul, teaching men that all these things had happened by way of example; that the Kingdom of God was not in the flesh but in the spirit; that the enemies of men were not the Babylonians but their

[14] The science of biblical interpretation by "types" is called Typology. It studies the foreshadowings of the Christian dispensation in the events and persons of the Old Testament. Christ Himself referred to Jonah as prefiguring His own Resurrection.

own passions; that God delighted not in a sanctuary made with hands, but in a pure and contrite heart; that the true circumcision is not external, of the body, but a matter of the heart, spiritual and not literal; that it was not Moses who gave them bread from heaven, etc.

But since the Jews were unworthy of such things, God did not make the revelation to them. Yet it was His will to foretell them so that they should be believed, wherefore He foretold the time of their fulfillment clearly; the events were at times described explicitly, but more often by means of symbols, so that those who loved the symbols might dwell on them, and those who loved what was symbolized might see it in the symbols.

All that does not tend toward charity is symbolical.

The sole object of Scripture is charity.

All that does not tend to this sole object is no more than a symbol of it. For since, as we have said, there is only one object, all that does not tend toward it, explicitly and literally, is but a symbol of it.

God therefore lends diversity to this one precept of charity in order to satisfy our curious minds, which are forever in search of variety; for we love variety, wherefore God satisfies our necessities by giving us variety even in the one thing needful, so that variety itself might lead us to that one necessary thing.

The Jews so loved the symbols, the things which symbolize, and placed their hopes so entirely in them, that when it came at the time and in the manner foretold, they failed to recognize the reality, the thing symbolized.

The Rabbis took the breasts of the bride (Song of Sol. 4:5) as symbols—as they do with everything that does not apply to their own sole object: temporal goods. And Christians take even the Eucharist as a type of the glory toward which they strive.

366. *Concerning types:* Nothing is so much like love as greed, and nothing is so contrary to it. Thus the Jews, loaded with benefits which stimulated their greed, were very like Christians, yet very much their opposite. In this way they were possessed of the two qualities which they essentially had to have: they were to be so like the Messiah as to be typical of Him, and so very unlike Him that their witness to Him could never be suspect.

367. Every religion is false if its belief does not, as part of its rule of faith, acknowledge one God as the principle of all things, and which in its moral system does not love that one God as the last end of all things.

368. But it is impossible that God should ever be the end if He is not the beginning. We may direct our gaze upward, but our feet are on the sand: the ground beneath us will crumble and we shall fall, even as we look at the sky.

369. There is a difference, complete and essential, between the acts of the will and all other acts.

The will is one of the principal organs of belief; not because it creates belief, but because things are true or false according to the standpoint from which we view them. The will, preferring one aspect to every other, diverts the mind from considering qualities in those things it does not choose to see; and so the mind, keeping step with the will, stops to examine the aspect of the matter that appeals to it; and so it forms its judgments according to what it finds.

370. The ordinary man has the power of not thinking about things he does not wish to think about. "Lose no time on thinking about the passages concerning the Messiah," said the Jew to his son. Our own people often do the same. This is how the false religions are preserved, and the true one also, for many folk. But there are some who cannot help thinking about them, and think the more, the more they are forbidden. Such men reject the false religions, and even the true one, if they find no solid arguments for it.

371. The true religion teaches us our duties and our weaknesses, our pride and concupiscence; and the remedies, humility and mortification.

372. The true religion should teach greatness and wretchedness; it should inculcate self-respect and self-loathing, love and hatred.

373. All the rules of right conduct are perfectly well known and we have only to apply them. For example:

No one doubts that one should not hesitate to risk life

in defense of the common good, and many do so; but not for religion.

Inequality among men is scarcely to be avoided; but once you grant that, you open the door not only to totalitarian rule but to absolute tyranny.

Some mental relaxation is necessary for the mind: but this opens the door to undisciplined thinking and other forms of excess. We ought to set a limit. But there *are* no limits in these matters. Philosophers have proposed laws for the control of our mental processes, but the mind will not accept them.

374. We are creatures of habit: whoever forms the habit of faith will rely upon it; he will no longer be afraid to confess that he fears Hell, he could not believe any other doctrine. He who is accustomed to believe that the king is to be feared, etc. Who can doubt then that our soul, accustomed as it is to the perception of number, space, movement, believes that, and nothing but that?

375. What are our natural principles but the results of habit? Children form their principles upon their fathers' habits, like hunting in animals.

We know from experience that a change of custom will introduce a different natural habit. And if there are some habits which custom cannot eradicate, there are also some habits contrary to nature, which neither nature nor a new habit can overcome. That depends upon a man's tendencies.

376. Fathers fear that the natural love of their children may disappear. What then is this natural thing that is liable to disappear? Habit is a second nature, and it destroys the first. But what is nature? And is habit not natural? I am much afraid that nature is itself no more than a first habit, just as habit is a second nature.

378. Memory and joy are intuitive; and even geometrical propositions may become so. For reason creates natural intuitions, and natural intuitions may be obliterated by reason.

379. *Sunshine sponges*[15]: When we observe that some

[15] The forty nine *Pensées* bearing the title *spongia solis* belong to a clearly defined group of fragments which had been worked over by

things happen every day, the same cause producing the same effect, we infer from it a law of Nature, as for example that there will be daylight tomorrow. But there are times when Nature asserts herself, and declines to be subject to her own laws.

380. If we do not recognize that we are full of pride, ambition, concupiscence, weakness, poverty, and injustice, we are blind indeed. And what shall we say of a man who, knowing this to be his condition, has no desire to be delivered from it?

We cannot do otherwise than respect a religion so well aware of the imperfections of men. And how can we do other than desire to participate in the truth of a religion, which gives assurance that she can provide the remedies so much needed for our human deficiencies?

381. There are some who see clearly that man has no enemy other than concupiscence, and that it is this which lures him away from God, for God is not his enemy. They also see that man has no higher good than God, who is better than a fat land. Those who believe that a man's good lies in the things of the flesh, and evil in anything that would draw him away from the pleasures of the senses, do

---

Pascal with special care. They all deal with topics of current interest which had made a strong appeal to him, and which were being discussed with animation in the salon of Mame. de Sablé, frequented by Pascal, Mersenne, La Rochefoucauld, and other learned men.

The *sponge* of the title has been interpreted in its ordinary pharmaceutical sense as "a body capable of absorbing and storing fluid into a cellular structure, and of discharging the whole of such fluid if sufficient pressure be applied."

Apart from his own scientific knowledge, Pascal would have been familiar with a current homiletic application of the idea, the popular *Heliotropium* of Jeremy Drexelius S.J., which had been published in French at Mons in 1642, and sold in thousands all over Europe.

From "the flower which turns with the sun, or, the complete conformity of the will of man with that of God," which is, broadly speaking, the theme of the *Imitation* and the *Pensées,* it would have been a step willingly taken by Pascal, the enthusiastic associate and leader of many great thinkers in his day, to the modern acceptance of photosynthesis, and the application of the old Jesuit's naïve theory in such modern advances as the solar furnace now being operated by the sun in the Pyrenees, and the sun-fed battery in a satellite. Bolometers, heat pumps and thermopiles are other illustrations of the catching, storage, and use of solar energy.

The translation "sun spots," occasionally found, is the conjecture or guess of a nineteenth-century editor.

indeed deserve to wallow in sensuality and to die of it. But they who seek God with all their heart, and whose sole misery is to be deprived of the sight of Him; they who have no other desire than to possess Him, and no other enemy than he who seeks to detach them from Him; who are grieved to find themselves surrounded by such enemies, and dominated by them—to these I say: Let them be comforted, for I bring them glad tidings. There is One who will redeem them; I will cause them to see Him; I will demonstrate that there is a God for them; but to those others I will not show Him. I will cause them to see that a Messiah was promised who should deliver them from their enemies: and that One such came who delivered them, not from their enemies, but from their sins.

When David foretold that the Messiah would deliver his people from their enemies, we may believe that, as to the flesh, these were the Egyptians; in which case, I cannot show that the prophecy was fulfilled. But we may also very fittingly believe that the enemies mentioned by David were their sins, for in truth their real enemy was not Egypt, but sin. This word "enemy" is therefore ambiguous. But when David says elsewhere, as he does with Isa. 43:25, and others, that "he will redeem Israel from all his iniquities," Ps. 130:8, all ambiguity disappears, and the double sense of "enemies" is reduced to the simple sense of "sins." For if he had "sins" in mind, he might very well describe them as enemies; but if he was thinking of enemies, he could scarcely describe them as "sins."

Now Moses, David, and Isaiah all used the same expression. Who then will say that their meanings were not the same, and that David's meaning when he spoke of "enemies" and obviously meant "sins," was not also the meaning intended by Moses when he spoke of "enemies."

Daniel (9) prays that the people may be delivered from being held in captivity by their enemies, but it is clear that he was thinking of his people's sins (Dan. 9:5), and he shows this when he says that Gabriel came to tell him that his prayer was heard: that he now had only seventy weeks of waiting, and that his people would then be delivered from wickedness; sin would have an end; and the Redeemer, the holy One, would bring in everlasting righteousness—not the righteousness of the Law, but eternal justice.

382. Heavens, what foolish talk! Would God have made the world only to damn it? Would He ask so much from men so weak? etc. Skepticism is at any rate a cure for an opinion as desperate as that: it will chase out *that* nonsense.

383. (It may well be that there are unanswerable arguments, but the thing is not certain. So all this objection proves is—that it is not certain that everything is uncertain . . . and skepticism wins again.)

384. The dogma of Original Sin is foolishness in the eyes of men, but it is preached upon that understanding. You must not then argue that it is not grounded in reason, since I make no claim that it is so. But this foolishness is wiser than the wisdom of men: "wiser than men," I Cor. 1:25. For how, without this dogma, should we describe man: his whole condition turns upon this one invisible point. And how should he arrive at such knowledge by his reason if it is a thing contrary to reason, and if his reason, so far from arriving at the fact by its own processes, recoils from it when it is proposed?

385. *On Original Sin. The strong tradition of Original Sin among the Jews:* On the saying in Gen. 8:21, "For the imagination of man's heart is evil from his youth."

R. Moses Haddarschan: This evil leaven is placed in man at the moment that he is conceived.

Massechet Succa: This evil leaven has seven names in the Scriptures. It is called evil, foreskin, unclean, enemy, scandal, heart of stone, the twisted thing, all of which signify the malignity staining the heart of man and hidden within it.

Midrasch Tillim says the same thing: that God will deliver what is good in man from what is bad. Malignity renews daily the attack upon man, as it is written in Psalm 36: 32–33, "The wicked watches the righteous and seeks to slay him. The Lord will not abandon him to his power." This malignity is a temptation to the heart of man in this life, and will be brought against him at the judgment in the next. All this is to be found in the Talmud.

Midrasch Tillim on Psalm 4, "Be angry but sin not": Tremble, and let your concupiscence be alarmed, and it will not lead you into sin. And on Psalm 36, "Transgression speaks to the wicked, deep in his heart," that is to say, the wickedness that is natural to man, said thus and thus to the wicked.

Midrasch el Koheleth: Better is a poor and wise child than an old and foolish king who cannot foresee the future. Here, the child is the virtue in man; the king is the evil that is in him. Evil is called king because all his members obey it; he is old, because he is in the heart of man from childhood to old age; and he is foolish, because he leads man into a road to ruin, which man cannot foresee.

The same thing is said in *Midrasch Tillim.*

Bereschit Rabba on Psalm 25, "All my bones shall say, 'O Lord, who is like to Thee, Thou who deliverest the weak from him who is too strong for him.' " And is there any greater tyrant than that evil leaven? And on Proverbs 25, "If your enemy is hungry, give him bread to eat": that is, if the evil leaven be hungry, feed it with the bread of wisdom, spoken of in Proverbs 9, and if it be thirsty, give it the water of Isaiah 55.

Midrasch Tillim says the same thing, and says that in this passage, Scripture speaks of our enemy and means the evil leaven; and that by giving him that bread and that water we shall be heaping coals of fire upon his head.

Midrasch el Koheleth on Eccles. 9:14, "A great king besieged a little city." This great king is the evil leaven, the great engines of war which he brings against the city are temptations, and the poor, wise man that was found in the city and who delivered it, was virtue.

And on Psalm 41, "Blessed is he who considers the poor," And on Psalm 78, "A wind that passes and comes not again." Which has led some into error as to the immortality of the soul. But the sense here is that the wind is that evil leaven, that travels along with man until his death, but will not return to him at the Resurrection. And on Psalm 103, the same thing.

Principles of the Rabbis. Two Messiahs.

386. Shall we say then that when they declared that justice had left the earth, men recognized the fact of Original Sin? "Let no man be called happy before his death." That is, they knew that eternal and essential Beatitude begins at death.

389. Memory is essential to all the operations of the reasoning faculty.

390. Chance suggests our thoughts, and chance dissipates them; there is no known method of retaining a thought in the mind—nor of lodging it there.

A thought has escaped me: I wanted to write it down, but instead I write that it has escaped me.

392. My thought sometimes escapes me, even in the very act of writing it down. But this keeps me in mind of my own weakness, which I am always forgetting: and the experience teaches me quite as much as that forgotten thought, since it disposes me to recognize that I am at best an unprofitable servant.

393. (A single thought occupies us wholly: we cannot think of two things at once; and a host of thoughts [assaults us] from the wordly side, crowding out the thought of God.)

395. *Fallen nature:* Reason is the very essence of man's being—and yet he never acts in conformity with it.

396. The corruption of reason appears plainly in the corruption of manners. It was necessary that the truth should come, so that man should no longer live for himself alone.

397. Part of the shamed embarrassment of the damned will be the discovery that they are condemned by their own reason—that very reason by which they claimed that the Christian religion stood condemned.

400. "Why do you want to kill me?" "Why not? Don't you live on the other side of the water? My friend, if you lived on this side, I should certainly be a murderer, and to kill you like this would be an act of injustice. But since you live on the other side, I am a good citizen and justice has been done."

400a. He lives across the water.

401. On what principle should a man[16] establish the

[16] The reference here may be to Montaigne.

economy of the world he is ambitious to govern? Upon the whim of the individual? But that would be chaos! Upon justice? He knows nothing about it.

It is certain that, even if he had known it, he would not have proposed that commonest of all the general principles known to men, that each should follow the customs of his country; [but] the light of true equity would have brought all nations under its rule, and lawgivers would not have preferred the whims and fancies of Persians and Germans to the pattern of even-handed justice. We should then have seen justice established in every nation of the world and in all ages; but instead of that we see no "right" or "wrong" that does not change its nature with a change of climate. Three degrees of latitude suffice to overturn the whole of jurisprudence; and a meridian decides what is the truth. A few years of tenure, and—the laws of nature have themselves changed: the law has its terms! And the conjunction of Saturn and Leo marks the time at which such and such an act was declared to be henceforth criminal. It is a strange justice that is bounded by a stream! Truth lies this side the Pyrenees, and error on the other.

Men admit that justice is not inherent in these customs, but in natural laws common to all countries. And they would certainly defend this opinion stubbornly if chance, when so casually distributing laws to humanity, had hit upon even one that was universal. But the joke is, that human caprice is so erratic that there is not even one such.

Theft, incest, infanticide, parricide have all in their time been regarded as virtuous acts. Could anything be more absurd than that a man should have a right to kill me because he lives on the other side of the water and his prince has a quarrel with mine, though I have none with him? Of course there are natural laws, but once this precious right-reason was corrupted, it corrupted everything: "Nothing belongs to us any longer; we call things 'ours' as a figure of speech," Cicero, *De finibus,* V. 21. "Crimes are committed by decree of the Senate and by vote of the people," Seneca, *Letters,* XCV. "Whereas we formerly suffered for our vices, we now suffer from our laws," Tacitus, *Annals,* III. 25.

This confusion of thought leads one man to declare that the essence of justice lies in the authority of the legislator, another, in the interests of the ruler, yet another, in the prevailing custom. This last is closest to the truth. To follow rea-

on only would mean that nothing is just of itself: since all
hings change with time. It is custom that creates all equity
imply because it is accepted. This acceptance is the mystical
asis of its authority, and anyone who sought to trace custom
ack to a principle would destroy it. Nothing is so defective
s the law passed to remedy an abuse: he who obeys such
aws because they are just, obeys a principle of justice which
e assumes to be present, but he does not obey law in its
ssence. He obeys an application of it, something self-con-
ained, *a* law, and nothing more. And anyone who sought to
xamine that man's motive would find it so weak, so trivial,
hat unless he is well used to the spectacle of the achieve-
nents of the human imagination, he will be amazed that a
ingle century should have sufficed to endow the doctrine
vith pomp and win it popular respect. The art of con-
piracy and of the overthrowing of governments is to ridicule
stablished customs, probing them to their very origins, so
s to show up their defective authority and their failure to do
ustice. "We must return," they say, "to the basic, primitive
aws of the state, which unjust custom has abolished." That
s certainly a losing game: nothing could be weighed cor-
ectly in those scales. Nevertheless, the people lend a willing
ar to such talk. They shake off the yoke as soon as they
eel it; and the great ones profit by the ruin of the estab-
ished order and that of the curious inquirers into received
customs. This is why the wisest of legislators said that men
nust often be deceived for their own good; and another, who
understood the government of men, wrote: "Since he knows
not the truth that would set him free, it is fitting he should
be deceived." Saint Augustine, *De civ, Dei,* IV, 27. The facts
about the conspiracy and the overthrow of the government,
he usurpation of power must not, of course, become known:
all that was something that happened some time ago, and
here was not much justice about it, but custom has cloaked
t in justice. You have to make a coup look authoritative
and permanent, and you have to keep its origins out of sight,
unless you want your new régime to come to a speedy end.

402. *Mine, thine:* "This dog is mine," those poor children
used to say, "and this is my place in the sun." There you
have the origin and the pattern for all the usurpations in
human history.

402b. "Rarely does a man respect himself sufficiently," Quintilian, X. 7. Montaigne, I, 39.

"So many deities, in tumult about a single head," Seneca, *Rhetor. Suesor*, i. 4.

"Nothing is more shocking than that assertion should go before knowledge," Cicero, *Acad.* 1, 45.

"I am not ashamed, as they are, to admit that I do not know what I do not know," Cicero, *Tusc.* 1, 25.

"It is better not to begin," Seneca, *Ep.* lxxii.

403. *Justice:* Fashion decides what is pleasing, and she also determines what is just.

406. I have passed a great part of my life in the belief that justice had a real existence; and in this I was not mistaken, for justice does indeed exist—to the extent that God has been pleased to reveal it to us. That is what I did not grasp, and that was how I ran into error: for I believed that our human justice is actually just in principle, and that I myself was equipped to recognize what justice required, and how to apply it. But I so often found that I had failed to arrive at a correct judgment, that I began to lose confidence, first in myself and then in others. I saw that all things and all men are subject to change. And so, after many times revising my own opinion as to the nature of true justice, I realized that our human nature is in a state of continual change, and on that subject I have not since then altered my mind. And indeed if I did so, that would only confirm my view of the matter.

The skeptic Arcesilaus, who reverted to dogmatism.

408. *True justice:* We have it no longer. If we had, we should not take the customs of our country as our rule of justice. Thus, having failed to find justice, we fall back upon force.

409. *Commitment leads to error:* It is deplorable to observe how all men argue about means, and never about ends. Each one considers how he shall behave in his particular state of life; but as for the choice of a state of life, or of native land, that is left to chance.

It is a pitiful thing to see so many Turks, heretics, and infidels following in the footsteps of their fathers, simply beause they have all been told by somebody or other that hat is the best way. And that is all that settles his state of ife for any man, be he locksmith or soldier.

That is why peasants have no use for Provence.

·10. It is not the custom of men to create merit, but only o reward it where they find it; and they judge God by themelves.

·11. Against those who are so confident of the mercy of God, that they remain lukewarm, and do no good works.

Since the two sources of our sins are pride and idleness, God has revealed to us two attributes of His own that will eal them: His mercy and His justice. The property of jusice is to beat down pride, however holy our works may be: Enter not into judgment," Ps. 143:2; and the property of nercy is to cure idleness by exhorting to good works, accordng to the passage which says, "God's kindness is meant to ead you to repentance," Rom. 2:4; and that other about the nen of Nineveh, "Let us repent, and see if He will have nercy on us," Jonah 3:8–9. And thus, so far from authorizng idleness, mercy is the attribute which directly attacks it; o that, instead of saying, "If there were no mercy in God, ve should have to make the most strenuous efforts after virue," we must say the opposite. Precisely because there is nercy in God we must spare no effort.

·12. It is absurd that there should be people in the world who have renounced all the laws of God and of nature, yet ave made laws for themselves which they obey very careully, as for instance, the soldiers of Mahomet, gangs of hieves, heretics, etc. It is the same with logicians. Apparently heir license must know neither bounds nor barriers, seeing hat they have rejected so many restraints that are both ust and holy.

13. *Injustice:* They had found no other way of satisfyng concupiscence than to do harm to others.

16. It is right that what is just should be obeyed; it is ssential that power should prevail and should be obeyed. ustice without power is helpless; power without justice is yranny. Justice without power is always disputed because

there are always wicked men; power without justice stands condemned. Our task must therefore be, to combine justice and power; to ensure that what is just is backed by power, and that the powerful are just.

Justice, however, is subject to dispute among men, whereas power is at once recognized, and where it exists it is obeyed. We have not been successful in making justice strong, because force is contrary to justice, and the powerful have asserted that only power is just. And so, having been unable to ensure that what is right should be strong, people have tended to act as though what was strong was right.

419. Why do we follow a majority? Because they have more right on their side? No, but because they have more power.

Why do we follow ancient laws and customs? Is it because they are more sound? No, it is because of their simplicity in principle. Because such laws are less likely to conflict with one another, they go straight to the root of the strife.

420. It is the result of power, not of custom. Men of an original turn of mind are rare. The majority only want to follow: they refuse honor to pioneers who seek it for their discoveries. And if the inventors are determined to win honors, and scorn men who are not original, these people will call them by offensive names and would very much like to set about them. Let no one therefore pride himself on his own quickness of intellect, or be too pleased with himself.

421. Power and not opinion is mistress of the world. But it is opinion that makes use of power. Power creates opinion Suppleness, in our opinion, is a fine thing—and why? Because a dancer on a *tight* rope would find himself alone, and I wil collect together a stronger party, to declare that such a practice has its perils.

423. We are unable to form any idea of the glorious state of Adam, nor of the nature of his sin, nor of the way in which it has been transmitted to us. These things had thei being in a state of nature entirely different from our own and transcending the present capacity of human understanding.

Even if we knew all about it, the knowledge would no bestow upon us the power to escape from our fallen condi tion. All that we really need to know is that we are wretched, fallen, separated from God but redeemed by Jesus Christ: and that is something of which we have marvelous proofs here on earth.

Thus, the two proofs of human corruption and of human redemption are derived from unbelievers who live indifferent to religion; and from the Jews who are implacable enemies of a Redemption.

424. *Proof:* 1° The Christian religion, by the manner of its establishment. It established itself so firmly and so gently, although so contrary to nature. 2° The holiness, the dignity, and the humility of a Christian soul. 3° The marvelous things in the holy Scriptures. 4° Jesus Christ, in particular. 5° The Apostles, in particular. 6° Moses and the Prophets, in particular. 7° The Jewish people. 8° The prophecies. 9° Perpetuity: no other religion has perpetuity. 10° Its doctrine, providing reasons for everything. 11° The holiness of the Law. 12° By the course of historical events.

There can be no room for doubt that, after considering the conditions of earthly life, and the nature of this religion, we ought not to refuse our inclination to follow it, if it makes an appeal to our hearts; and certainly there is no reason to ridicule those who do follow it.

425. *Proofs of religion:* Morality, doctrine, miracles, prophecies, types.

426. *Proof of both Testaments together:* To prove the truth of both Testaments together it is only necessary to see whether the prophecies of the one are fulfilled in the other. To examine the prophecies we need to understand them. For if we believe them to have one meaning only, then it is certain that the Messiah has not yet come. But if they have two meanings, it is certain that he came in the person of Jesus Christ.

The whole question then is to know whether they have two meanings.

Here are the proofs that Scripture has two meanings, and that these meanings were conveyed by Jesus Christ and the Apostles:

1. Proof from the Scriptures themselves.

2. Proof from the Rabbis: Moses Maimonides says that the Scriptures have two faces, and that the Prophets were only foretelling Jesus Christ.

3. Proofs from the Kabbala.

4. Proofs from the mystical interpretation applied to the Scriptures by the Rabbis themselves.

5. Proof, from Rabbinic principles, that there are two senses [of Scripture]; two advents of the Messiah, one glorious and one humble, according to the expectations of those who wait for Him; that the Prophets foretold only the Messiah; that the Law is not eternal, but will of necessity be changed with the coming of the Messiah; that when He comes, no one will remember the Red Sea, that Jews and Gentiles shall be mingled.

6. Proof from the key provided by Jesus Christ and the Apostles.

428. Two men are telling silly stories. One makes free use of the *double entendre*, which is supposed to conceal his meaning from anyone "not in the know," while the other talks in a simple style. If a third party heard them talking in this way and was not in the secret, he would judge both speakers by the same standard. But if, in what followed, one of them spoke with the tongue of angels, while the other uttered nothing but the flattest of commonplaces, the hearer would conclude that one man spoke in mysteries, but not the other. For the one speaker would have shown that he was incapable of such silliness, but was capable of profundity; the other, that he could not rise to an exalted plane, but could sink to a low one.

The Old Testament is a cipher.

430. Adam, *the form of Him that was to come*. Six days to create one, six ages to create the other. The six days that Moses speaks of for the creation of Adam are nothing but a type of the six ages that were necessary to prepare for Jesus Christ and His Church. If Adam had never sinned, and if Jesus Christ had never come, there would have been but one Covenant, one age of men, and the work of the Creation would have been represented as though it had been a single act.

431. When the Creation had receded into the past, God

raised up one chronicler, and entrusted a whole people with the guardianship of his record, so that this book might be the best authenticated in the world, and that all men might learn of a thing so necessary to be known, yet which could only be made known to them in this way.

432. The two oldest books in the world are Moses and Job; one was a Jew, the other a heathen, yet both look to Jesus Christ as their common center and object. Moses, by recording God's promises to Abraham, Jacob, etc., and by his prophecies; and Job, when he says, "Oh, that my words were written . . . for I know that my Redeemer lives," Job 19: 23b–24.

434. One word out of David or Moses, such as, "God shall circumcise the heart," gives the clue to their spirit. Though it be said that all their other sayings are ambiguous, and make us wonder whether to be philosophers or Christians, yet a saying like this strikes the keynote for all the others, whereas one word from Epictetus will throw everything else he says into disorder. Ambiguity can deceive us up to a certain point, but not beyond it.

436. The only religion which goes against our human nature, is contrary to "common sense," and opposed to our pleasures, is also the only one which has a continuing existence.

438. No other religion than ours has taught that man is born in sin, no sect of philosophers ever said so, hence none of these has told the truth.

No other sect or religion has existed upon earth from the beginning, but only the Christian religion.

439. *Perpetuity:* Our religion comprises the belief that man has fallen from a state of glory and of communion with God, into a condition of sorrow, penance, and estrangement from God; but that after this life we shall be restored by a Messiah who was to come. And this belief has always existed upon earth. All [other] things have passed away, but this religious belief persists; for it and because of it all things have their being.

In the first age of the world, men were swept off their feet into every kind of sin, and yet there were holy men, such as Enoch, Lamech, and others, who waited patiently for the Christ promised from the beginning of the world. Noah saw the wickedness of humanity at its height, and he was found worthy to save the world in his own person, through the hope of the Messiah, whom he foresaw from afar. In the time of Isaac and Jacob, abomination was spread throughout the world, but those holy men lived by faith; and Jacob, when he was dying, and as he blessed his children, interrupted his words of blessing to cry in exultation: "I wait for thy salvation, O Lord," Gen. 49:18. The Egyptians were infected with idolatry and magic, and even the people of God were led astray by their example; yet Moses and some others believed in Him whom they saw not, and worshiped Him as they looked beyond, to the enduring good things that He was preparing for them.

The Greeks, and after them the Romans, set up false gods, their poets created a hundred different theologies, their philosophers divided into a thousand different sects; and yet there were always to be found, in the heart of Judaea, certain chosen men who foretold the coming of a Messiah known to them alone.

In the fullness of time at length He came; and since His coming we have witnessed the birth of schisms and heresies without number, the overthrow of States, and universal change. Yet this Church, adoring Him who has been worshiped from the beginning, has continued in being without interruption. And it is a wonderful fact, without parallel and altogether divine, that this same religion, while it endures forever, has never been free from attack. A thousand times it has been brought to the very eve of total destruction; and on each occasion, God has intervened to save her by some extraordinary manifestation of His power. This is an amazing thing, as is also the fact that she was enabled to endure without yielding or bending to the will of tyrants. For it is not strange that a state should continue, where its laws are made to be adaptable as conditions may require; but that . . . (see the passage marked in Montaigne) [I, 23 on Fortune].

442. *Perpetuity:* People have always believed in a Messiah. The tradition of Adam was still fresh in the time of Noah and Moses, and since their time He has been foretold by Prophets, who spoke of Him when declaring events that

were to come—events which, as they duly occurred from time to time in the sight of all men, marked the authenticity of the prophetic mission, and gave additional support to their promises concerning the Messiah. Jesus Christ performed miracles, as did also the Apostles who converted all the heathen; thus all the prophecies being fulfilled, the Messiah is proved for all time.

443. *Perpetuity:* We must bear in mind that the expectation or worship of the Messiah has persisted without interruption from the beginning of the world; that there have always been found certain men who said that God had revealed to them that a Redeemer was to be born who would save His people; that there then came Abraham, saying it had been revealed to him that this Redeemer was to be born of his own line through a son he was to have; that Jacob declared that the Messiah should be born of the house of Judah, one of his own twelve sons; that Moses and the Prophets followed, declaring the time and manner of His coming; and how they said that the Law as it stood was to be observed only until the time of the Messiah; that their Law was to be strictly observed until that time, but then the other law, the law of the Messiah, would endure forever; that thus a rule of law, either their own or that of the Messiah, of which theirs was a promise, would endure upon earth forever; that it has in fact never ceased; and that finally Jesus Christ came; and that all the circumstances of His coming did in point of fact fulfill the prophecies. This is a wonderful thing.

444. *To show that true Jews and true Christians have one and the same religion:* The religion of the Jews appears to consist essentially in descent from Abraham, in circumcision, in sacrifices, in ceremonies, in the Ark [of the Covenant], in the Temple, in Jerusalem, and finally, in the Law, and the covenant with Moses.

But I say, that it consisted in none of these things, but only in the love of God, and that God rejected all those other things.

That God did not in fact accept the posterity of Abraham.

That if the Jews offend Him, God will punish them as though they were strangers: "And if you forget the Lord your God and go after other gods and serve them and worship them, I solemnly warn you . . . that you shall surely perish.

Like the nations that the Lord makes to perish before you, so shall you perish," Deut. 8:19–20.

That if they love Him, strangers shall be received by God as though they were Jews: Let not the foreigner who has joined himself to the Lord say, "The Lord will surely separate me from his people," Isa. 56:3. "The foreigners who join themselves to the Lord, to minister to him, to love the name of the Lord, and to be his servants . . . these will I bring to my holy mountain, and make them joyful in my house of prayer; their burnt offerings and their sacrifices will be accepted on my altar," Isa. 56:67.

That the true Jews believed all their merit to derive from God rather than from Abraham: "For thou art our Father, though Abraham does not know us and Israel does not acknowledge us; thou, O Lord art our Father, our Redeemer from of old is thy name," Isa. 63:16.

Moses himself told them that God is no respecter of persons: "God is not partial, and takes no bribe," Deut. 10:17.

The Sabbath was only a sign, Exod. 31:15; and a memorial of the exodus from Egypt, Deut. 5:19. Thus it is no longer necessary, since we must forget Egypt.

Circumcision was only a sign, Gen. 17:11. Hence, while they were in the desert the Jews were never circumcised, because there they could not mix, nor be confused, with other peoples; and because after the coming of Jesus Christ it is no longer necessary.

That the circumcision of the heart is commanded: "Circumcise therefore the foreskin of your heart, and be no longer stubborn. For the Lord your God is God of gods and Lord of lords, the great, the mighty and the terrible God, who is not partial and takes no bribes," Deut. 10:16–17.

That God said He would one day perform it: "And the Lord your God will circumcise your heart and the hearts of your children, so that you will love the Lord your God with all your heart," Deut. 30:6.

That the uncircumcised in heart shall be judged: "Behold, the days are coming . . . when I will punish all those who are . . . uncircumcised . . . and all the house of Israel is uncircumcised in heart," Jer. 9:25–6.

That the outward is worth nothing without the inward: "Rend your hearts and not your garments," Joel 2:13, Isa. 58:3, 4.

The love of God is commanded throughout Deuteronomy: "I call heaven and earth to witness against you this day, that I have set before you life and death, blessing and curse; therefore choose life, that you and your descendants may live," Deut. 30:19.

That the Jews, since they lacked this love, would be rejected for their sins, and the Gentiles chosen in their place: "And he said, I will hide my face from them, I will see what their end will be, for they are a perverse generation. . . . They have stirred me to jealousy with what is no god; they have provoked me with their idols. So I will stir them to jealousy with those who are no people; I will provoke them with a foolish nation," Deut. 32:20, Hos. 1:10, Isa. 65:1.

That temporal goods deceive us, and that the true good is to be found in being at one with God, Ps. 143:15.

That their feasts are displeasing to God, Amos 5:21.

That the sacrifices of the Jews are displeasing to God, Isa. 66:1–5, 1:11, Jer. 6:20; David's "Have mercy on me, O God . . ." Even those of the good ("I looked for justice," Ps. 49:8–14).

That he established those sacrifices solely on account of their hard hearts, Mic. (admirably) 6:6, I. Sam. 15:22, Hos. 6:6.

That the sacrifices of the Gentiles will be accepted by God, and that He will take no pleasure in the sacrifices of the Jews, Mal. 1:11.

That God will make a new covenant through the Messiah, and that the old will be annulled, Jer. 31:31.

"Statutes that were not good," Ezek. 20:25.

That the things of old shall be forgotten, Isa. 43:18, 19, 45:17, 18.

That the Ark will be forgotten, Jer. 3:15, 16.

That the Temple will be rejected, Jer. 7:12–14.

That the sacrifices will be rejected, and other pure sacrifices introduced, Mal. 1:11.

That the order of Aaron's sacrificing priesthood would be deposed, and that of Melchizedek introduced by the Messiah, "The Lord says to my lord . . ." Ps. 110:4.

That this sacrificing priesthood would be forever, Ps. 110:4.

That Jerusalem would be rejected, and Rome accepted, Ps. 110.

That the name of Jew would be rejected, and a new name given, Isa. 56:15.

That the new name would be better than that of "Jew," and would endure forever, Isa. 62:5.

That the Jews were to be without prophets (Amos), without king, without princes, without sacrifice, and without an idol.

That the Jews will nevertheless always exist as a people, Jer. 31:36.

445. *Republic:* The Christian republic, and the Jewish also, had God for sole ruler, as is observed by Philo the Jew, in his book, *On Monarchy*.

When they fought, it was for God alone, and their main hope was in Him; they regarded their cities as belonging to Him only, and they preserved them for him, I. Chron. 19:13.

446. The Synagogue preceded the Church, and the Jews preceded the Christians; the Prophets foretold the Christians, just as Saint John announced the coming of Jesus Christ.

447. Worldly Jews stand halfway between Christians and heathens. The heathen do not know God, and they love this world only. The Jews know the true God—but they love this world only. Christians know the true God, and have no love for the things of this world. Jews and heathens love the same earthly things, while Jews and Christians know the same God.

The Jews were of two kinds: some had only pagan dispositions, while others had tendencies that might be called Christian.

448. Worldly Jews and heathens have their sorrows, as Christians have also. There is no Redeemer for the heathen; they do not even hope for one. There is no Redeemer for the Jews; for them, this hope is vain. There is no Redeemer for any but for Christians only. (See the fragments headed *Perpetuity*.)

449. The Jews, who were called upon to subjugate nations and kings, were themselves the slaves of sin; and Christians, whose vocation it has been to serve and to be subject, are the children of the household.

450. There are two kinds of men in every religion: among the heathen, the worshipers of animals, and others worshiping one God in the religion of Nature; among the Jews, the worldly and the spiritual, the latter being the Christians of the old Law. Among Christians, the cruder, unrefined kind are, as it were, the Jews of the New Law. The worldly Jews looked for a worldly Messiah. The crude type of Christian believes that the Messiah has dispensed them from the duty of loving God. True Jews and true Christians worship a Messiah who teaches them the love of God.

451. Anyone who judges the religion of the Jews by its cruder representatives will gain but an imperfect understanding of it. Their religion is clearly seen in their sacred books and in the prophetic tradition: The Prophets made it perfectly clear that they did not interpret the Law in a literal sense. Thus our own religion is divine as taught in the Gospels, by the Apostles and by tradition, but it is brought into contempt by those who pervert its teaching.

According to the worldly type of Jew, the Messiah was to be a great temporal prince. According to worldly Christians, the coming of Jesus Christ has dispensed them from the love of God, since He gave us the sacraments, which do everything for us, working a perfect work without our help. Neither of these types represents either the true Christian or the true Jewish religion.

True Jews and true Christians have always waited for a Messiah who would teach them the love of God, and how by this love they might triumph over their enemies.

453. *Proofs of Jesus Christ:* No man who knows with certainty that at the end of seventy years he will be free, can be called a prisoner. No prisoner nowadays has any hope of freedom. God promised [the Jews] that, even though He should scatter them to the ends of the earth, if they remained faithful to His Law, He would bring them together again. They have indeed continued to observe the Law with the greatest fidelity, and yet they remain oppressed.

454. It is an astonishing fact, worth very special attention, that the Jewish people are seen to survive for so many years, yet always in a state of misery. These things were necessary as proofs for Jesus Christ: that they should survive

the centuries to witness to Him; and that they should be always in misery because they crucified Him. And although continued survival in conditions of wretchedness implies a contradiction, these people nevertheless continue to survive, despite their misery.

455. It is clear that these people were raised up expressly to bear witness to the Messiah, Isa. 43:9, 44:8. They preserve the sacred books and they love them, but they do not understand them in the least. And all this was foretold: that the judgments of God were entrusted to them, but as a book that is sealed, Isa. 49:11.

458. The Jews reject Him, yet not all of them. The true Jews receive Him, but not the worldly. And so far is this from diminishing His glory, that it is the finishing touch, which completes it: since the reason they gave for this rejection, the only one found anywhere in their writings, in the Talmud and the Rabbis, is simply that He did not subdue the nations by force of arms, "Gird your sword upon your thigh, O mighty one, in your glory and majesty," Ps. 45:3. Is that all they have to say? "Jesus Christ was killed," they say. "He failed. He did not subdue the heathen by the use of His power. He did not bestow their spoils upon us. He gave us no riches." Have they nothing more to say? It is by this that He commands my love. There would for me be nothing compelling about such a figure as they expected. It is plain that nothing but wickedness[17] prevented them from accepting him. This refusal makes them unshakable witnesses; and what is more, they also thereby fulfill the prophecies.

460. "If all these things were plainly foretold to the Jews, how is it that they did not believe? Or how did they escape destruction when they resisted a thing so clear?"

I answer, first: It was foretold that they would not believe, however plain the thing might be; and also, that they would not be destroyed. Nothing is more to the glory of the Messiah. For it was not enough that there should be Prophets: their prophecies had also to be preserved, and they had to be above suspicion. Now . . .

[17] Adopting the reading, *vice*, from Chevalier and a majority of texts.

461. If all the Jews had been converted by Jesus Christ, we should be left with only unreliable witnesses. And if they had [all] been destroyed, we should have had no witnesses at all.

462. The Jews were accustomed to great and startling miracles. In the mighty works of the Red Sea and the land of Canaan, they saw examples of the [yet mightier] deeds that would be done by their Messiah, and so they looked forward to other and still more impressive miracles, beside which those of Moses would be but as the model to the finished work.

463. *Prophecies:* Great Pan is dead.

464. The prophecies are the strongest proofs of Jesus Christ; they are also the proofs with which God was more lavish, because the event that fulfilled them is a miracle that endures from the birth of the Church until the end. Moreover, God raised up Prophets for sixteen hundred years; and for four hundred years after that, he caused all those prophecies, and the Jews who had preserved them, to be scattered into every corner of the world. Such was the preparation for the birth of Jesus Christ, and since His Gospel was to be believed throughout the world, it was necessary that there should be prophecies demanding belief in Him, and also that those prophecies should have been spread all over the world, so that all the world might accept Him.

465. But the mere fact of prophecies was not sufficient. The knowledge of them had to be carried to every quarter, and they had also to be preserved in the records for all time. Further, in order that the eventual fulfillment of prophecy [18] should not be called coincidence, the result of a series of accidents, it was necessary that details of time and place should form part of the prophecy. It redounds even more to the glory of the Messiah that the Jews themselves should be the witnesses and even the means of His triumph, apart from the fact that they should have been preserved by God for this very purpose.

[18] i.e., the birth of Christ, as in Fragment 464.

466. *Prophecies:* If one man alone had composed a book of prophecies concerning Jesus Christ, the time and manner of His coming; and if Jesus Christ had indeed eventually come in conformity with the details of those very prophecies, the fact would have carried enormous weight.

But here we have much more than that: we see a whole succession of men who follow one another, without a break and without variation of message for four thousand years, to prophesy concerning this same coming. We see an entire people, with a tradition unbroken throughout four thousand years, who render collective testimony to this belief, from which they were not to be diverted by all the menaces and all the persecutions they have had to suffer. These are facts which carry a great deal more weight.

467. We only understand the prophecies when we see them fulfilled: thus the arguments from withdrawal from the world, from discretion, and from silence, would only carry weight with those who already know and believe.

Joseph, an example of the interior life under a law that was entirely external, Heb. 11:22.

External penances tend to dispose us to interior penance, just as humiliations develop humility. Thus the . . .

483. During the lifetime of the Messiah . . . "Propound a riddle," Ezek. 17:2. His forerunner, Mal. 3; Unto us a child is born, Isa. 9; He will be born in the city of Bethlehem, Mic. 5; He will appear chiefly in Jerusalem, and will be born of the family of Judah and of David.

He is to shut the eyes of the wise and the learned, Isa. 6, 8, 19, etc.; to preach the Gospel to the poor among men, Isa. 29; to open the eyes that are blind, restore the sick to health, bring out the prisoners from the dungeon, Isa. 42.

He is to teach the perfect way, and to be a teacher of the Gentiles, Isa. 55, 42:1–7.

The prophecies shall be unintelligible to the wicked, Dan. 12:10; but full of meaning for the wise, Hos. 14:9.

The prophecies which describe Him as poor, also represent Him as Lord of the nations, Isa. 52, 53, 54; Zech. 9:9.

The prophecies which foretell the time of His coming describe Him only as Lord of the Gentiles, and as suffering; and not as coming in the clouds, as judge. And those that represent Him as a judge, and as coming in glory, say nothing of the time.

That He is to be a sacrifice for the sins of the world, Isa. 39, 53, etc. He is to be a precious cornerstone, a sure foundation, Isa. 28:16.

He is to be a stone of offense and a rock of stumbling to both houses of Israel, Isa. 8:14. The builders will reject this stone, Ps. 118:22. God is to make this stone the headstone of the corner. And this stone shall become a great mountain and fill the whole earth, Dan. 2:35.

He is therefore to be rejected, refused recognition, and betrayed, Ps. 109:2–12, Zech. 11; spat upon, buffeted, mocked, afflicted in countless ways, and given gall to drink, Ps. 69; pierced, Zech. 12; pierced through hands and feet, killed, and lots cast for his raiment, Ps. 22:16–18.

That He would rise again, Ps. 15, on the third day, Hos. 6:3.

He will ascend into the heavens and sit on the right hand of God, Ps. 120; the kings of the earth set themselves against Him, Ps. 2; that He will sit at the right hand of His Father, and be victorious over His enemies, and that kings shall come to the brightness of this rising, and the wealth of the nations, Isa. 60:3, 5.

That the Jews will continue as a nation, Jer. 31.

They shall dwell many days without king or prince, as wanderers, Hos. 3; without Prophets, Amos; looking for salvation, but not finding it, Isaiah.

The calling of the Gentiles by Jesus Christ, Isa. 52:15, 55:5, 60; Ps. 81.

Hos. 1:9, 10: And the Lord said, Call his name, Not my people, for ye are not my people, and I am not your God. Yet the number of the people of Israel shall be like the sand of the sea. In the place where it was said to them, "You are not my people," it shall be said to them, "Sons of the living God."

484. Amos and Zechariah. They have sold the just, and therefore they shall never be recalled; Jesus Christ betrayed; Egypt shall be forgotten, Isa. 43:16–19, Jer. 23:6–7.

485. *Prophecy:* The Jews shall be dispersed and shall fill the whole world, Isa. 27:6.

A new law, Jer. 31, 32.

Malachi. Grotius.[19] The glory of the second temple. Jesus Christ will visit it, Hag. 2:7–10.

The calling of the Gentiles, Joel 2:28, Hos. 2:24, Deut. 32:21, Mal. 1:11.

486. The Jews are witnesses to God, Isa. 43:9, 44:8. *Prophecies fulfilled.* II. Sam. 13:2, I. Kings 23:16, Josh. 6:26, I. Kings 16:34, Deut. 23.

Mal. 1:11. The sacrifice of the Jews rejected, as is also pagan sacrifice everywhere, even outside of Jerusalem.

Before he died, Moses foretold the calling of the Gentiles and the rejection of the Jews.

Moses foretold what would be the destiny of each tribe.

Prophecy: "You shall leave your name to my chosen for a curse . . . but his servants he will call by a different name," Isa. 65:15.

"Make the heart of this people fat," Isa. 6:10. And how? By flattering concupiscence, and planting in them the hope of satisfying it.

487. Hos. 3, Isa. 42, 48, 54, 60, 61: "I foretold it of old, that they might know that it is I." Jaddus and Alexander (*see* Josephus, *Antiquities* xi, 8).

488. *Prophecies:* It is prophesied that in the time of the Messiah, He would come to make a new covenant which should make them forget the flight from Egypt, Jer. 23:5, Isa. 43:16; which should make His law to reside in the heart, and not in external observances, and which should admit the fear of Him (hitherto aroused by external things) deep in the heart. Who does not see the Christian law in all this?

489. That then idolatry should be overthrown; that this Messiah should cast down all the idols, and bring men to worship the true God.

That the temples of the idols should be cast down, and that among all nations and in every place on earth there

[19] *De veritate religionis Christianae,* V. 14, where Grotius quotes Mal. 3:1, in support of Hag. 2, describing the glory of the second Temple.

should be offered Him a pure, and not an animal, sacrifice.

That He should be king of Jew and Gentile. And behold this king of Jew and Gentile, oppressed by both, both plotting His death, supreme Lord of both, and destroying both the worship that had been taught by Moses, whereon He had established His earliest Church, in Jerusalem its center; and the worship of idols in Rome, center of idolatrous cults, in place of which He established there His true Church.

490. *Prophecies:* That Jesus Christ will be seated at the right hand of God, while God subdues His enemies.

Therefore He will not Himself subdue them.

491. That "after those days . . . no longer shall each man teach his neighbor and each his brother, saying, 'Know the Lord,' for they shall all know me," Jer. 31:34, "your sons and your daughters shall prophesy," Joel 2:28, "and I will plant my Spirit and my fear in your hearts," Jer. 31:33.

All these passages convey the same thing. To prophesy is to speak of God, not in terms of external proofs and signs, but in the language of interior and immediate feeling.

492. That He would teach men the perfect way. And neither before Him nor after Him was there ever any that taught divine truth as this man taught it.

493. *Prophecies:* That the Jews would reject Jesus Christ, and that then the Jews would be rejected by God, for the reason that the chosen vine gave only wild grapes. That the chosen people would be unfaithful, ungrateful, and unbelieving, "a disobedient and contrary people," Rom. 10:21. That God will strike them with blindness, and that they will grope in broad daylight as though they were blind; that a forerunner would go before Him.

494. Moses was the first to teach the doctrines of the Trinity, Original Sin, and the Messiah. David was a great witness: a king, good and merciful, a noble soul, of a sound intellect, and wielding great power. He prophesied, and the miracle that he foretold came to pass: a fact of infinite significance.

Suppose that his pride had suggested it: he had only to announce that he was the Messiah to be accepted as such—

for the prophecies pointed more plainly to him than to Jesus Christ. The same applies to Saint John [the Baptist].

495. *Prophecies:* The time [of the coming of the Messiah] was foretold in relation to the condition of the Jewish people, the situation in the Gentile world, the advanced state of the rebuilt Temple, and in terms of the passage of time.

496. It requires considerable confidence in the message to foretell the same event in so many different ways: the four idolatrous or heathen kingdoms, the fall of the Kingdom of Judah, and the seventy weeks—all these had to happen together, and all before the destruction of the second temple.

497. "Him whom they have pierced," Zech. 12:10. That a deliverer should come who would crush the devil's head, who would deliver his people from their sins, "from all his iniquities," Ps. 129:8; that there should be a New Covenant, which would be eternal; that there should be another priesthood "after the order of Melchizedek," Ps. 110:4, which should be forever. That the Christ should be glorious, powerful, strong, and yet so poor that He would not be recognized, that He would not be accepted for what He is. That He would be rejected and put to death, that His people, having denied Him, would no longer be His people, that idolaters would receive Him, would gather together, would come to Him, that He would leave Zion, to reign in the midst of idolaters, that the Jews would nevertheless survive, and continue forever, and that He would be of the house of Judah, but after the monarchy had ceased.

504. To show that the Old Testament is figurative only, and that when the Prophets spoke of temporal goods, they meant goods of another kind; which we proceed to demonstrate as follows:

1. A literal meaning would be unworthy of God.

2. Their teaching very evidently contains a promise of temporal blessings; and yet they say that their announcements are cryptic, and their meaning will not be understood. Whence it appears that the secret meaning was not that which they expressed openly, and that therefore they must be understood to be speaking of other sacrifices, an-

other liberator, etc. They say that these things will only be understood in the latter days, Jer. 30:24.

3. The third proof is, that their teachings are contradictory, and mutually destructive; so that, if we assume that by the words "law" and "sacrifice," they meant only what Moses meant, i.e., the Mosaic Law and sacrifice, we at once encounter an obvious and gross contradiction. Therefore they understood something quite different, sometimes contradicting themselves in one and the same chapter.

Now, to understand an author's meaning . . .

507. Two errors: 1. To take everything literally. 2. To take everything spiritually.

509. *The extravagances of the Apocalyptics, Pre-Adamites, Millenarians, etc.:* Anyone who wishes to do so, can base extravagant opinions upon Scripture; take, for example, the words, "This generation shall not pass away until all these things take place," Matt. 24:34. Upon this point I would say, that one generation will follow another, and so on, in unbroken succession.

In II. Chron. 1:14–15, Solomon and the king are mentioned as though they were two different persons. I would say they were in fact two different persons.

511. Some types are clear, and they indicate what is meant without ambiguity, but others seem almost to have been dragged in by the hair, so that they convey nothing to anybody except those already persuaded. They are like the imagery we meet in the Apocalyptic writers, with the difference, however, that they do not carry conviction; so that it is the height of absurdity to claim that their imagery is, in general, as striking and correct as any of ours [i.e., in the New Testament]. The odds are not even. The two classes of imagery cannot be compared, and they must not be confused. They may be comparable in this or that feature, but they differ basically in other respects. In all things pertaining to the Divine, the limpid clarity of what is plain compels us to treat the obscure passages with respect.

(Just as, where men are speaking in cryptic language, anyone hearing them thinks they are talking nonsense.)

The symbolism [in the Old Testament writers] is sufficiently explicit to be intelligible to the elect, though there is enough of obscurity to hinder them in some degree, and so to humble them. The obscurity is sufficient to blind the reprobate, yet there is clarity enough to render them culpable and without excuse. Saint Augustine, Montaigne, Sabunde.[20]

The ancestry of Jesus Christ, as recorded in the Old Testament, is so mixed up with other records which are not to the purpose as to escape notice. Suppose that Moses had kept a separate record of the genealogy of Jesus Christ, the thing would look extremely artificial. If, on the other hand, there were no record of the Lord's ancestry in the Mosaic writings, then His descent would have been difficult to trace. But if the Old Testament record be closely examined, the descent through Thamar, Ruth, etc., can be quite clearly distinguished.

The men who ordained those sacrifices knew that they were vain; yet the men who declared them useless continued to offer them.

If God had sanctioned one religion only, it would have been too easily identified. But if you examine the [Christian religion] closely, it is possible to perceive the truth among all the confusing elements.

Premise: Moses was a man of intelligence. If then he was governed by reason, by the power of his own mind, he would obviously not have said anything that was directly contrary to reason.

Thus all the very obvious weaknesses are in fact elements of strength. For example, the two genealogies, one in Saint Matthew, the other in Saint Luke. What could be plainer, than that there was no conspiracy behind them?

514. If there were only one religion, God would be clearly revealed in it. Similarly, if there were no martyrs except in our own religion.

Since God is thus hidden, any religion that does not declare Him to be a hidden God is not true; and any religion that does not give the reasons for this hiddenness is not a

[20] Saint Augustine and Sabunde are both quoted by Montaigne (*Essais,* II, 12.) The *Theologia Naturalis Raymundi de Sabunde Hispani, viri subtilissimi,* was first printed at Venice in 1484. It had been translated into French by Montaigne and was very familiar to Pascal, whose thought is steeped in its ideas, many of which are derived from the Cabalists and from Ramòn Lull.

teaching religion. Our religion satisfies these requirements: "Truly thou art a God who hidest thyself," Isa. 45:15.

515. If there were no obscurity, man would not be aware of his own corruption; if there were no light, man could never hope to be healed. Thus it is not only right, but even for our gain in moral strength, that God should be in part hidden from us, yet not unknown; because it is as dangerous for man to know God without knowing his own wretchedness, as it is for him to know his own wretchedness without knowing God.

517. People who find it difficult to believe in anything, try to justify themselves by an appeal to some belief which the Jews rejected: "Now if this point were so clear," they argue, "how is it that the Jews would not believe it?" And they seem almost to wish that the Jews *had* believed, so that their denial should not be a stumbling block to themselves. But it is just this fact of the Jewish denial which is the basis of our own belief. We should be much less disposed to believe, if the Jews were on our side. Since they are not, the grounds of our own belief are the more secure. It is a remarkable thing that the Jews should have become so proficient in prophecy, so strong in defense of things prophesied, and such uncompromising enemies of the thing prophesied when it came to pass.

519. *Contradiction:* You cannot paint a good portrait unless you reduce to order all the features that are normally in conflict: it is not enough to record a series of harmonious qualities, unless you also harmonize the discords. If we are to understand the meaning of a writer, we have to compare and reconcile those statements in which he appears to contradict himself.

Similarly, if we are to understand the Scriptures, we must find an interpretation by which all the conflicting passages are harmonized. It is not enough to select a single meaning—though it may well suit several passages which happen to be already in agreement—for it is essential to find a single meaning capable of reconciling passages which appear to contradict one another.

Every author has a standard of values, according to which

everything he says must be assessed, however perverse it may appear. In the absence of such a scale of values, nothing that he said would have any meaning.[21] Now it cannot be said of the Scriptures, least of all of the Prophets, that they are meaningless, for they undoubtedly abound in good sense. We must therefore look for a single meaning which will reconcile all the contradictory sayings.

The true meaning of the Scriptures therefore is not that given to it by the Jews, but it is in Jesus Christ that all the contradictory passages are reconciled.

The Jews found it impossible to reconcile the failure of the royal and princely line (foretold by Hos. 3:4) with the prophecy of Jacob, that "The scepter shall not depart from Judah, nor the ruler's staff . . . until he come to whom it belongs; and to him shall be the obedience of the peoples," Gen. 49:10.

If we take the Law, the system of sacrificial worship, and the Monarchy to be the essential features of revealed religion, it is impossible to reconcile all the relevant passages.[22] Of necessity therefore, we have to say that they are only types. There are times when we cannot even reconcile all the statements of a single author, nor of a single book, nor even, at times, of a single chapter. Such conflict provides abundant evidence of an author's intention, as when Ezekiel says that man should walk in the statutes of God, Ezek. 20:19, and should not walk in them, Ezek. 20:25–26.

520a. A type implies a thing absent and a thing present, pleasure and frustration; [23] a cipher has two meanings, one which is clear to the initiate, leading him to the secret meaning.

521. If the Law and the sacrifices are the true religion, they must be acceptable to God, and must not displease Him

[21] This is an ordinary principle of criticism, and it applies to the writings of any satirist, who only survives his generation if he satisfies the requirement. G.B. Shaw abides our question, but Swift and Pascal are free.

[22] Because all three features had collapsed and disappeared before the advent of the Messiah.

[23] The visible symbol is a mere emblem to the stranger; but the initiate holds the key, which leads him directly to the thing signified.

in any particular. If they are types only, they must please and displease Him.[24]

Now, the typology used throughout the whole of Scripture is at once pleasing and frustrating. It is said that the Law shall be changed, that the sacrificial system shall be changed, that the people shall be without the Law, without a prince, without a sacrifice, that a new covenant would be made, that the precepts they have hitherto received are not good, that their sacrifices are an abomination, and that God does not, nor ever did, require any of them.

On the other hand, it is said that the Law shall abide forever, that the covenant is forever, that the princely scepter shall never be taken from among them, since it shall by no means depart from them until the coming of the eternal King.

Are all these passages to be taken literally? No. Are they then only symbolism? No, but they are to be understood either literally or symbolically. Where the passages in our first group [it is said that the Law shall be changed, etc.] will not bear a literal interpretation, they are to be understood symbolically.

Not all of the passages cited in our first group are to be understood literally, but all may be understood as symbolism; therefore they were not spoken as applying to historic fact, but as symbolism. "The Lamb that was slain . . . before the foundation of the world." Rev. 13:8.[25] The judge who also sacrifices.

522. Once the key to the mystery is known, it is impossible not to see how everything fits into the plan. Let us but read the Old Testament with this interpretation in mind, and we shall soon see whether the sacrifices were acceptable, whether descent from Abraham was absolutely necessary to gain the friendship of God, whether the Promised Land was the place of final rest. No. Therefore they were only types. Let us but examine in the same way all the ceremonial ordered by the Law, all those commandments which do not

24 According to the principle laid down in fragment 520a, that the use of a symbol implies absence and frustration, whereas the truth is fruition—pleasure in a thing present. True worship is not satisfied by symbols.

25 The Lamb of God is the eternal sacrifice, of which the sacrificial system is only a type.

make for an increase of charity, and we shall see that they are no more than symbols.

All those sacrifices and ceremonies were therefore either symbols or nonsense. Now some things that happen to be clear are altogether too noble to be regarded as nonsense.

We ought to inquire whether the outlook of the Prophets was confined to the world of the Old Testament, or whether they saw beyond it.

525. *Objection:* The Scriptures are obviously full of things that were not dictated by the Holy Spirit.

Answer: But these things do no harm to the faith.

Objection: But the Church has declared that everything in the Scriptures is the work of the Holy Spirit.

Answer: My answer is in two parts: That the Church has never made any such pronouncement; and that, supposing she were to do so, her position could be defended.

Those prophecies that are cited in the Gospels as having been fulfilled—do you suppose they were put there to compel your belief? Certainly not. They were intended to put an edge on your belief by making you inclined [26] to skepticism.

526. *Reasons for the use of types:* The Prophets had to deal with a materialist people, and to make that people the fit trustee of a spiritual covenant. To instill the hope of a Messiah, it was essential that there should be antecedent prophecies, declared by men who were above suspicion, diligent, faithful, singularly zealous, and recognized by all.

That all this might be accomplished, God made choice of this race of materialists, to whom He entrusted prophecies which foretold the Messiah not only as a deliverer, but also as one who would bestow the earthly benefits beloved of their people. Thus the Jews developed an extraordinary enthusiasm for their line of Prophets, calling the attention of the whole world to the prophetic books in which their Messiah was foretold, and proclaiming to all peoples that He was to come precisely in the manner described in those writings, which were there for all to read. This is why the Jews were disappointed by the poverty and the ignominious circumstances of His coming, and why they became His bitterest enemies. In the result, the very race which, of all the races of the

[26] Interpreting the verb *éloigner* in the weaker meaning of La Bruyère and Ménage, the common usage of the seventeenth century.

vorld, was least likely to listen to the Christian claim, was een to comprise the most strict observers of His Law and the nost zealous protagonists of His Prophets, and to have preerved the records of both without corruption. Thus those who ejected and crucified Jesus Christ because He was an occasion f scandal to them, were the very possessors of the holy ooks, which not only foretold Him, but also prophesied that Ie would be rejected as a scandal. Thus [further] by their ery rejection of Him they implied recognition that this was He that should come." Therefore his claims were recognized y the behavior of two opposed parties: the righteous Jews vho received Him, and the unrighteous who rejected Him; nd the acceptance and the rejection were both foretold.

This is why there is in the prophecies a hidden and spirtual meaning to which this people would have been hostile, nderlying the symbolism which they so zealously protected. Even if the spiritual meaning had been revealed to them hey would have been incapable of loving it; and since they vould have found it unacceptable, they would have had no nterest in preserving the books of the Law, nor would they ave provided for the scrupulous observance of their ceremonial. Similarly, if they had set any value on the spiritual lessings that were promised, they would have persevered in ope until the Messiah came: their testimony would therefore have lacked force, since they would already have been His friends.

Therefore it was well that the spiritual meaning should e hidden; but on the other hand, suppose the spiritual meanng had been so cunningly concealed that no reader could ver detect it, how could it have served to prove the Messiah? What then was done? The spiritual meaning was hidden beeath the symbolism of a great many passages, and it was nly allowed to find clear expression here and there. Further, he time of His appearing, and the state of the world into vhich He was to come were so clearly indicated that the ircumstances were as clear as daylight. The spiritual meanng is in some passages so obvious, that only a spiritual lindness, like that inflicted on the mind by the indulgence f sensuality, could prevent a man from seeing it instantly.

We see then the divine plan. In innumerable passages the piritual sense is concealed beneath another, and only very arely is it immediately clear, but even where the spiritual neaning lies concealed, the passage is so ambiguous that it may well conceal both meanings, whereas the passages which contain only a spiritual meaning are perfectly clear, and can only be understood in the spiritual sense.

Such passages could never therefore lead us into error, and only a people as worldly as the Jews could be deceived by them.

For where blessings are promised in abundance, what was to prevent the Jews from understanding that the true benefit of spiritual blessings was intended—except their own greed, which limited the meaning to material things. But those whose only rest was in God, referred such blessings to God alone. For the two principles between which the human will is divided are concupiscence and charity: not that concupiscence is incompatible with the faith in God, nor that the possession of material things necessarily excludes charity, but concupiscence seeks to make use of God while it takes its pleasures in the world, while charity finds its delight in God, and merely makes use of the world.

Now the name of a thing is determined by its last end, and whatever prevents us from attaining that end is a hindrance. Thus all creatures, however good, are hindrances to the just if they distract them from God; and God Himself is a hindrance to any man who prefers his own concupiscence to the love of God.

Thus this word "hindrance" depends for its force upon our last end; so that to the just their own passions were hindrances, and to the materialistic Jew the enemy was the Babylonian. Thus such terms were obscure only to the unrighteous; wherefore Isaiah said, "Bind up the testimony, seal the teaching among my disciples," Isa. 8:16; saying also that Jesus Christ would be a stumbling block. But "blessed are they that shall not be offended in Him." Hosea expresses it perfectly, "Whoever is discerning, let him know them; for the ways of the Lord are right, and the upright walk in them, but transgressors stumble in them," Hos. 14:9.

527. This covenant, then, was made in terms which were obscure [27] to one party, the unrighteous, but clear to the just.

[27] Adopting for the whole of this fragment the reconstructed text of Zachary Tourneur (Cluny I, page 345), where an attempt is made to explain the textual obscurities, and which in particular restores the continuity of fragment 527 with fragment 526. The separation was accidental, due only to the scissors of the original preserver of the *Pensées*.

Yet even for the unrighteous it threw into relief the truth that was to be made increasingly clear to the just. For God rewarded the just among the Jews with so many material blessings of so miraculous a nature, that He was clearly able also to bestow not only such blessings as were invisible and spiritual, but also a Messiah.

For Nature is an image of grace, and visible miracles are images of invisible ones: "But that you may know that the Son of man has authority on earth . . . I say to you: Rise . . . ," Mark 2:10, 11.

Isa. 51:10, says that the Redemption will be like the passage through the depths of the Red Sea.

God has therefore demonstrated, by the events of the Exodus from Egypt, of the passage of the Red Sea, by the defeat of the kings [of Egypt and Amalek], by the manna, by the multiplication of the descendants of Abraham, Gen. 22:17, that He was able to save them, able to send them bread from Heaven, etc. Thus the rebellious people are a type and symbol of that same Messiah who was to come and reign over them,[28] etc.

God has shown, finally, that all these things are but types, and what it means to be "truly free," "an Israelite indeed," what is "the true circumcision," and what "the true bread from Heaven," etc. . . . Kircher and Ussher.[29]

In these promises, every man may find his heart's desire: worldly advantage, spiritual blessings, God or creatures, but with this difference, that they who look for creatures therein will certainly find them—together with a number of limiting conditions and an absolute ban upon loving them; they will also find a command to love and worship God alone—which amounts to the same thing; and an explicit declaration that when the Messiah shall at last appear, it will not be to them that He comes. They, on the other hand, who find in His

28 Adopting Tourneur's conjectural reading, *reigneront.*

29 Athanasius Kircher S.J. (1601–1680), a scholar of international renown, celebrated for his knowledge of the natural sciences and mathematics, oriental languages, and Egyptology. Like Pascal, he invented a calculating machine. He wrote a concordance of the Greek and Hebrew texts of the Old Testament.

James Ussher (1581–1656) Protestant Abp. of Armagh, and a close friend of Laud. No royalist surpassed him in deference to the divine right of kings, and all parties marveled at his learning.

Both men were learned in cabalism and the typology of the Old Testament.

promises only a foretaste of God Himself will certainly find Him there, and that without any challenger to dispute His kingdom; they find also the command to love Him alone; and that there shall come at the time foretold a Messiah, to give them those blessings for which they have prayed.

Thus the Jews had their miracles, and prophecies were fulfilled in their sight. They had the Law, and it contained the teaching that one God, and He alone, was to be given love and worship; this Law was in force forever. Thus the Jewish Law had all the marks of the true religion, and the true religion it was. But here we must distinguish between the teaching of the Jews and the teaching of the Jewish Law. Now despite the fact that it possessed miracles, prophecy, and perpetuity, the teaching of the Jews was invalidated by the fact that it lacked the additional commandment, to worship and love God alone.

529. What do the Prophets say concerning Jesus Christ? That He will be publicly acknowledged as God? No: but that He will be in the truest sense a hidden God; that He will not be recognized; that nobody will believe that this can be He; that He will be a stone of stumbling on which many will fall, etc. Let no one therefore reproach us with lack of clarity, since we ourselves confess to it.

"But," you will say, "there certainly are obscurities."—And if there were not, nobody would have found Jesus Christ a stumbling block—and it was one of the formal intentions of the Prophets that they should do precisely that: "Shut their eyes; lest they see." Isa. 6:10.

534. Charity is not a "type" precept—a commandment under the Law. Jesus Christ came to abolish types and establish the truth; and to say that He came only to impose a "type" precept of charity, and to do away with the reality which was there before, is a dreadful thing. "If then the light in you is darkness, how great is the darkness!" Matt. 6:23.

535. Isa. 51, The Red Sea an image of the Redemption: "That you may know that the Son of man has authority on earth to forgive sin . . . I say to you, Rise," Mark 2:10, 11. God willed to demonstrate that He had power to raise up a holy people sanctified by a holiness invisible and spiritual, and to endow that people with eternal glory. He therefore

willed the Creation of the visible world. Since Nature is an image of grace, God first performed in the works of Nature that which He was afterward to perform in the order of grace, so that men might see how, having power to bring into being the visible Creation, so also He was able to bestow invisible spiritual blessings. This was why He saved His people from the Flood, why He raised up Abraham to be their father, why He redeemed them from the power of their enemies, and provided for them a place of rest.

It was not God's purpose to save those people from the Flood, and to decree that an entire nation should trace its descent from Abraham, solely in order to bring that nation to the possession of a fat land. Even grace itself is but the image of glory, for it is not in itself that last end. Grace itself had been typified by the Law, and is itself a type of glory, its principle or cause. Saints and common men have the same lives to live upon earth: both are seeking satisfaction, and they differ only in the object wherein they find it. They both describe as obstacles all such things as frustrate their quest, etc. Thus God demonstrates His power to bestow spiritual gifts by the power that He exercises over the visible Creation.

538. *The blindness of the Scriptures:* According to the Jews, the Scriptures say that "when the Christ appears, no one will know where He comes from," John 7:27. Also, "We have heard from the Law that the Christ remains forever," John 12:34; yet the Son of man has just declared "by what death He was to die," John 12:32, 33. And yet, says Saint John, "they did not believe in Him, though He had done so many signs before them," that the saying of Isaiah might be fulfilled: "He has blinded their eyes, and hardened their heart."

539. *Greatness:* Religion is so great a thing that it is but right, that those who will not take the trouble to inquire into it when it becomes difficult, should be deprived of it. Of what would such people complain, if religion were so easy that all the questions could be answered, merely for the asking?

540. All things work for good for the elect—even the obscurities of Scripture: they value these for the occasional flashes of divine enlightenment. For other men all things turn to evil—even those flashes of light: these indeed they

even curse, because of the obscure passages which they do not understand.

541. God has turned the blindness of this people to the advantage of the elect.

542. When we observe that some men are reduced to despair by their own lack of faith, we say that God has not [yet] enlightened them; in the case of the other men who have rejected the faith, we say that God has withdrawn His light from them.[30]

543. We can only know God through Jesus Christ. Without this Mediator, all communication with God is broken off. It is through Jesus Christ that we know God. All those who have claimed to know God, and who have sought to prove His existence without reference to Jesus Christ, have had to fall back upon very inadequate proofs. But to prove Jesus Christ [in the first place] we have the prophecies, and these are reliable proofs which can be tested. These prophecies were fulfilled—they were authenticated by the event. They thus establish the certainty of the truths they announce and also, *a fortiori*, the divinity of Christ. In Him and through Him, then, we know God. Without such certitude, without the Scripture and the doctrine of Original Sin, without the necessary Mediator who was promised and who came, it is not possible to produce conclusive proof of God, or to teach either sound doctrine or good morals. But through Jesus Christ and in Him we can prove God, and we can teach both faith and morals. Jesus Christ is therefore the true God of men.

But at the same time we become aware of our wretchedness, for this God is also the Redeemer who heals it. We can scarcely know God therefore unless we recognize that we ourselves are sinners. Also, those who have come to know God without an understanding of their own wretched condition if they continue without Him, have not glorified God, but themselves. "For since, in the wisdom of God, the world did not know God through wisdom, it pleased God through

[30] i.e., the greatness of man is to be measured by his wretchedness, which forces him to perceive by contrast. One of many passages indicating the debt of Pascal to Sabunde.

the folly of what we preach to save those who believe," I. Cor. 1:21.

544. Wretchedness leads to despair, and pride leads to presumption. By showing man how great a remedy was required, the Incarnation shows man the depth of his wretchedness.

545. For a man to know God and not to know his own wretchedness, leads to pride.

Awareness of wretchedness without the knowledge of God leads to despair.

Knowledge of Jesus Christ offers a middle way, because in and through Him we find God, and learn our misery without Him.

548. Jesus Christ, to whom both the Testaments look—the Old as its hope, the New as its pattern, and both as their center.

555. The conversion of the heathen was reserved for the application of the grace of the Messiah. The Jews fought against them for a long time, but without success. All that Solomon and the Prophets had said about them was in vain. The sages, such as Plato and Socrates, were unable to persuade them.

556. Jesus Christ taught men the simple truth about themselves: that they were selfish; enslaved to their appetites; blind, sick, unhappy, sinners; that it was laid upon Himself to deliver, enlighten, bless, and heal them; and that this would be brought about by hatred of self, and by following him through poverty to the death of the Cross.

557. Without Jesus Christ, man is of necessity left in a condition of sin and misery; in Christ a man is redeemed from sin and misery. In Him are to be found all our strength and all our happiness. Apart from Him there are only sin and wretchedness, error, darkness, and despair.

558. *The names of Christ:* Saviour, father, sacrificing priest, victim, food, king, wisdom, lawgiver, afflicted, poor; one that should come to form a people, to lead and feed it, and bring it into His own country.

The office and work of Christ: He, and He alone, was to raise up a great people, elect, holy, and chosen; He was to lead and feed them, and bring them into a place of rest and holiness; He was to make them holy unto the Lord, make of them the Lord's temple; reconcile them to God and save them from His anger; deliver them from that bondage to sin which so evidently reigns in the heart of man; give His people a law, and engrave that law upon their hearts; offer Himself to God for them; sacrifice Himself for them, a victim without blemish, and Himself the sacrificing priest; He was to offer up Himself, His own body and blood, yet He was to offer to God bread and wine.

"When Christ came into the world, He said . . . ," Hebr. 10:5. "One stone upon another," Mark 13:2.

What went before, and what followed. All the Jews surviving, and yet wanderers.

559. *Origin of contradictions*: A God humiliated, even to the death of the cross; a Messiah, by his own death victorious over death; two natures in Jesus Christ; two advents; the dual nature of man.

560. When the Jews asked Him concerning His divinity, they demonstrated His humanity.

561. *We have no king but Caesar:* Therefore Jesus Christ was the Messiah, since they no longer had any king of their own, but a foreigner, and would accept no other.

562. Of all the things of earth, He shares only the sorrows, not the pleasures. He loves His neighbor, but His charity is not limited to him: it is extended to include His enemies, and then the enemies of God.

563. The Church has had just as much trouble in defending the humanity of Jesus Christ against those who denied it, as in proving His divinity. And the arguments were equally strong.

564. I contemplate Jesus Christ in all men, and in ourselves: Jesus Christ as father, in His Father; Jesus Christ as brother, in His brethren; Jesus Christ as the poor man, in His poor; Jesus Christ as rich, in the rich; Jesus Christ as

doctor and priest, in His priests; Jesus Christ as sovereign Lord, in all princes, etc. For Christ in glory is all that is great, since He is God; and in His earthly life He was all that was poorest and mean. He took upon Himself that condition of poverty and misfortune, that He might be found in every person, and be a pattern for all conditions of men.

565. Jesus Christ lived in such obscurity (as the world reckons obscurity), that historians, who record only the important affairs of state, have scarcely noticed Him.

566. *On the fact that Josephus, Tacitus, and other historians have not spoken of Jesus Christ.* So far from telling against Him, this is an argument in His favor. For it is certain that Jesus Christ existed, that His religion was noised abroad, and that those historians heard about it. It is therefore clear that they were quite deliberately silent concerning Him; or it may be that they wrote of Him, but the record was suppressed or altered.

567. Had ever any man more brilliant fame? Before His coming, He was foretold by all Jewry, and when He had come, the Gentiles worshiped Him. Both peoples, Jewish and Gentile, look to Him as to their center.

And yet, was there ever a man that less enjoyed such fame? Of His thirty-three years, thirty were spent before He made any public appearance. Within three years, He is being called an impostor, and the priests and the elders disown Him: His friends and kinsmen distrust Him. In the end He dies, betrayed by one disciple, denied by another, forsaken by all.

What benefit did He have, then, from all that fame? No man ever had greater glory, no man ever suffered greater shame. All the glory was for our sakes only, that we might be able to recognize Him; for Himself He kept nothing.

568. The infinite distance between bodies and minds is a type of the infinitely more infinite distance between minds and charity: for charity is supernatural.

Greatness, with all its glamour, has no luster for men who are inquiring into the things of the mind.

The real greatness of men of intellect is not perceptible

to kings, to wealthy men, to military leaders, to any of those men who are great only in respect of material things.

The majesty of wisdom (and wisdom itself is of no account unless it be from God), is unrecognized by those whose concern is with material things.[31] And to men of intellect there are three orders of greatness, differing in kind.[32]

There are the men of great intellect. These enjoy an empire of their own, their own splendor, greatness, victories, and luster. They have no need of material greatness, in which they are not at home. They are observed,[33] not by the outward eye, but by the mind, and that is enough for them.

Good men have their empire, their splendor, their victory, and luster: they have no need whatever of material greatness, nor do they value human respect on account of spiritual gifts; from this order of greatness, therefore, which bestows nothing and takes nothing away, they are completely detached. They are seen, not by the human eye, nor by the inquisitive mind, but by God and His angels; and that is sufficient for them.

Archimedes, though he had no princely title, would appear to have received due reverence: he did not win any dazzling victories, but he made his discoveries available to the mind of humanity. And with what dazzling splendor did he appeal to the minds of men.[34]

Jesus Christ possessed no material wealth, and made no contribution to the physical sciences, yet He stands in His own order of holiness. He made no scientific discoveries, nor did He reign over men; but He was humble, patient, holy—holy before God, terrible to evil spirits, and altogether with-

[31] Adopting for this paragraph of the fragment the punctuation of Tourneur (Éd. Pal.), who here begins a new sentence.

[32] At this point we reach the goal of Pascal's argument, pursued throughout the *Pensées:* the order of charity, resplendent in the joy of a rehabilitated human nature. The whole of this fragment is intended to refute a common objection to the divinity of Jesus Christ —that He was of humble origin and obscure condition.

[33] i.e. they are reverenced, even by their peers, as kings receive homage from their subjects.

[34] Archimedes (287–212 B.C.), greatest scientist of the ancient world, and creator of the theoretical part of the sciences of statics and hydrostatics. He made important contributions to geometry and to the theory of numbers. Pascal himself was hailed in his lifetime as "another Archimedes"; but the point of the mention here is, that although Archimedes was related to the royal house, he was never given any princely title.

out sin. Oh, with what pomp, with what transcendent majesty, does He appear to the view of those hearts that can discern wisdom!

Even though Archimedes had been styled a prince, it would have been pointless for him to pose as such in treatises on geometry.

It was quite unnecessary for our Lord Jesus Christ to appear in earthly glory in order to compel attention to His Kingdom of holiness. But He certainly came in all the majesty proper to His own order!

It is perfectly ridiculous to be scandalized by the lowly condition of Jesus Christ, as though this lowliness were of the same order as the greatness which He came to reveal. When we consider the greatness that He showed in His life, in His Passion, in His obscurity, in His death, in the calling of His disciples, in their forsaking of Him, in His mysterious resurrection, and the rest, we find it so stupendous that there is no reason to make a scandal of a lowliness which in point of fact is not present.

But there are some who can only admire worldly greatness, as though there were no greatness of the mind, and others who admire only the intellect—as though there were not another order of greatness which is altogether higher, in the order of wisdom.[35]

All material things taken together—the firmament, the stars, the earth with its kingdoms—are not to be valued against the lowliest of human minds; for the mind is aware of all these things, and it knows itself, whereas material things know nothing.

All material things taken together, with all the minds of men and all that those minds have achieved, are not to be compared with the smallest impulse of charity, for the least of such actions is of an infinitely higher order.

From the whole of the material creation taken together, no man can extract a single thought, even the smallest: the thing is impossible, for thought is of another order; nor can all the material things and all men's minds together produce a single impulse of true charity: it is an impossibility, for charity is of another order, which is supernatural.

[35] The true humility of the mind of Pascal comes out clearly in this passage. His concept of the three orders of things involves the recognition that they are heterogeneous and therefore discontinuous.

569. Just as Jesus Christ dwelt unknown among men, so His truth lies hidden among the common opinions, which look so very like it that they might be taken for Gospel. So also with the Eucharist and ordinary bread.

571. The spurious justice of Pilate served only to inflict suffering on Jesus Christ; for by a pretense of justice, Pilate first had Him scourged, and then put to death. It would have been better to have had Him killed immediately. It is always the same with those who make a show of justice: they do both good and evil to please the world, and to demonstrate that they do not belong entirely to Jesus Christ—for they are ashamed of Him. And in the end, when the great temptations come, and the occasions of sin abound, they consent to His death.

572. Why did not Jesus Christ come in a public and obvious manner, instead of relying upon the testimony of antecedent prophecies? Why did He cause Himself to be foretold by means of types?

574. If Jesus Christ had come only to sanctify, all Scripture and all the attendant circumstances would have pointed to the fact, and it would be very easy to convince unbelievers. If Jesus Christ came only to deceive, then all His conduct would be ambiguous, and we should have no argument to convince unbelievers. But since He came to "become a sanctuary" as well as a "stone of offense," as Isaiah says (8:14), we are unable to convince unbelievers, nor they us. Yet by this very fact we convince them, since we are able to say that there is, in the whole of His personal conduct, no overwhelming proof one way or the other.

575. Jesus Christ wrought miracles, and so did His Apostles after Him, and the primitive saints in great number; this was because the prophecies were not yet accomplished in full: they were actually in process of being fulfilled by those early saints themselves, so that miracles were the only effective testimony. It was foretold that the Messiah would convert the nations, but how should this prophecy be fulfilled unless the nations were in fact converted? And how could the nations be converted to the Messiah, unless they

also witnessed that one final fulfillment of prophecy which was to prove Him? Therefore all things were not fulfilled until He had died, risen again, and converted the nations: and throughout that period therefore, miracles were necessary. They are no longer necessary as testimony to be used against the Jews, for with respect to them, the fulfillment of so many [of their own] prophecies is a standing miracle.

577. No other religion has proposed that we should hate self. No other religion, then, can satisfy those who hate themselves, and who seek a being worthy of their love. And these, if they had never heard of the religion of a God who humbled Himself, would embrace with eagerness such a faith, as soon as it was offered to them.

578. The true, the solitary virtue, then, is hatred of self (for we are hateful by reason of our concupiscence), and the search for a being who is truly lovable, that we may love Him. But since we cannot love what is external to ourself, we must love a being who is within us and yet not ourself, and this is true for each and every man. Now only the universal being is of this kind. The Kingdom of God is within us; the universal good is within us, is ourself, and yet is not ourself.

580. That which mankind has only been able to understand by a great effort of the intellect, has been taught by our religion to its little children.

581. Philosophers have consecrated the vices, by attributing them to God Himself; but Christians have consecrated the virtues.

582. Jesus Christ condemned no man unheard. Even to Judas He said, "Friend, why have you come?" Matt. 26:50. And similarly to the man who had no wedding garment.

583. Jesus Christ is a God whom we approach without pride, and before whom we humble ourselves without despair.

584. This is not the kind of self-abasement which renders a

man incapable of good, nor is it a holiness beyond the reach of sin.

585. Not only do we not know God save through Jesus Christ, but we do not know ourselves except through Him. We do not understand the meaning of either life or death, unless through Jesus Christ. Apart from Jesus Christ we do not know what our life is, nor our death; nor what God is, nor what we ourselves are.

The Scriptures themselves look to Jesus Christ alone, and they have Him only for their object. Apart from the Scriptures we know nothing and we see nothing but confusion in the nature of God and in our human nature.

588. There are very few true Christians, even with regard to the faith: there are many who believe, but their beliefs are superstitious; there are many who have no beliefs at all, but are freethinkers. Apart from these two classes, there are not many.

590. The "humbling of the heart"[36] may be said to express Saint Paul's view of the Christian character; but *Albe vous a nommé, je ne vous connais plus,* sums up the non-Christian, the inhuman character. But the humane man is quite the opposite.[37]

591. There are only two kinds of men: the just, who believe themselves to be sinners; and sinners, who believe themselves to be good.

593. No man is so happy as the true Christian, nor as reasonable, virtuous, or lovable.

594. Only the Christian religion makes a man both lovable and happy. A man of mere good feeling cannot be both.

595. There is nothing on earth that does not serve to demonstrate either the misery of man, or the mercy of

[36] *See* Ephes. 4:2; Col. 3.

[37] The allusion is to Corneille, *Horace,* II.3, where the young Horace represents the inhuman character, Curiace the humane man of good feeling; but there is a third type superior to both, and this is the man who has learned Christian humility.

God; the weakness of man without God, or his strength when God is with him.

596. *Proof of Jesus Christ:* The allegation that the Apostles were impostors is quite absurd. Let us follow the charge to its logical conclusion: let us picture those twelve men, meeting after the death of Jesus Christ, and entering into conspiracy to say that He has risen. That would have constituted an attack upon both the civil and the religious authorities. The heart of man is strangely given to fickleness and change; it is swayed by promises, tempted by material things. If any one of those men had yielded to temptations so alluring, or given way to the more compelling arguments of prison, torture, death, they would all have been lost. Follow up that argument.

598. "The Apostles were either deceived, or deceivers." Both accusations present difficulties: for how is it possible to arrest a man, and then learn that he has risen from the dead . . . ?

While Jesus Christ was with them, He was able to sustain them; but afterwards? If it were not He that appeared to them, who was it that inspired their activity?

600. The style of the Gospel is admirable in so many ways; one striking feature is that they never utter one word of invective against the executioners and enemies of Jesus Christ. There is not a word of reproach in any of the Evangelists against Judas, or Pilate, or any of the Jewish leaders.

Now, if this moderation in the Gospel writers had been merely assumed along with their many other admirable characteristics, and if it were an affectation, put on merely to attract that comment which they themselves dared not venture to make, they could not have failed to gain friends, who would willingly have performed the service for them. But since their behavior was quite without affectation and their motives entirely disinterested, the moderation of their behavior passed without notice. It is my belief that several other features of this kind have gone without notice until this very day—a fact which testifies to the absence of rancor in the narrative of the Gospels.

601. An ordinary workman talking about wealth; a con-

tractor, talking about the war, or about royalty, etc.; but a rich man speaks about wealth with discretion, as a king speaks calmly of some great gift he has just made. And God speaks with authority concerning God.

602. Who was it that taught the Evangelists the qualities that belong to a completely heroic soul, so that they were able to depict the perfect example of such a soul in Jesus Christ? Why do they make Him weak in His agony? (Luke 22:41–44). Do they not know how to describe a resolute death? Yes, for this same Saint Luke describes the death of Saint Stephen as more courageous than that of Jesus Christ (Acts 7:59).

They therefore show Him as capable of fear when the moment of death was as yet in the future, but thereafter as completely courageous. When they describe Him as "very heavy," it is when His own soul is troubled (John 12:27); but when other men afflict Him He is perfectly calm.

605. *Light, darkness.* If the truth had not its distinguishing signs, the darkness would be too intense. It is a wondrous mark of the truth, that it has always been preserved in one Church, one visible community. And if within this Church there were only one opinion, the light would be altogether too brilliant. The true opinion is the one which has always prevailed: for the truth has been present from the beginning, but no error can be said to have persisted in the Church.

606. The history of the Church should properly be called the history of truth.

607. Then Jesus Christ came to tell men that they had no other enemy but themselves; that it is their own passions that separate them from God; that He had come to destroy those passions, to bestow on them His grace, and so make of them all, one holy Church; that He had come to bring into this Church both heathens and Jews—destroying the idols of the one, and the superstitions of the other. Now, all men naturally opposed such a design as this, and not only by reason of the instinctive reaction of concupiscence; and among the first to oppose it were the kings of the earth, who united to suppress this religion at its birth, as had been foretold: "Why do the nations conspire? . . . the kings of the earth set them-

selves, and the rulers take counsel together against the Lord and his anointed," Ps. 2:1–2.

All the great ones of the earth joined forces—the learned, the wise men, and the kings. Some wrote against Him, others rejected Him, and kings destroyed Him. And notwithstanding all those forces that were opposed to them, those weak and simple men [the Apostles] resisted the powers arrayed against them, bringing even kings, those wise and learned men, to submission, and at last driving away all idolatry from the earth. And all this was done by virtue of the power that had foretold it.

609. *Limbs. Begin here:* To regulate the love that a man should have for himself, we must imagine a body made up of thinking limbs [38] (since we are all parts of a whole), and see how each member ought to love itself, etc.

610. Let us imagine a body made up of limbs that think.

611. If the feet and hands had wills of their own, they would never be able to function properly within their own order, except when they submitted their individual private wills to the primary will that governs the whole of the body. Without the control of that primary will, the "private" wills would fall into a state of disorder and distress; but when their one united desire is for the good of the body, all that they do in harmony also achieves the separate well-being of each member.

612. If the members are to be happy they must possess a unified will, and it must conform to the single will which controls the body.

613. The example of the noble deaths of Spartans and others no longer has much effect on us. What lesson could it teach us? But the example of the deaths of the martyrs touch us closely, for are we not "members one of another"? We have a common bond with them; their resolution can help to build up our own fortitude, not only on account of their example, but also perhaps because we owe it to them that we ourselves should be resolute. This in no way applies

[38] This idea is adopted from Descartes. *See* the *Discourse on Method,* § 5, and fragment 614 below.

to the example of the heathen: with them we have no bond. One does not become rich by merely meeting a wealthy stranger: if he becomes one's husband, or if one has a wealthy father, then one may be described as rich.

614. *Morality:* Having created the heavens and the earth, which are unable to know the happiness of their being, it was the will of God to create beings who would be able to know happiness and who would be *thinking limbs* —intelligent members, that is, of a body. For our limbs do not of themselves feel any happiness in their state of association with the body, in their marvelous responses to sense perception, in the care that nature takes to infuse into them the animal spirits [39] and to make them grow—and acquire strength. How happy our limbs would be, if they could but perceive and feel all that! But in order to do so, they would require intelligence, so as to know the facts, and a rightly ordered will with which to give assent to the will of the universal soul. And if, having received intelligence, they were to make use of it only to retain nourishment within themselves and to prevent it from passing to the other limbs, they would not only commit an injustice, but they would in the end involve themselves in the suffering they had inflicted on those other members; and they would come to hate, rather than to love, themselves. For their happiness, no less than their duty, lies in consenting to be guided by that "universal instrument of the reason" of which they are all part,[40] and which loves them better than they love themselves.

615. To be a member is to have no life, being, or move-

[39] What Pascal calls the "intelligence" of the limbs is an idea borrowed from Descartes and adapted to the doctrine of the Mystical Body of the Church. See also fragment 609. The Cartesian doctrine speaks of "the animal spirits, which resemble the most tenuous vapors, or rather, extremely pure and lively tongues of flame, which . . . as the animal spirits are distributed through the muscles, cause the limbs of the body to move in different ways, according to the variety of sense perception and internal feelings." Descartes, *Méthode,* 5.

[40] Pascal's "entire soul" may have been suggested by the passage in which Descartes describes the relation between the nerves and muscles of the body: "For the reason is a universal instrument, which can be adapted to all sorts of occasions, but the organs [of the body] have need of some particular disposition for each particular action." *Méthode,* 5.

ment, except through the spirit that causes the limbs of the body to move for the service of the body.

A severed member can no longer see the body to which it belonged,[41] and has nothing in prospect but a state of wasting away and dying. Yet it fancies itself to be a self-contained and self-sufficient body; and seeing no other body upon which it depends, it fancies that it depends only upon itself, and it seeks to constitute itself its own center and body. But having no vital principle within itself, it only goes astray, and it loses itself in astonishment that its existence is so uncertain: for it is well aware that it is not a body, and yet it does not perceive that it is a member of a body. When at last it comes to know itself, it is as if it were returning home, and it no longer loves itself except for the sake of the body. It repents of its past strayings. Such a member would be unable of its own nature to love any other thing, save for its own ends and to have dominion over that thing, because each thing loves itself above every other thing. But when it has learned to love the body to which it belongs it loves itself, having no being but in the body, through it and for it: "But he who is united to the Lord becomes one spirit with Him," I Cor. 6:17.

The body loves the hand; and the hand, if it had a will, should love itself in the same degree as the body loves it. Any love in excess of this would be an injustice.

"He who is united to the Lord becomes one spirit with Him." We love ourselves because we are members of Jesus Christ. We love Jesus Christ because He is the body of which we are members. All is one, each is contained in the other, like the Three Persons.

616. What is the ego?

A man stands at the window to watch the passers-by. If I happen to pass, can I say that he placed himself there to see me? No, for he is not thinking of me in particular. But if a man loves someone because of her beauty, does he really

[41] A direct reference to a curious passage in the *Discourse on Method;* Descartes writes: "I had shown what the structure of the nerves and muscles of the human body must be in order that the animal spirits within should have the power to make the limbs move; as we see a severed head continue to move and to bite the ground, even though it is no longer animate." It is known that Descartes and many of his contemporaries, including the Solitaries of Port Royal, practiced vivisection in the furtherance of their scientific investigations.

love her? No; for the smallpox can destroy the beauty without destroying the person, and that will put an end to his love for her.

And suppose someone loves me for my judgment, or for my memory, is it really *I* that am loved? No; for I may lose those faculties without losing *myself*. Where then is this "I," if it is neither in the body, nor in the mind? And how can we love either body or mind at all, save perhaps for certain qualities only which are perishable, and therefore do not constitute the ego? Now, could we love a person on account of his soul (in the abstract), and also for certain qualities we were able to perceive therein? No: that is impossible, and it would be wrong. We never love a person, therefore, but only qualities.

Let us then laugh no more at men who are honored for reasons of rank and office, for no one is loved except for borrowed qualities.

619. The two arguments in conflict with one another. We must begin with that: otherwise we shall understand nothing, and everything we say will be heresy. And even when one truth is established, we must be careful to add that we bear in mind the truth opposed to it.

623. When all is said, we have to admit that there is something astounding about the Christian religion. "That is because you were born in it," someone will say. Not at all. I react against it for that very reason, lest preconceived ideas should bias my judgment. And yet, although I was born in it, I never cease to find something astounding about Christianity.

624. Without all this heavenly knowledge, how could men have avoided falling into one or other of the natural errors —either that of vanity, a root of pride remaining in them from the memory of primeval innocence, and indulged as they view their own earthly achievement; or of humiliation as they contemplate their actual weakness? For they are unable to perceive the whole of truth, and so they have not been able to attain to perfect virtue. One half of mankind

---

Pascal could make use of even so gruesome an illustration, to drive home his concern for the corporate element in Christian living. The same idea was exploited in a contrary sense by C. S. Lewis in his novel, *That Hideous Strength.*

regards Nature as uncorrupted; the other half, as beyond redemption. Thus all have fallen into either sloth or pride, the twin sources of all the vices, and they are left with scarcely any option: either they must abandon themselves to "the dominion of appetite," out of mere lax living, or they must crush all their natural instincts by the exertion of the will. Thus those who have recognized the nobility of human nature have taken no account of the corrupt elements in it, and so, while they avoided idleness, they fell through pride; whereas those who acknowledged the weakness of humanity were unable to admit that it had any dignity: these were well able to avoid vanity, but they fell into despair. Hence there arose a variety of sects: Stoics, Epicureans, dogmatists, Aristotelians, etc.

Only the Christian religion has been able to cure these two excesses, not by using one to expel the other, as worldly wisdom might suggest, but by applying the "simple mysteries of the faith" to drive out both. For the Christian faith lifts up the just to the very threshold of the knowledge of things divine; and to them it imparts the conviction that even in that enlightened state they still carry within themselves the root of all corruption, and that it will render themselves to error throughout their earthly lives, subject always to misery, sin, and death. And to the sinner she cries that he is capable of acquiring and increasing the grace of the Redeemer. Thus Christianity causes even the just to tremble, while the sinner, whom she does not acquit of blame, she nevertheless consoles. Thus carefully does she moderate men's fear by instilling hope in the measure that it is deserved, reminding the sinner that, as was his capacity for sin, so now is his capacity for grace (Rom. 5:20); that this twofold capacity for sin and grace is common to us all, and the Christian religion humbles a man far more effectively than any more reasoning could do, yet without reducing him to despair; while it confirms him in hope far more securely than his natural pride could ever do, and yet without presumption. Thus does the Christian religion teach men that she alone is free from error and from sin, and that to her alone therefore does it belong to instruct them and reform them.

Who then can refuse to believe in and to adore this heavenly light? For is it not clearer than the day that we are conscious of indestructible elements of greatness in ourselves? And is it not also true, that at every moment we experience the consequences of our actual pitiable condition? What then does this state of chaos, this monstrous confusion, cry aloud, but the reality of those two states, and in a voice so powerful that we are obliged to listen to it?

625. This is the point at which I reject all other religions. In this religion I find an answer to every objection. It is but right that so pure a God should reveal Himself only to those whose hearts have been purified. Henceforth this religion commands my love, and for me, its divine system of morality is alone sufficient to bestow authority. But I find more besides.

I find it a very convincing argument that, from as far back as men can remember, there have constantly been Prophets who told them that they were tainted by a corruption that was universal, but that a Redeemer would come; that the message was not brought by one man only, but by many men, and indeed by a whole people, producing a line of Prophets —as they were expressly created to do—for four thousand years. Here is a people still subsisting, yet more ancient than any other. Their books have been known to all the world for four hundred years past.

The more I examine these books, the more truths do I find in them. A whole people foretell Him before His coming; a whole people worship Him at His advent; and what went before that advent and came after it. And in the end, the Synagogue, as also was foretold, and this very people frequenting it, without idols, without kings, wretched and prophetless. Since the Jews are our enemies, they are admirable witnesses of the truth of those prophecies in which their own wretchedness and even their blindness were foretold.

Such a chain of events and such a religion, its authority, its power of survival, its perpetuity, its morality, the behavior of its followers, its doctrine and effects—all this I find entirely divine. The darkness of the Jews was fearful, and that too was foretold: "And you shall grope at noonday, as the blind grope in darkness," Deut. 28:29; "The words of a book . . . which men deliver to one that is learned . . . and he saith, I cannot read," Isa. 29:11–12. The scepter, still in the hands of the first foreign usurper; the rumor of the coming of Jesus Christ.

Therefore I stretch out my arms to my Redeemer, who

had been foretold for four thousand years, and came to earth to suffer and die for me, at the time foretold and with all the attendant circumstances; and by His grace I wait for death in peace, in the hope of being eternally united with Him. Yet I live my life with joy, either in such prosperity as He is pleased to give me, or in the adversity He sends me for my good, and which by His own example He has taught me how to suffer.

626. The heart has its reasons, which the reason knows not, as we see in a thousand instances. I say that the heart naturally loves the Universal Being, and that it loves itself naturally, according to the measure in which it gives itself to one or the other—to reason, or to God; and it hardens itself against one or the other, as it pleases. You have cast away the one, and kept the other: do you love by reason?

627. It is the heart that is conscious of God, and not the reason. This, then, is faith: God sensible to the heart, not to the reason.

628. Heart, instinct, principles.

629. Faith is a gift of God: do not believe that we could ever call it the result of a reasoning process. Other religions make no such claim for their faith: they claim only that their faith resulted from a reasoning process—although their reasoning process does not exactly lead to that belief.

630. We know truth, not by a reasoning process only, but also by the heart. It is in this way that we know first principles; and reasoning, which plays no part in establishing first principles, tries in vain to shake them. Skeptics, whose one aim in life is to do that, find they have wasted their labor. We know that we are not deceived as to first principles, however incapable we may be of proving them by a reasoning process: our helplessness proves nothing but the weakness of the reason. It does not (as the skeptics maintain) prove the fallaciousness of all knowledge. For our knowledge of first principles, such as the existence of space, time, movement, number, is as certain as any other knowledge attained by the use of reason. It is upon the knowledge gained by the heart and the instinct that reason relies, and on which it must

base all its arguments. (The heart feels that there are three dimensions in space, and that numbers are infinite; then reason demonstrates that there are no two square numbers, one of which must be twice the magnitude of the other. Principles are felt, propositions are deduced, and both with certainty, although by different ways.) It is as useless as it is absurd for the reason to require the heart to prove its first principles before it will accept them; just as it would be absurd if the heart demanded from reason a *feeling* for all propositions demonstrated before accepting them.

Such an absurdity could only serve to belittle reason, which must always be free to form a judgment. It does not shake certainty—as though it were only reason that could instruct us. On the contrary—would to God that we never needed reason, but could understand all things by instinct and feeling! But Nature has refused us this gift. On the contrary, she grants us very little knowledge of that kind, and everything else has to be acquired by the use of reason.

This is why those to whom God has given the grace of religion by infusing it into their hearts are indeed most happy, and are quite legitimately certain of their faith. But to those less fortunate we can only give faith by appealing to reason, in the hope that the appeal to the heart will be made by God; for until that response is made, faith is only a human act, and does not guarantee salvation.

631. Do not wonder, that certain simple people believe without reasoning. God brings them to love Him and to hate themselves. He inclines their hearts to believe. Belief is never strong nor faith unquestioning, except where God Himself has touched the heart. And at the moment that He touches the heart, then—and thenceforward—a man believes. David knew this very well: "Incline my heart to thy testimonies," Ps. 119:36.

632. Those who believe without having read the Testaments do so because they have a simple, interior goodness, and because all that they have heard of our religion is in keeping with it. They feel that God made them; their one desire is to love God; they desire to hate none but themselves; they feel that in themselves they do not possess the requisite strength, and that they are incapable of going to God [alone, and without help]; and that unless God

comes to them, they are incapable of any communion with Him. Also they hear it said in our religion that God alone is to be loved, and self alone hated; but that since we are all fallen beings, and so incapable of God, God became man to unite Himself with us. Where men possess this disposition and have so clear a knowledge of their duty and of their own incapacity to fulfill it, nothing more is needed to convince them.

633. Those whom we see to be Christians, yet without any knowledge of prophecies and proofs, are as well able to form a judgment in matters of religion as those who have that knowledge. They judge it by the heart, as others judge it by the mind. It is God Himself who disposes them to believe, so that they are very effectively convinced.

I am perfectly willing to admit that such a Christian, who himself believes without the use of proofs, will perhaps be unable to convince an infidel, who can make out a good case for his own ideas. But those who are familiar with the proofs of Christianity[42] will have no difficulty in proving that such a believer is truly inspired by God, even though the believer himself is unable to prove it.

For God has said, in prophecies which are undoubtedly genuine, that in the reign of Jesus Christ He would pour out of His spirit upon the nations, and that the sons and daughters and children of the Church should prophesy: wherefore there is no doubt that the Spirit of God rests upon these believers, but is certainly not to be found among those infidels.

637. This religion is so proportioned as to appeal to every type of mind. The first type stops short at the mere institution: and this religion is such that the institution alone is sufficient proof of its truth. Others pursue it as far back as the Apostles. The more learned are able to trace it back to the beginning of the world. The angels have a still better view of it, since they can see it from infinity.

640. The Scriptures provide passages of consolation—and of warning—for all conditions of men. Nature seems to have

[42] To a French Catholic in the age of Pascal, *la Religion* meant only one thing: the Christian faith as taught by the Catholic Church.

done the same, with her two infinites, natural and moral: for we have the higher and the lower; the sagacious—and the less wise; the most exalted and the very mean, to bring down our pride and to take away our sadness.

642. Instead of complaining that God has hidden Himself, you should thank Him that He has revealed so much concerning Himself. You should also thank Him that He has not revealed Himself to proud scholars, who are not worthy to know so holy a God.

There are two kinds of men who know [God]: those who are of a humble heart, who love humility, whatever their intellectual capacity, great or small; and those who have sufficient understanding to recognize the truth, however averse they may be to accepting it.

643. The prophecies, and even the miracles and the proofs of our religion are not of such a nature that we may call them absolutely convincing. But they are sufficiently persuasive, so that nobody could say that it is contrary to reason to accept them. Thus we have enough of both evidence and obscurity to enlighten some and to confuse others. But the evidence in favor is of such a nature as to counterbalance, if it does not actually outweigh, the evidence against religion. So that, since it is certainly not the reason which persuades us to reject religion, it can be nothing else but concupiscence and the malice of the heart. When we use these particular arguments, therefore, there is sufficient evidence to condemn [a stubborn unbeliever], yet not enough to win him over. Thus it becomes evident that those who accept this argument do so by grace rather than by a conviction of the reason; and that concupiscence, rather than any reasoning process, causes the stubborn to reject it.

646. We make for ourselves an idol out of the truth itself; for truth without charity is not God, but an imitation of Him and an idol, which we may neither love nor worship; and even less may we worship or love His opposite, which is the lie.

It might well be that I found myself loving total darkness. But if God should be pleased to lead me by a path of shadows, of half-darkness, the twilight condition vexes me; because I do not gain the merit of walking in complete darkness, I am displeased. This is a defect, and a sign that I have made for myself an idol, a proud desire for darkness, which is not according to the divine ordinance. And it is in walking in the way of *His* testimonies that we ought to delight.

648. The world exists for the exercise of mercy and judgment. It is not as though the men living in it had but just come, new-made, from the hands of God; rather are they His enemies, to whom of His grace, He gives light sufficient to find their way back to Him, if it be their desire to seek Him out and to follow Him; but sufficient also to warrant punishment, if they should refuse to seek and follow Him.

650. "A miracle," says one of them, "would strengthen my will to believe."[43] He says this when he sees no miracle. Reasons seen from a distance seem to limit our vision; but when we look into them more closely we begin to see beyond them. Nothing soothes the clamor of the mind. "There is," say they, "absolutely no rule without exception, no truth so universal, that it has not some one aspect in which it fails." It is sufficient to show that the proposition does not apply universally; the exception can then be advanced, and they can say, "It is not always true, therefore there are cases in which it is not so." Nothing then remains, but to show that the present case is one of them; and they are either very unskillful or very unlucky if they do not find some way of penetrating the defenses.[44]

651. "If I had seen a miracle," they say, "I should be converted." How can they be sure they would do a thing of which they know nothing? They suppose that this conversion is just an act of adoration of God, a business transaction, as it were, or a conversation, with God Himself as the other

[43] This was the ordinary meaning of the word *créance* for the contemporary reader of Pascal, and it is appropriate to the sense of the Fragment cp. Provinciales 13. The word has the force of "a willingness to be convinced upon presentation of sufficient evidence," and expressed the attitude of the "free thinkers."

[44] The whole of the *Apology* is addressed to a highly intelligent opposition for which Pascal has a great respect. This Fragment is indirect speech in the third person, and the sense of it is, that the believer must be very sure of his ground before entering into debate with unbelief. The last sentence, in particular, is a warning expressed in *the third person plural.*

party. Whereas true conversion is an act of self-annihilation before the universal being, since that being has been provoked, times without number, and those who have angered Him He may at any moment lawfully destroy; it consists also in the recognition that we can accomplish nothing without His aid, and have deserved nothing but His displeasure; and it consists, finally, in the realization that there is between ourselves and Him an impassable barrier, so that if we were without a mediator there could be no communication with Him.

656. Whether there is one single principle of all things, one single end, all by Him, all for Him . . . ? Well, then, true religion must teach us to worship and love Him alone. But we are incapable of worshiping what we do not know, or of loving anything other than ourselves; wherefore the religion that teaches us those duties must also make us realize our own powerlessness, and show us the remedies for it. Christianity does in fact tell us that by one man all was lost, and that therefore communication was broken off between God and ourselves; and that by one Man, communication was restored.

We are born into a world so far alienated from the love of God (and yet that love is so necessary), that we must have been born into a state of guilt, or else God would be unjust.

659. The mark of a true religion should be the obligation to love its God: that would be no more than justice. Yet no other religion has commanded it, and ours has done so. A true religion should also have some knowledge of concupiscence and weakness: our religion possesses such knowledge. It must also have provided remedies for them, and one such remedy is prayer. No other religion makes it a matter for prayer, that its adherents should love Him, and follow Him.

661. Two errors; to exclude reason, and to admit no argument but reason.

663. *Submission*: We must know when we ought to doubt, when we may be certain, and when to submit. Whoever does otherwise, does not understand the capabilities of reason. There are some who fail to apply these three rules, either

because they do not understand the principles of demonstration and assert that such and such things are obvious when they are not so; or by suspending judgment about everything, because they do not know when they ought to submit; or by submitting on all points, because they do not know that there are some matters on which they ought to exercise their reasoning powers.

664. Submission, and the right use of reason: this is the essence of Christianity.

665. Saint Augustine said, reason would never submit if it did not conclude that there are some matters on which it ought to do so. It is therefore right that reason should submit, whenever it concludes that it ought to do so.

667. If we submit everything to the test of reason, our religion will have nothing of mystery or of the supernatural about it. If our religion violates the rules of reason, it will be absurd—and it will rightly be ridiculed.

668. It certainly takes grace to make a man into a saint. Anyone who doubts this does not know what a saint is—nor what a man is.

669. Be comforted, it is not on account of any actions of your own that you can expect grace; on the contrary. If you look for nothing as due to you by merit, you may hope that your prayer will be heard.

671. The law has not destroyed nature: it has controlled her by imposing rules. Grace has not destroyed the law, it has caused the law to be respected and applied.

The faith received in baptism is the source of life for every Christian, every convert.

672. The Law compelled obedience to something which it did not bestow. Grace gives what it imposes.

673. There is no doctrine better adapted to the human condition than Christianity. It teaches man his twofold capacity, for receiving grace and losing it, on account of the twofold

danger to which he is always exposed: the temptations to pride and to despair.

674. The whole of the faith is summed up in Jesus Christ and Adam; just as all morality is included in the terms "concupiscence" and "grace."

676. Let no man say that I have said nothing new: my arrangement of the matter is new. When we play tennis, we both serve the same ball, but one of us places it better.

I would just as soon be told that I have used an obsolete terminology: as if the same mental images, or reasoning processes, would not serve to establish a completely different argument if they were arranged in another order, or as if the same words in a different order would not express an entirely different thought.

677. The last thing we decide when writing a book, is what to put at the beginning.

SELECTED WORKS

Religious Writing

The Memorial

On the evening of November 23, 1654, Pascal underwent a mystical experience which influenced his entire life. In his room in the rue des Francs-Bourgeois-Saint-Michel, he began to meditate on the Passion of Christ, using as a text the translation prepared at Louvain. In the course of his meditation, Pascal was overcome with anguish for his faults and with the assurance of Divine forgiveness. At 10:30 he seized pen and paper and wrote the Memorial *which recalls his experience. This he sewed into his clothes so that at any instant, for the rest of his life, he could find beneath his hand the record of his ecstasy.*

In the Year of Grace 1654,
On Monday, 23rd November, Feast of Saint Clement, Pope and Martyr,
and of others in the Martyrology.
and Eve of Saint Chrysogonus and other Martyrs.
From about half past ten at night until about half past twelve.

Fire
"God of Abraham, God of Isaac, God of Jacob,"[1]
not of the philosophers and scientists.
Certitude. Certitude. Feeling. Joy. Peace.
God of Jesus Christ
"My God and your God,"[2]
Thy God shall be my God,
Forgetting the world and all things, except only God.

[1] Exod. 3:6, Matt. 22:32. The words that Moses heard from the Burning Bush were quoted by our Lord when He rebuked His tempters.

[2] Ruth 1:16.

He is to be found only by the ways taught in the Gospel.
Greatness of the human soul.
"Righteous Father, the world has not known Thee, but I have known Thee." [3]
Joy, joy, joy, tears of joy.
I have fallen away from Him.
"They have forsaken me, the fountain of living water." [4]
"My God, wilt thou forsake me?"
May I not be separated from Him for all eternity.
This is life eternal, that they know Thee, the only true God, and Jesus Christ, whom Thou has sent.
Jesus Christ.
Jesus Christ.
I have fallen away from Him; I have fled from Him, denied Him, crucified Him.
May I not be separated from Him for eternity.
We hold Him only by the ways taught in the Gospel
Renunciation total and sweet,
Total submission to Jesus Christ and to my director.
Eternally in joy for one day of trial upon earth.
I will not forget thy Word.[5] Amen.

The Mystery [of the Agony of Jesus]

It was customary at Port Royal for those who were just beginning to think on heavenly things to keep a record of their meditations. "The Mystery of the Agony of Jesus" is one of Pascal's written reflections. Pascal's meditation has the concrete details that Saint François de Sales recommended to his spiritual clients to incorporate into their prayer as a remedy for distraction. "The Mystery of the Agony of Jesus,"

[3] John 17:25.
[4] Jer. 2:13.
[5] Ps. 118:16.

long ignored by Pascalian scholars, is one of the finest pieces of religious writings in French.[6]

Jesus suffered in His Passion the torments that men inflict upon Him; but in His Agony He suffered torments that He inflicted upon Himself: "He was deeply moved in spirit, and troubled," John 11:33. This was a torment inflicted, not by a human, but by an Almighty hand; and He had need to be Almighty, to bear it.

Jesus sought some comfort from the three dearest of His friends—but they were asleep. He prayed them to watch with Him awhile—and they left Him, with total indifference, with so little compassion that not for a moment were they held back from their sleep. And so Jesus was left alone with the wrath of God.

Jesus was left alone upon the earth, without a single one that could either feel or share His suffering, or even know of it. Heaven and He were alone in that knowledge.

Jesus was in a garden—not in a garden of delights, like the first Adam, who there destroyed himself and all the human race, but in a garden of suffering, where He saved Himself and all humanity.

He suffered this pain and this abandonment amid the horror of the night.

I believe that Jesus never uttered a complaint but this once; but this time He cried aloud, as though He could no longer contain that bitter sorrow: "My soul is very sorrowful, even to death," Mark 14:34.

Jesus sought the moral support of the companionship and comfort of men. I believe this was the sole occasion in the whole of His life that He did so. But He found none, for His disciples were asleep.

Jesus will be in agony until the end of the world, and during that time we also must not sleep.

In the midst of this general abandonment, when He found even those friends sleeping whom He had chosen to keep watch with Him, He was deeply perturbed because of the danger to which they had exposed [not Him, but] themselves. Despite their ingratitude, He admonished them with tender affection concerning their salvation and their eternal

[6] In the manuscript as it is today, the completion of the title appears on the back of the Fragment, which is a meditation according to the fourth method of Saint François de Sales, on the Sorrowful Mysteries of the Rosary.

good, warning them that "the spirit indeed is willing but the flesh is weak," Matt. 26:41.

Jesus came again, and again He found them sleeping as though no anxiety either for Him or for themselves, could keep them awake. He of His mercy therefore did not wake them, but left them to their rest.

Jesus prayed, as one uncertain of the Father's will, and as dreading death; but when He knew that will, He leaped forward to submit to it: "Rise, let us be going," Matt. 26:46. "Jesus, knowing all that was to befall him, came forward . . . ," John 18:4.

Jesus asked of men, and was not heard.

While His disciples slept, Jesus wrought their salvation. This He has done for every righteous man while he slept, either in the void before he was born, or in his sins after he was born.

He prayed but once that the cup might pass from Himself, and this He asked in a spirit of submission. And twice He prayed that the cup might come, if it must.

Jesus in weariness.

Jesus, seeing all His friends asleep, and all His enemies on the watch, committed Himself entirely into His Father's hands.

Jesus did not allow Himself to be swayed by the enmity in Judas: He saw therein the working of the divine dispensation —and *that* He loved. So far was He from being shaken by the depth of that malice, that in such a moment He could call him "Friend," Matt. 26:50.

Jesus tore Himself away from His disciples to enter upon His agony. We also must detach ourselves from our closest and most intimate friends, if we are to imitate His example.

Jesus was in an agony, He suffered the most bitter sorrow: let us, likewise, pray the more earnestly.

We implore the mercy of God, not that He may leave us in peace with our vices, but that He may deliver us from them.

If God were to give us masters with His own hand, how necessary would it be to obey them with goodwill! Now, necessity[7] and the things that happen[8] are such masters.

[7] Extreme human need, adverse circumstances.

[8] "God discloses His will to us in the things that He allows to happen." Letter III to Mlle de Roannez, 1656.

"Take comfort, you would not be seeking me, had you not already found me.

"I thought of you in my Agony; I shed those drops of blood for you.

"It is tempting me, rather than proving your own wisdom, to wonder whether you would acquit yourself well in some hypothetical situation. If it should arise, I will act in you.

"Be guided by my Commandments: consider how well I guided the Virgin and the Saints, who allowed me to act in them.

"The Father loves all that I do.

"Would you have me pay forevermore with the blood of my humanity, while you yourself contribute never a tear?

"Your conversion is my affair. Fear not, and pray with confidence, as you would for me.

"I am present with you by my word in the Scriptures, by my Spirit in the Church and in inspiration, by my power in the priests, by my prayer in the faithful.

"Doctors will not heal you, for in the end you must die. But it is I that will heal you, and make your body immortal.

"Suffer then the bondage of the flesh, and the servitude of life in the body. For the present, I deliver you only from the reprobate mind.

"I am a better friend to you than this man or that, for I have done more for you than they have done; and they would not have borne what I have suffered at your hands. They would not have died for you at the time of your very infidelities and cruelties, as I have done and am ready to do, and as I am doing throughout time, in my elect, and in the Blessed Sacrament.

"If you knew your sins, you would lose heart."

I shall lose heart, then, Lord; for on Thy assurance I believe in the malice of my sins.

"No. For I, who show you that malice, can heal it in you; and the fact that I show it you is a sign of my will to heal it. To the extent that you expiate your sins, you will recognize the evil in them; and you shall hear it said: 'Your sins are forgiven.' Do penance therefore for your secret sins, and for the hidden malice of all the sins known to you."

Lord, I give Thee all.

"I love you more than you have loved your own uncleanness: 'The sow that was washed turned back to wallow in the mire,' II Pet. 2:22.

"And for this be glory given to me, and not to you, who are worm and clay.

"Confess to your director that my very words are an occasion of sin to you, of vanity and curiosity."

I see the depth of my pride, my curiosity, my concupiscence. I have no communion with God, nor with Jesus Christ the righteous. But He was made sin for me: [9] "All thy plagues are fallen upon Him." [10] He is made more hateful than I; yet, far from hating me, He holds it an honor that I should go to His aid.

But He healed Himself, and so much the more will He heal me. I must add any wounds to His, and join myself to Him. And in saving Himself He will save me. But henceforth I must add no more.

"You shall be like God, knowing good and evil," Gen. 3:5. Every man plays the god when he passes judgment that this or that is good or bad, and when he allows himself to be depressed or overjoyed by the things that happen.

Do small things as though they were great, because of the majesty of Jesus Christ who does them in us, and who lives in our lives. And do great things as though they were small and easy, because of His omnipotence.

Fragments

11. I love poverty because He loved it. I love wealth because it bestows the power to help the needy. I keep faith with all men. I do not return evil to those that have injured

[9] II Cor. 5:21: "For our sake he made him to be sin who knew no sin." And see Zachary Tourneur's reading, and his note, *Cluny II, Pensées de Blaise Pascal*, p. 14, 1941.

[10] Isa. 53:6. "We have turned every one to his own way, and the Lord has laid on him the iniquity of us all."

me, but I wish them to be in a condition like my own, in which neither good nor evil can be suffered at the hands of men. I try to be just, true, sincere, and loyal to all men, and to show affection to those to whom God has more closely bound me. And whether I am alone or in the sight of men, I do not lose sight of God, who will be the judge of all my actions, and to whom I have consecrated them all.

Such are my feelings, and every day of my life I bless my Redeemer, who planted them in me, and who made of me—a man full of weaknesses and shortcomings, concupiscence, pride, and ambition—one free from all these evils by the power of His grace, to which all the glory is due, since in myself there is only misery and error.

15. The conditions in which, according to the world, it is easiest to live, are the most difficult in which to live according to God; and vice versa. From the worldly standpoint, nothing is so difficult as the religious life, nothing so easy as to live without God. Nothing is easier, in the worldly sense, than to occupy high office and possess great wealth; but nothing is more difficult than to live a good life in such a situation, and to develop no interest in the way of the world, nor the taste for it.

17. Let God not hold us guilty of our sins—that is to say, of all the consequences of our sins; for these are terrible—even of our smallest faults, if we were willing to trace them without pity to the end.

25. *Probability:* They have a few sound principles, but they misapply them in order to deceive.[11] Now such misuse of truth ought to be punishable with the same severity as lying.

As though there could be two Hells, one for sins against charity, the other for sins against justice.

34. Men like to be certain: they like the Pope to be infallible in matters of faith, and learned men to be so in matters of morals. Thus we have certitude.

[11] Interpreting *s'en abuser* according to the ordinary usage of La Bruyère, La Fontaine, and Pascal.

94. *Miracles:* A miracle is an effect beyond the natural power of the means used [S. Theol. I.q. 105, 8]; the non-miraculous is an effect which does not exceed the result expected from the ordinary power of the means used. Thus, those who heal by invoking the devil do not work a miracle, for miracles are not beyond the ordinary power of the devil. But . . .

95. The miracles were worked, not to convert, but to condemn, [S. Theol. la 2aeq. 113, a 10, ad 2; cp 3a. q. 43, a 3, ad 3.]

96. *First objection:* "Even an angel from Heaven . . . ," Gal 1:8. We must not judge truth by miracles, but miracles by truth. Therefore miracles are useless. "Now, miracles are not useless: they serve a purpose, but they must not be in conflict with truth. Hence the saying of Fr. Lingendes.[12] "God will not permit that a miracle should lead into error." Where a controversy arises within the one Church, miracle will decide the issue.
Second objection: "But Antichrist will work miracles." Pharaoh's magicians did not succeed in leading men into error. So we cannot, upon the testimony of Antichrist, say to Jesus Christ that He has led us into error (for the miracles of Antichrist will be worked against Jesus Christ, so that they cannot possibly lead into error). Either God will not permit false miracles, or He will provide for still greater ones.[13]

Jesus Christ subsists from the beginning of the world, a fact which argues more convincingly than all the miracles of Antichrist. If within the Church itself there were to be a miracle in support of error, we should [necessarily] be led into error. Schism is visible, a miracle is visible. But schism is a plainer mark of error than miracle is of truth. Therefore such a miracle could not lead into error. But short of schism, the error is less striking than the miracle, so that the attendant miracle might lead into error.

"Where is your God?" Ps. 42:3–10. Miracles reveal Him—like the lightning flash.

[12] Père Claude de Lingendes, S.J., a famous preacher of Pascal's time. He died in 1660.

[13] As was done in the case of Pharaoh's magicians. [Exod. 7.]

98. This is not the homeland of truth: truth wanders unknown among men. God has covered her with a veil, which prevents her from being recognized by those who do not hear her voice. A way is thus open to blasphemy, even against such truths as are at any rate very probable. If the truths of the Gospel are proclaimed, so also are many things which are in conflict with them; and disputed questions are wrapped in obscurity so that people cannot discriminate. And they ask: "Why should we believe you, rather than another? What sign do you give? You have only words, and so have we. If you had miracles, well and good." It is true that doctrine ought to be supported by miracles—even though men twist the meaning of the miracle so that they may revile the doctrine. And if miracles happen, they then say that these are not enough without doctrine—which is another truth, and they twist it into an attack upon miracles.

Jesus Christ healed the man born blind, and He wrought a number of miracles on the Sabbath. Thus it came about that He blinded the Pharisees, who declared that miracles must be supported by doctrine. "We know that God spoke by Moses, but as for this man, we know not whence he is . . . Why, this is a marvel, that you know not whence he is," John 9:29–30, and yet He has worked such miracles.

Jesus Christ never spoke against God, nor against Moses.

Antichrist and the false prophets foretold by both Testaments will speak openly against God and against Jesus Christ. God will not allow the secret enemy, the man who is careful not to be openly His adversary, to work miracles in public. Never was it known, in any open controversy where both parties claimed to be speaking for God, Jesus Christ and the Church, that miracles were worked in support of the false Christians, while the other, the orthodox side, was left without miracles.

"He has a demon. Others said . . . Can a demon open the eyes of the blind?" John 10:20–21.

The proofs which Jesus Christ and the Apostles drew from Scripture are not conclusive, for they simply say that Moses foretold the coming of a prophet. They do not prove that He Himself was that prophet—and that is the crux of the matter. These passages therefore served only to show that Jesus Christ and His Apostles were not running counter to Scripture—that Scripture is not self-contradictory; they do not suggest perfect agreement on all points. The exclusion of strife, and the presence of miracles, are sufficient.

There is such a thing as a reciprocal obligation between God and man—which would explain such sayings as, "What more was there to do for my vineyard, that I have not done in it?" Isa. 5:4, and, "Come now, let us reason together, says the Lord . . . ," Isa. 1:18. For,

1° "God must perform what He has promised," etc.

Men owe it to God to accept the religion which He sends them. God owes it to men not to lead them into error. Now they would be led into error, if miracle workers[14] were to preach doctrines which could not be seen to be clearly false by the light of common sense, and if a greater worker of miracles had not already appeared, to warn mankind against believing in them.

Thus, if schism were to occur in the Church, and the Arians, for example (who claimed, as the Catholics did, the support of Scripture), had performed miracles, while the Catholics had performed none, men would have been led into error.

For a man who claims to declare the secrets of God to us does not deserve credence on his private authority, unbelievers refuse to listen to him; similarly, when a man raises the dead, prophesies things to come, divides or calms the waters, heals the sick, in testimony of his communion with God, there is no unbeliever who will not go and hear him (Luke 19), and the skepticism of such as Pharaoh and the Pharisees is due to a supernatural hardening of the heart. When, therefore, we see both miracles and sound doctrine on the same side, there is no difficulty. But when we see miracles allied with bogus teaching, we have to make up our minds which teaching is the more clear. Jesus Christ Himself was suspected.

Bar-Jesus blinded (Acts 13:11): the power of God overwhelms that of His enemies.

The itinerant Jewish exorcists who were overcome by the devil they had themselves challenged, who overpowered them with the cry: "Jesus I know, and Paul I know, but who are you?" Acts 19:11–20.

Miracles are for the support of doctrine, not doctrine for the support of miracles.

[14] Religious impostors.

If the miracles are authentic, will they suffice to persuade all men concerning doctrine? No, that will not happen, for, "Even if . . . an angel from heaven . . . ," Gal. 1:8.

Rule: We have to judge of the doctrine by the supporting miracles, and also of the miracles by the doctrine which they support. Both parts of the rule are true, and they do not contradict one another. You have to fit the rule to the occasion.[15] How pleased you are, indeed, whenever you come across a general rule, and can apply it to a particular case, hoping to stir up a bit of trouble, create a dilemma, and conceal the truth a little longer! We shall have to put a stop to that little game, Father! [16] Truth is one, and is secure. Now the "obligation" of God to men makes it impossible that He should ever allow them to be permanently deceived by an error.[17] Therefore it is impossible for any teacher having the ability to deceive, to conceal indefinitely the error in his doctrine behind an appearance of good, while he proclaims meanwhile his obedience to God and the Church; nor is it possible that he should be able to support his teaching with miracles, in order insensibly to instill a doctrine that is as false as it is subtle. These things are out of the question. Still less is it possible that God Himself, who knows the hearts of men, should work miracles to support the teaching of such a man.

99. If the devil were to promote a form of teaching which was his own ruin, he would, as Jesus Christ said, be divided

[15] *Il faut distinguer les temps.* This is a perfectly ordinary idiom in the language of Racine, Bossuet, La Bruyère and other seventeenth- and eighteenth-century writers, who used the expression in the same way as Pascal. No "juggling with words" is involved.

On the whole of this fragment and its apparent contradictions see the remark of Leon Brunschvicg: "Where doctrine is ambiguous, miracles provide a test; where miracles create perplexity, doctrine is the touchstone." Pére Beurrier testified that Pascal was undoubtedly strongly orthodox, perfectly submissive to the Church and to the Holy Father, and that he undoubtedly died a good Catholic. Chevalier pointed out that Pascal always "outstripped and dominated" the Port-Royal Jansenists with whom he found himself accidentally associated, and in whose notions he had certainly become entangled. And we may note his remark to Mlle Roannez, that "the body is no more alive without the Head, than the Head without the body."

[16] This is probably a reference to P. Annet, whose *Rabat-joie des Jansénistes* had lately been published.

[17] Descartes, *Méditation IV*.

against himself. If God were to support teaching which tended to the destruction of the Church, He would be divided against Himself. "Every kingdom divided against itself is laid waste," Matt. 12:25. For Jesus Christ worked against the devil, and destroyed his power over the hearts of men, that He might establish the Kingdom of God. Exorcism symbolizes this fact. Therefore He added, "If I by the spirit of God cast out demons, then the Kingdom of God has come upon you," Matt. 12:28.

102. *Begin here:* Miracles are the test of doctrine, and doctrine is the test of miracles.

There are false miracles and true, and we require some sign by which we may distinguish them, or both will be useless. But they are by no means useless—on the contrary, they are basic to Christianity. Now a true miracle provides proof of what is true, and our rule must be one which does not impair the proof of the truth, for such proof is the chief end of miracles.

Moses gave two rules: the nonfulfillment of a prophecy, Deut. 18; and that the miracles do not lead to idolatry, Deut. 13; and Jesus Christ gave one, Mark 9:39.

If doctrine determines the validity of the miracle, miracles are useless to doctrine. But if miracles form the criterion . . .

Objection to this rule: Differences of time. One rule under Moses, another rule today.

Every religion is false if its creed fails to adore one God as the principle of all things, and if its moral teaching fails to inculcate the love of the one true God as the end of all.

105. If there were no false miracles there would be certainty. If there were no rules by which to discriminate them, miracles would be useless and there would be no reason to believe in them. Now, humanly speaking, there is no such thing as certitude in this world, but we have our intelligence.

129. Having considered whence it comes that there are so many false miracles, bogus revelations, divinations, etc., it seems to me that the real reason is that there are true ones. For so many false miracles would not be possible if there were not also some true ones, nor so many false revelations, if there were not also some that were true, nor so many false

religions, if there were not one that is true. For, supposing there has never been anything of that kind [i.e., conflicting religious claims], it is virtually impossible that men could have imagined it, and still less possible that so many others should have been persuaded to believe it. But there have been many things both important and true, and these have been believed by men of greatness; so that the habit of belief has become natural—and it makes men capable of believing also what is false. Thus, instead of concluding that since there are so many false miracles, there cannot be any true ones, we must on the contrary say that there must be some true miracles, since there are so many that are false; and that there are some fake ones simply because there are some that are true, similarly, that there are even some false religions because there is one that is true. Some would object to this: that savages have a form of religion, but this is because they have heard something of the true religion, as appears from the tradition of the cross of Saint Andrew, of the Flood, of the rite of circumcision, etc. The reason is, that the mind of man is naturally inclined to admit all the ideas proposed to it, and so is exposed to every falsehood of that [kind as well as to ideas that are true].

131. It is impossible to disbelieve miracles on rational grounds.

247. The difference between the mathematical mind and the intuitive mind.

In the first, the principles can be grasped very easily, but they are remote from everyday life, so that it does not readily occur to us to apply them, simply because we have never become familiar with the method. But when we give them even a little attention, the principles are plain enough, and only a person willfully in error would proceed to draw a false conclusion from principles so plain that it is scarcely possible for him to mistake them.

But in the case of the intuitive mind the rules are drawn from common experience, and all eyes can see them. We have only to turn the head—and that requires no effort. It is only a question then of good eyesight, but *that* we must have. For the principles in this case are so many and so raveled together, that it is almost impossible not to miss some of them. Now the omission of a single principle leads to error, so that we have to be very clear-sighted, so as to see them all;[18] and we need also a considerable degree of mental alertness if we are not to draw false conclusions from the premises, once these are known.

All mathematicians would therefore have intuitive minds if they were also clear-sighted, because they do draw false conclusions from known principles and people with intuitive minds would be mathematicians if their sight could be trained upon the unfamiliar disciplines of mathematics.

What prevents many intuitive persons from being mathematicians is that they completely lack that flexibility of mind necessary to grasp the principles of mathematics; but the reason why mathematicians are not intuitive is that they cannot see what is before their eyes. They are accustomed to the exact and simple principles of mathematics, and they only proceed to reason when they have carefully examined and tested the premises. Thus they are lost in matters of intuition, where the arguments cannot be tested in this way, where they are indeed scarcely visible, felt rather than seen, and only with infinite difficulty conveyed to those who have not felt their immediate impact. The principles underlying intuition are so many, and of such delicacy, that great insight is required to perceive them, and much sensitivity is necessary to make honest and accurate deductions from them once they are understood. For it is as a rule impossible to demonstrate them step by step, as would be done in mathematics, because intuitive minds have not the same grasp of mathematical principles, and it would be an endless business for them to acquire it. In some of its aspects the issue must be seen at a glance, and not worked out by a reasoning process. Thus it is that mathematicians are rarely endowed with intuition, and perceptive people are seldom also mathematicians. Mathematicians always want to approach these delicate questions as though they were theorems in geometry, and they make themselves look silly when they start from definitions and proceed to axioms which is not at all the right way to handle a problem of this kind. It is not that the mathematical mind cannot grasp such issues, but it can only do so silently, simply, and when free from the control of technical rules; for true felicity of expression is be-

[18] A keen eye and a trained judgment see more in a great painting than is visible to the amateur.

yond the reach of most of us, and genuine feeling belongs only to a few.

Intuitive minds, on the other hand, are well accustomed to forming a judgment at a single glance, and they are so completely disconcerted when they are confronted with propositions, that they recoil from them, and are discouraged. Such propositions can only be approached by way of barren principles and sterile definitions, which they are not used to studying in such detail.

But the mind that delights in error is neither intuitive nor mathematical.

Mathematicians, then, who are merely mathematicians possess right judgment, so long as everything is carefully explained to them in terms of definition and axiom. Otherwise they run into error, or are extremely tiresome in other ways, because they are only able to arrive at correct conclusions if they are furnished from the start with principles which have been carefully explained to them.

And the intuitive mind which has no equipment but its "instinct" lacks the patience to argue from first principles when dealing with speculative questions or with the realm of the imagination—which they do not encounter in daily life and which are completely foreign to their experience.

248. A kind of eloquence that knows how to persuade by sweetness and not by mere strength of will.

249. *Mathematics and intuition.* True eloquence sets little store by the play upon words, and true morality is not taken in by any mere "spiritual morality," which [19] is not under the control of rules.

For goodwill [20] belongs to the judgment, as knowledge belongs to the intellect. Intuition is a faculty of the judgment, mathematics, of the mind.

To take philosophy lightly is the mark of a true philosopher.

250. There are various kinds of right judgment: some have it in a particular range of ideas, but not in another, where they are liable to talk nonsense.

[19] According to Brunschvicg, the punctuation of the manuscript justifies this reading.

[20] Adopting a meaning of *sentiment* common in La Bruyère and Racine.

Some men are skillful in reaching sound conclusions from a few premises, and this is evidence of a right judgment.

Others are able to reach sound conclusions where they have a good number of premises.

Some, for example, have a good knowledge of the properties of water where the principles involved are few (though the application of these principles is a matter of such complexity that only a trained mind can grasp it).

Such persons might not make clever mathematicians, because this is a science involving a great number of elements, and a mind may be such that, while it is well able to investigate to the full a small number of principles, it cannot in the least understand a subject where the principles involved are many.

There are then two kinds of understanding: one is capable of a clear grasp of principles and speedy deductions from them, and this is the precise mind; the other, of versatility, of understanding a great number of principles without confusing them, and this is the mathematical mind. The first has strength and exactness; the other, comprehension. Now, one quality may well exist without the other, for a mind may be strong, but also narrow, or it may be broad and weak.

251. Infinite movement: the point which fills all things, movement in a state of rest; the infinite without quantity, indivisible, yet infinite.

252. What a difference there is between knowing God and loving Him!

254. These people have no heart. One should not make friends of them.

255. There is a certain standard of grace and beauty which consists in a certain relation between our own nature, such as it is, weak or strong, and the thing that we like.

Everything which conforms to this standard pleases us, whether it be a house, a song, a sermon, verse or prose, a woman, birds, streams, trees, rooms, clothes, etc. Anything which does not conform to this standard is displeasing to men of taste. And just as there is a perfect relationship between a song and a house which are made to good models, because they conform to these same models, each after its kind, so also there is a perfect relationship between things made after bad models. Not that the bad model is unique, for there are plenty of them; but every bad sonnet, for example, on whatever bad model it may be made, is exactly comparable with a woman who dresses in a style which is equally bad.

Nothing shows more clearly how ridiculous a bad sonnet is than a careful comparison with its model; and then to imagine a woman or a house dressed or designed according to an equally bad model.

256. It is amusing to note that there are people in the world who renounce all the laws of Nature, and then make laws for themselves which they obey strictly, as for example the soldiers of Mahomet, robbers, heretics, etc. And logicians too. It seems their particular license has to be entirely without limit or bar, seeing that they have broken through so much that is so just and sacred.

257. *Poetic beauty:* Just as we are accustomed to speak of poetic beauty, so ought we also to speak of mathematical beauty, and medical beauty; but this we do not do, and the reason is that while we know quite well what is the object of mathematics, which is a matter of proofs, and what the purpose of medicine, which consists in healing, we do not know what it is that makes a thing pleasing, and to please is the purpose of poetry. In this case we do not know what natural model we should imitate, and for want of that knowledge, certain extravagant terms have been invented: "Golden age," "the wonder of our times," "fatal," etc., and this jargon is called poetic beauty.

But if anyone were to describe a woman in this way, that is, by describing trivialities in long words, we should have a pretty miss tricked out in mirrors and chains; and this would make us laugh, for we have a better idea of what constitutes female charm than we have of poetic beauty. But people who did not know any better might admire her in such trinkets, and in many a village she would be voted queen. And that is why we call sonnets made to such a pattern, "village queens."

258. Nobody passes in this world as a judge of verse unless he has first hung out his sign as a poet, a mathematician, etc. But men with a general culture see no need of such a sign, for they see scarcely any difference between the craft of a poet and that of an embroiderer.

Persons possessed of a general culture are not described as poets, mathematicians, etc., but they are indeed such, and good judges of the matter, too. You cannot guess what they are: they will talk on whatever subject was in hand when they came into the room. One does not observe in them any one quality rather than another, except when they need to use it. Then we recall that they have it; for it is so perfectly in character that we never describe them as good speakers when there is no occasion for oratory, but when a speech is required, we remember that they speak well.

So it is false praise to say of such a man as he comes into the room, that he is a very skillful poet; but it looks bad if no one asks his opinion when poetry is under discussion.

259. All the spurious purple patches that you and I detest in Cicero have had their admirers, and plenty of them.

260. We ought not to want to say of anyone that he is a mathematician, or a preacher, or an eloquent speaker, but that he is a *good man*, a man of breeding. Only this universal quality pleases me. When, as soon as you see a man, you think of his book, that is a bad sign. I should prefer that no one of his qualities should be noticed until it is needed and the occasion arises for its use. *Nothing in excess,* for fear that some one quality should be seen to predominate, and he get a name for it. Let nobody think of him as a good speaker except when a speaker is required—but then let everyone remember him.

261. When we want to correct a person for his own good, and to show him that he was in error, we must take note of the viewpoint from which he looks at the thing, for from that angle he is generally right. Such truth as there is in the thing we must admit, but we have to show him where he is wrong. Such treatment pleases him, since it shows him that he was not altogether mistaken, but only failed to see all sides. Now nobody is annoyed not to have seen everything, but nobody likes to realize that he has been mistaken. The

reason for this may be that a man naturally cannot see everything; and that he naturally thinks he cannot be mistaken about the standpoint from which he sees the thing, since his sense perceptions are always true.

262. Man is full of needs; he cares only for such people as can satisfy them all. "He is a good mathematician," someone might say—but I have no business to speak about mathematics: he might deal with me as though I were a proposition.

"He is a good soldier." Am I then a town under siege? What I really need is some one man of parts who can himself supply all my requirements.

263. The style of writing of Epictetus, Montaigne, and Salomon de Tultie is a flowing, familiar style, very persuasive, very easy to remember and to quote, because it is made up entirely of thoughts suggested by the ordinary small talk of everyday life. For example, when people mention the vulgar error that the moon is the origin of all things, they will defend it by appealing to Salomon dc Tultic, who says that "where the truth of a matter is unknown, it is a good thing to have a vulgar error . . . ," etc., for which, see the fragment overleaf.

264. A poet, but not a man of any attainments.

265. Certain authors, when they speak of their works, say, "My book, my commentary, my history," etc., like a commoner who owns his own house and is forever talking of "my place." It would be better if they said, "Our book, our commentary, our history," etc., since there is usually more of other people's work than their own in what they write.

Provincial Letter Number 4

Of Actual Grace—of Sins of Ignorance—of Responsibility

Paris, February 25, 1656

Sir,

There are no people in all the world like these Jesuits. I have met Dominicans in plenty, as well as professors of theology, and learned men of that kind; but the visit from which I have just returned has certainly filled a gap in my education. Other men do but copy the Jesuits. Information is so much more likely to be authentic if you get it at the fountainhead, and so I have been to see one of their most learned Fathers; I was accompanied on this occasion also by the same faithful Jansenist friend as had been with me to see the Dominicans.

I particularly wanted to find out something about this quarrel they are having with the Jansenists about *actual grace*. So I said to this good Father that I would be very much obliged if he would explain the matter to me, that I did not even know what the expression meant, and that I begged him to enlighten me. "Very willingly" said he, "for I like to meet an inquiring mind. Here is the definition: 'Actual grace is an inspiration of God, by means of which he makes known to a man His will, and by means of which he strengthens that man to do it.' " "And what," I inquired, "is the point at issue on this subject, between yourselves and the Jansenists?" "It is this," he answered. "We hold that God gives actual grace to every man upon every occasion of temptation; because we maintain that, if we had not the actual grace requisite to preserve us from sin in every temptation then, whatever sin we committed, it could never be imputed to us. But the Jansenists say something different: that sins committed without actual grace will be just as certainly imputed; but in this they are mere dreamers." I saw the drift of his argument, but I wanted to induce him to express himself more clearly. I therefore said: "This expression, 'actual grace,' perplexes me, Father. I find it unfamiliar, please be so kind as to repeat the definition without using this term, and I shall be greatly obliged." "Certainly," said the Father, "you wish to have the definition instead of the thing defined: this can be done without the slightest change of meaning,[1] and I shall be most happy. We maintain then, as an unchallengeable principle, that 'no action can be imputed as a sin,[2] if God does not give us, before we commit it, the knowledge that it is sinful, and an inspiration from Himself which strengthens our will to avoid it.' Do you understand me now?"

I was astonished by this statement, according to which all sins of surprise, and all such as are committed in entire forgetfulness of God, will not be imputed. I turned to my Jansenist friend, and saw plainly enough from the expression on his face that he, at any rate, understood nothing of the kind. But he uttered not a single word; so I said to the Father: "I might certainly be very much relieved, Father, if what you say were really true, and you could bring some strong arguments to support it."

"You ask for arguments?" he promptly answered, "I can find you plenty, and very sound ones, too, depend upon it." Upon which, off he went, to look for his books.

While he was gone, I said to my companion, "Can there be any other writer, then, who ventures to speak as this man does?"

"Do you find it a novelty?" he said. "Bear in mind that neither Fathers of the Church, nor popes, nor councils, nor the Scriptures, nor any devotional book (even of the kind we are getting today), have ever said anything of the sort. But as to these new casuists and our neo-Scholastics, he will find you any number."

"But what nonsense!" I said. "I can refute any of these modern writers, the moment they go against tradition."

"You are right there," he said.

As he spoke, the good Father came into the room, loaded with his books. He handed me one from the top of the pile.

1 A tilt at the pedantries of the Scholastics.

2 Provided it be free.

"Here, read this," he said. "It is Father Bauny's *Somme des péchés*,[3] and the fifth edition, too, which shows you that it must be a good book."

"Rather a pity, though," said my Jansenist in my ear, "that this particular book should have been condemned at Rome, as well as by the French Bishops."

"Look at page nine hundred and six," said the father.

I read the passage he had marked, and read the following words: "For an act to be sinful, and to be deemed guilty in the sight of God, we must know that the act we propose to commit is worthless; or at least we must either doubt or fear that it may be so; or, though we have reason to believe that the act proposed is displeasing to God and is forbidden by Him, yet we persist in doing it, kick over the traces, and insist on breaking a law we know to be divine."

"This begins well enough," I remarked. "Wait a moment, however," said he, "and see what malice will do. It was because of this very passage that M. Hallier (before he became a friend of ours), made a mockery of P. Bauny, and said of him: 'Ecce, qui tollit peccata mundi.' It is certainly true," I admitted, "that we have here a new method by which to be redeemed—one devised by Père Bauny."

"Would you now like to go on to an authority still more respectable?" he went on. "Take this book by P. Annat,[4] his latest work against Arnauld. Turn to page thirty-four, which I have turned down, and read especially the lines I have marked there with a pencil: they are pure gold."

I accordingly read as follows: "He who has no thought of God, nor of his sins, nor any apprehension (as far as I can discover), and no consciousness of his duty to practice the love of God; nor any contrition, has no actual grace to direct and strengthen his will to perform such acts. But it is also true that he commits no sin by omitting them; and if

[3] A "catalogue of sins" which had already been condemned at Rome by a Decree dated 6 October 1640. The Jansenists were, however, scarcely entitled to plead this condemnation, since most of their own works were already on the Index. The whole of this letter brings out the subtlety and malice of the Jansenist attack, and the *false imputations* they were prepared to bring against the teaching authority of the Church.

[4] Annat was Confessor to the King. The book mentioned was the *Réponse à quelques demandes touchant la première lettre de M. Arnauld,* 1655. It was one of the books to which Arnauld referred in his *Seconde lettre à un duc et pair.*

he should be damned, it would not be a punishment for such ommission." And a few lines further down: "The same may also be said of a culpable act." [5]

"Can you not see for yourself," said the Father, "how this author deals with sins of omission, as well as of commission? For he leaves out nothing. What do you think of it?"

"Oh, I am indeed pleased," I answered, "for I can already see some very pretty consequences of such reasoning; and as I look into them, new mysteries are added to the faith. It is clear that far more people, very many more, will be justified because they plead ignorance or forgetfulness of God, than by grace and the sacraments. But, my dear Father, are you not perhaps deluding me? Is there not something here that resembles a satisfaction which does not satisfy? I am terribly afraid of the distinction here, for I have already been taken in by it. Do you really mean it?"

"What!" explained the father, with some heat, "this is no laughing matter. There is no question of equivocation here."

"I am not joking," I said, "for my anxiety to learn is almost as great as my dread of the answer."

"Well, then," said he, "to set your mind at rest, take a look at these books by Le Moine, who taught these doctrines with all the authority of the Sorbonne. He learnt them from us, as a matter of fact, but he has expounded the subject very well, and settled the point beyond dispute. He teaches that for an act to be sinful, all the following factors must be present to the mind.[6] Read them through, and weigh every word."

I proceeded to read through the Latin text, which I here translate: "1. God imparts to the soul a measure of love, which inclines it to do the thing commanded; but the opposed force of concupiscence solicits the contrary act. 2. God imparts to the soul a knowledge of its own weakness. 3. God imparts to the soul the knowledge of the medicine which can heal its disorder. 4. God inspires in the soul the desire to be

[5] Both writers are perfectly correct, if their words be understood of inadvertence or of invincible ignorance.

[6] Either explicitly or implicitly. But the passage cited is only a textbook analysis of a perfect moral act, based upon the ordinary procedures of morals and philosophy. Nobody supposes that such a sequence of ideas is always present, nor in the order given, nor with such comprehension, clarity, and precision.

healed. 5. God inspires the soul to pray, and to implore His assistance."

"And," said the Jesuit, "if all these things are not present to the mind, the act is not properly a sin, and cannot be imputed as such; as M. le Moine says on the same page, and throughout the whole of his book. Do you want still more authorities? Here they are, then."

"But every one of them is modern," murmured my Jansenist.

"So I see," I said, and turning to the Father, observed: "My very dear Father, this is going to be excellent news for certain people that I know; for you can scarcely have met anyone with fewer sins to their account than they. For they give never a thought to God, and their sins have ruined their power of reasoning. These have no knowledge of their own weakness, nor of the medicine that can heal their disorders. They have never reflected upon their souls' welfare, and still less would they desire to engage in prayer, or to ask God for any assistance. According to M. le Moine, therefore, these souls are still in a state of baptismal innocence. They have never thought of the love of God, nor been moved to sorrow for their sins. Therefore, according to Père Annat, they have not sinned through defect of charity or lack of contrition, although their lives are spent in the quest of pleasures without end, and not a trace of remorse or compunction has ever interrupted that search. All of which excesses have led me to believe till now that these souls were doomed to perish everlastingly. But you now assure me, father, that these very excesses make their salvation certain. May Heaven bless you, my Father, for assuring me of the justification of such people! Other men teach that souls are saved by being afflicted with austerities, but you have shown that those whom we might suppose to be most desperately ill, are really in quite good health. Oh, for the broad way to happiness in this world and the next! I had always believed that the less God occupied our thoughts, the more sinful would be our condition; but from what you now tell me, once we achieve such self-mastery as enables us to dismiss Him altogether from our minds, all things become pure to us forevermore. No more sinners by halves, with a little love left for the good life: your half-sinners will certainly all be lost. But your free and easy sinners, your hardened sinners, your sinners without sorrow, perfect and finished in their very wickedness—Hell will never hold them, for they cheated the devil in the very act of giving way to him!"

The good Father could see plainly enough that these consequences followed directly from his own premises, but he slipped out of the difficulty very cleverly without showing the slightest annoyance (whether from prudence or from a natural mildness of disposition, who shall say? [7]) by remarking: "We are not unacquainted with the unhappy cases you mention. We say that, if they had never at any time adverted to God, and never at any time entertained a thought of changing their ways by repentance, then those evil living persons would be without sin. But we assert that they have all, in fact, done both these things, and that God never abandons a man to his sins without first showing him the evil of what he proposes to do, and inspiring in him the desire to avoid doing it, or at least praying for divine help, that his will may be strengthened to resist it. And the only people who deny this are the Jansenists." [8]

"What, Father," I cried, "is it *this* that constitutes the heresy of the Jansenists, the idea that everytime we sin, remorse troubles the conscience, and that despite that warning we do not hesitate to sin, but persist in it and kick over the traces, as P. Bauny puts it. If that be all, it is a very odd kind of heresy! I have always believed that a man might well be damned for not developing a good condition of mind and heart, a well-ordered, rightly directed will; but, that he might be damned for believing that the rest of the world does not have them,[9] has certainly never occurred to me. I feel bound in conscience, father, to undeceive you, and to inform you that there are thousands of people who are never con-

[7] One of the occasions on which Pascal is not quite straightforward, because he is "writing for effect." At no time has any authority ever taught that any man who deliberately indulges vicious habits so as to close his understanding to the divine will, and his heart to those holy inspirations which move him to avoid the occasions of sin, is free of responsibility, and that his acts are not sinful; nor that he becomes *less* guilty as he takes one step after another toward sinful indulgence, i.e., as his will is weakened by his own fault. The wit of the challenger is here keen, yet clumsy: to make one's adversary look absurd, yet to leave his case unanswered, is not a good procedure in serious argument.

[8] Grace is given, and the requisite increase of grace may be merited. Moreover, every man has, up to a given time, the means in his power to avoid sin and grow in grace.

[9] Adopting a reading found by Faugère in the manuscript.

scious of any such good inspirations; who sin without remorse, who sin with satisfaction—and are proud of the fact. Who should be better informed on this subject than yourself? You have probably yourself heard the confessions of some of these very persons—for it is among people of distinction that they are usually found.[10] But be on your guard, father, for dangerous consequences may flow from this principle of yours. Do you not perceive the effect it will have on our libertines,[11] whose one object it is to shake the authority of religion? What a handle you give them, indeed, for this very purpose, when you tell them, as an article of faith, that every sin they commit is accompanied by the knowledge that it is evil and, an interior desire to abstain from it. For is it not obvious that their own experience has satisfied them of the fallaciousness of your teaching on the subject—teaching which you claim to be of faith—and that they will extend their skepticism to all your other beliefs? Will they not say that, if you are not to be relied upon as to one article, you must of necessity be suspected as to them all? So that you will compel them to form one of two possible conclusions: either that religion is false, or that you yourself are not well informed about it."

My Jansenist friend now lent his support to my contention: "If you wish to protect the coherence of this doctrine of yours, Father, it might be as well to go into less detail. You might perhaps be content with less precision than you have used with us, in your explanations of what you understand by 'actual grace.' For how can you openly teach (without losing entirely the respect that people have for you), that 'no man is guilty of sin unless he have a prior knowledge of his own weakness and of the remedy for it; also a desire to be delivered from it, and an interior inspiration moving him to ask for the help of God'? Will anyone believe you when you say, that men who are abandoned to avarice, lust, blasphemy, dueling; men who actively seek to avenge their own wrongs;

[10] Pascal was himself of considerable social position, Bauny was an eminent professor, Annat was spiritual director of the greatest ruler of the century.

[11] The *libertines,* freethinkers or Pyrrhonians of Pascal's time were men of powerful but undisciplined mind who, while professing to be Christians, were really saturated with the atheistic rationalism of Giordano Bruno, Paracelsus, and Charron. It was at such men that the *Apology* of Pascal was aimed.

who rob other men, and commit sacrilege, have in fact 'a true interior desire' to practice chastity, humility and other Christian virtues? [12]

"Will anyone believe that those libertines we spoke of, who go about proclaiming that Nature is the only power, would listen for a moment to any charge that Nature herself is disordered, and indeed diseased and in need of cure? Are you going to tell me that men who firmly believe it proven that 'God bestows no power, nor did anyone ever ask Him for it,' would dream of asking Him for it for themselves?

"The Epicureans deny that there is any such thing as divine Providence: who then can believe that they ever felt any 'inspiration' to engage in prayer, since they themselves have said that—'it is an affront to God that we should petition Him in our need'—as though He were capable of even a passing thought for such creatures as ourselves.

"Finally, do you maintain that idolaters and atheists have any desire to pray to the true God (with whom they are unacquainted), to bestow upon them virtues (of the power of which they know nothing), in every single temptation which lures them toward sin—on numberless occasions, that is, throughout their life on earth?" [13]

"Yes," said the Father firmly, "we do maintain all these doctrines; and rather than admit that men sin without any consciousness of wrongdoing, and without some desire for the opposite virtues, we declare that every living being, including the hardened sinner and the unbeliever, has such knowledge and experiences, such desires to pray, every time he encounters temptation. For you cannot show me that this is not so—at any rate, not from Scripture."

Upon this, I intervened. "My dear Father, need we go to Scripture, when the thing is self-evident? This is no question of a matter of faith, nor even of reasoning; this is a matter of *fact*. We can see it, we know it, we feel it."

My Jansenist, however, was all for pursuing the argument according to the Father's own terms: "If you want us to

[12] Pascal's satirical intention again leads him into error. No moralist teaches that sin disappears where the moral sense has been impaired or destroyed by bad habit.

[13] Pascal is writing in a spirit of keen mockery. He comes close to an allegation that all the acts of an infidel are sins, the virtues of the philosophers no better than vices, and the entire ancient world certainly damned; but the tenor of his thought as a whole redeems him from Madame de Sévigné's charge that he was "a good Jansenist."

argue from Scripture only, Father, by all means let it be so, but do not try to resist its authority. For we read that 'God hath not revealed His judgments to the Gentiles, whom He left to wander in their own ways.' Do not say, therefore, that God Himself does in fact enlighten such men, for (as the Scriptures tell us), they 'are abandoned to darkness and the shadow of death.'

"Is it not evidence sufficient that your principle is erroneous, to remind you that even Saint Paul calls himself 'the chief of sinners,' and that was on account of a sin which he says was 'committed out of ignorance and an excess of zeal?' Is it not enough to learn from the Gospel that those who crucified Jesus Christ stood in need of the pardon that He Himself pleaded on their behalf, although they *knew not* the extent of the wickedness they were committing—for had they realized, they would not (as Saint Paul said) have crucified the Lord of Glory?

"Does it not suffice to overthrow this principle of yours, that Jesus Christ should Himself have warned us, that there will arise persecutors within the Church, who think they do God a service when they bring about her ruin? He warned us against such people to make us understand that this sin (which according to the Apostle is the greatest sin of all), may be committed by men who not only do not know that the act they contemplate is sinful, but who would sincerely believe themselves to be sinners, if they were to abstain from that act? [14] And, finally, does not Jesus Christ Himself teach us that there are two kinds of sinners: [15] those who sin deliberately, and those who sin without knowledge, and that both will be punished though in different measure?"

The Father found himself hard put to it by all these arguments from Scripture, to the authoriy of which he had himself appealed, and began to flounder a little as the debate continued. He appeared willing to leave wicked men to pursue their sins, without the knowledge of evil and the divine inspiration to avoid it that he had alleged; and changing his ground slightly, said, "At any rate you will not deny that the

[14] A direct reference to the disastrous schism of Luther, from the fearful results of which Pascal's own country was still suffering severely, and which had been justified by the plea of "I can no other."

[15] Luke 12:48. "But the second servant was not culpably ignorant, and where the mind does not advert to the malice of the act, the consent of the will is diminished, and with it the malice of the sin."

just never fall into sin without [a knowledge of evil given them by God]."

"You are backing out of it, father," I cried, interrupting him. "You are deserting your own general principle. You find you cannot press it home with respect to freethinkers; so you want to compromise, and to preserve this rule of yours for the just.[16] This being so, I can see that its application will be considerably restricted: it will apply to so few, that I may safely leave you in possession, for such a rule is scarcely worth an argument."

My Jansenist, however, was so well informed on all the points at issue that he might well have studied the subject that very morning, and he now intervened to say: "Your change of front, Father, is the last ditch. All your people fall back upon it when they see they are getting the worst of it. But you are on no better ground now than you were before: the condition of the just will be no stronger argument for you than the state of the wicked. Who can doubt that the just also fall frequently into sin through inadvertence and surprise? Do we not learn that even holy men are burdened by the flesh, that concupiscence baits traps for them, and that it often happens that, however ascetic they may be, they give way to concupiscence and disguise it as necessity? Saint Augustine admits this of his own behavior, in his *Confessions* (III, 9).

"How often have we seen the best of Christians yield to acrimony, when they do not immediately get their own way in a dispute? Yet their conscience, instead of making them aware of their wickedness and uneasy about it, justifies their anger as a perfectly proper zeal for truth; and they may not realize their error until long afterwards.[17]

"And what is to be said of people who turn with zest to behavior which is in fact wrong, but which they have persuaded themselves is good? Their erroneous belief does not

[16] Pascal was determined upon overthrowing his opponent, but he sought an easy victory by making his Jesuit a simpleton and a slightly ludicrous figure. The Jesuit had no need either to withdraw or to change his ground: he had but to defend a perfectly valid principle on the lines of footnote 15.

[17] The Jansenist is here confusing trivial and venial sins (which even the good cannot always avoid) with grave sins, against which the just are armed. Moralists are concerned only with formal mortal sin.

justify the offense, and according to the Fathers such actions would remain sinful. The history of the Church supplies an abundance of examples.[18]

"Apart from this error, how is it that the just commit so many secret sins; and how can it be true that these are so numerous that God alone knows how many they are, and how great? So that nobody can know with certitude whether he deserves love or hatred? And so that the holiest of men must always be in a state of fear and trembling, even though they are not conscious of guilt in any particular matter, as Saint Paul says of himself.

"Do you not see, then, Father, that these examples of both just men and sinners dispose of the principle you have proposed, that sin requires knowledge of the evil involved, and love of the opposite virtue; because the addiction of the wicked to sin proves plainly enough that they have no desire for virtue, and the love of the just for virtue is clear evidence that they do not have that knowledge of evil in their sins of every day; as the Scriptures testify.

"And so true is it that the sins of the just are of this nature, that very holy men seldom sin in any other way. For they are souls of a very great purity: they take the greatest care to avoid the slightest sin, and they shrink with a sensitive prudence from the least thing that might be displeasing to God; and yet they necessarily sin daily in more ways than one. Are we to believe that such holy souls advert to God before each imperfection, with 'the knowledge that a particular act proposed to their will is sinful, and that a remedy for the temptation is available; with a desire to be saved from it, and an inspiration from God to pray for this aid,' and are we to believe that, despite this sequence of disclosures and inspirations, these zealous and watchful persons should still not be saved from the secret snare, but should find it possible to throw off the restraint of conscience and good habit, and fall into the sin?

"Let us then conclude, Father, that neither sinners nor good men are always, and upon every occasion of temptation, conscious of such convictions, desires, and inspirations; that is (to use your own expression), they are not aware of the presence of 'actual grace' before each offense. And never again must you say, as your innovating moralists do, that

18 The examples to which Pascal appeals have not been identified.

where there is no knowledge of what is right, sin is impossible; but say rather, with Saint Augustine and the old fathers, that 'It is impossible for a man not to fall into sin, when he knows not what is right.' "

The good Father could see that his teaching was now being challenged in respect of the just as well as of sinners; but he did not lose courage. After a moment's thought, "I'll show you something here that will certainly convince you," he cried, and opening his Father Bauny at the very same page he had shown us before, he proceeded: "Look here, and you will see the reasoning on which his line of argument is based. I knew he would have some good proofs! Read what he cites from Aristotle, and you will admit that if he can claim the support of so ancient an authority, you will either have to burn the books of that prince of philosophers, or else come over to our opinion. Observe now exactly what are the principles laid down by Father Bauny. He says, firstly, that 'an act cannot be called sinful if it is involuntary.' "

"I admit that," said my friend.

"This is the first time," I remarked, "that I have found you two people to be in agreement. And if I were you, Father, I should stick to that rule, and go no farther."

"That would do us no good at all," said the Father, "for we need to know what are the necessary conditions in which an act may be called voluntary."

"I am very much afraid," I said, "that you will get into difficulties on that point."

"Never fear," said he, "for this at least is certain—Aristotle is for me. Listen carefully to what Father Bauny says: 'An act is voluntary when it is performed by a human being capable of perceiving, knowing, and understanding all the good and all the evil involved in that act. Following the philosopher' " ("Aristotle, of course, as you know," said he to me, with a sly squeeze of the hand), " 'we generally say *that a voluntary act is one done by one who knows from the beginning all that is contained in that act;* so that when the will is impelled, spontaneously and without any deliberation, to will or to reject, to do a thing or to leave it undone, before the understanding has been able to consider that act, and to reach a judgment as to whether there be any evil in such desire or rejection, in such doing or leaving undone, then that act is neither good nor bad. Thus, in the absence of such consideration and inquiry, this viewing and consideration by the mind, of the good and evil qualities of the act in question, the said act is not voluntary.' "

"Well," said the Father, "are you satisfied now?"

"It certainly looks as though Aristotle is of the same opinion as your Father Bauny," I said, "though I must say I am surprised at that. Do you really mean to say, Father, that to be aware of what we are doing, and to do it because we desire to do it, are not sufficient to constitute a voluntary act, but that it is also necessary 'to see, to know, and to understand fully all the good and evil qualities of the act in question'? If this be the case, scarcely any act in life can be called voluntary, for it is scarcely possible to advert to all those considerations in respect to every act of every day. How many oaths are uttered in gaming, what excesses are committed in debauch, what license do we see at the Carnival, and none of these things are voluntary, so consequently they are neither good nor bad, because they were not preceded by this deliberation of the mind as to the good or bad qualities of the act! How is it possible, Father, that Aristotle could have formulated such a doctrine as that—for I have heard it said that he was an exact thinker!"

"That is a point that I can clear up for you," said my Jansenist friend. He asked the Father to hand him the *Moralia,* and he opened the book at the beginning of Book III, which contains the passage cited by Father Bauny. "You may be forgiven, Father, for assuming, upon the authority of Father Bauny, that Aristotle was ever of this opinion. You would have revised your own ideas if you had read Aristotle for yourself. It is certainly true that he teaches that, 'for an act to be voluntary, all the parts of the act must be known.' [19] But what does he mean by this, if not that we must know the special circumstances of every such act, as is clearly indicated by the examples he gives; for he supports his argument by citing only instances which contain an unknown factor involving ignorance, as in the case of the man who was demonstrating the power of a catapult. The prisoner pleaded that he only intended to show how it worked, but the bolt he let fly injured a bystander; or of Merope, who killed her own son by mistake, instead of her enemy, and so on.

[19] Aristotle, *Eth. Nic.* III, i.e., a man must know the nature and number of the circumstances of the act, and the things and persons affected by it.

"You can see from these instances, then, what kind of ignorance is required to render an act involuntary: it is what theologians call ignorance of the fact—as you, my dear Father, must know perfectly well. But as for ignorance of the law, ignorance, that is, of the moral value of the act, the good or evil contained in it (with which alone we are at present concerned), let us see whether Aristotle is of the same opinion as Father Bauny. The Philosopher says: 'Bad men always close their eyes to what they ought to do and what they ought to refrain from doing. It is this circumstance that renders them wicked and vicious. We therefore cannot say that because a man deliberately ignores what he is in duty bound to do, that his action is involuntary. For such closing of the eyes when he makes his choice between the good act and the bad, does not make his act involuntary: it only makes it vicious. The same may be said of a man who is ignorant of the laws governing his own duties, since such ignorance makes him worthy of blame, and nobody thinks of excusing him. Therefore an act is only called involuntary, and is only free from blame, where there is particular ignorance, ignorance of the circumstances of the act and of the things and persons that may be affected by it. In such cases a man is pardoned, excuse is found for him, and he is deemed to have acted against his will.'

"After a passage like that, Father, will you still say that Aristole supports your opinion? And who will not be astonished to find a pagan philosopher who is more enlightened than your own learned men, in a matter of such consequence to the entire fabric of morals and the cure of souls, as is a knowledge of the conditions which make an act voluntary or involuntary, and consequently either sinful or not sinful in intention? Expect nothing more then, Father, either from 'the prince of philosophers' or from the greatest of theologians who, in his *Retractations*, Book I, c. 15, settles the matter thus: 'They who sin through ignorance still act with intent, and they commit a sin even though they did not intend a sinful act. Therefore even a sin of ignorance cannot be committed without an act of the will in him who commits it; but the will is directed to the act, and not to the sin involved. This does not however prevent the act from being a sin, since it is sufficient to make an act a sin, to have done a thing we were under an obligation not to do.' "

The Father seemed to me to be surprised, and even more at

the passage from Aristotle than at the one from Saint Augustine. But as he was considering his answer, it was announced that Madame la Maréchale de . . . and Madame la Marquise de. . . were waiting to see him. As he made haste to leave us, he said: "I will talk to our fathers about this matter. They will certainly have a satisfactory answer to the difficult points you have raised."

We agreed to this very willingly, and when I was alone with my friend, I expressed astonishment at the overthrow of all morality implied in such teaching as we had just heard. He answered that he was surprised I should be astonished.

"Do you still not know that their sophistries are even more notorious in morals than in doctrine?"

He gave me one or two striking instances, and promised more at our next meeting. I hope that what I learn from him can be made the subject of my next letter.

I am, Sir, etc.

Moral Works

Comparison of Christians of the Earliest Times with Those of Our Times

This little treatise probably dates from the time when Pascal was engaged in the controversial Provincial Letters *and manifests the same profoundly earnest moral concern. Its thesis is simple: Christianity had in Pascal's day become bourgeois. It was accommodated to the spiritual tepidity of the day and no longer manifested that world-conquering sincerity and depth which once characterized it. The spirit of the New Testament seemed to have evaporated and been replaced with an easier morality. Contemporary Christianity had hardly any suspicion of the great demands of authentic Christianity. Instead of being the salt of the earth, a light to the world, it had become a quiet social group, compromising with the spirit of the world.*

1. In the primitive Church there were only well-informed Christians—men and women who had been very carefully instructed in all things necessary to salvation;[1]

Instead of which we find nowadays an ignorance so vulgar that any Christian with a real love for the Church must sigh for a return to that ancient discipline.

In those days, no candidate was baptized until he had received a thorough course of instruction; baptism had to be merited: it was the recognition by the Church of the long-sustained effort of a convert to amend his life;

[1] As in the case of the *Pensées,* this short essay has come down to us in three different versions, and scholars do not agree upon the order of the paragraphs. The order here given is that proposed by Lafuma. Some paragraphs (e.g., number 15) seem to be drafts for sections which appear elsewhere in the essay in a rewritten form.

Whereas nowadays a man can come into the Church without the slightest difficulty, without inconvenience, and without any studies at all.

In those days, a catechumen was only received after he had passed through a very searching examination.

But now, any man may be received, and he need not even be ready for any kind of examination.

In those days, no man was ever baptized unless he abjured his former way of life, and made an act of renunciation of the world, the flesh, and the devil.

But men may now come into the Church before they are in a condition to do any of those things.

Finally, it was in those days essential to come out of the world if one desired to be received into the Church; whereas nowadays we enter the world and the Church almost simultaneously.

This discipline was in those days the essential distinction between the world and the Church.

4. In those days, the Church and the world were irreconcilable opposites, like two mortal foes in never-ending conflict. But it was believed that, of these two foes, the one who appeared to be the weaker would one day triumph over the one who was apparently the stronger, with the result that there was constant movement, with people leaving the one embattled group to enter the other. The precepts of one party would be rejected, the precepts of the other adopted in their stead. A man had to divest himself altogether of the ideas of the one party, and adopt the way of life of the other.

2. In a word, a man left the world, he renounced it altogether; he abjured the environment into which he had been born as a human being, to devote himself entirely to the Church, which he entered by a kind of second birth. He thus became fully conscious of the terrifying difference between the one world and the other.

3. Instead of which, we nowadays find ourselves members of two worlds at one and the same moment; and the hour of our birth into the world is not far removed from the moment of our rebirth into the Church. In consequence, no directive of the reason can any longer intervene (to guide choice or strengthen purpose), or to make any distinction between two

states and two modes of birth which are in fact absolutely opposed. Reason develops and is formed in both states simultaneously: we frequent the sacraments, but this does not prevent our enjoyment of the pleasures of the world, etc.

Thus, whereas in early times the essential difference between the Church and the world was perfectly obvious, they are nowadays so mixed and confused that it is scarcely any longer possible to distinguish the one from the other.

7. In the time of the infant Church, catechumens (those who sought baptism), were only admitted to the Christian community after very full instruction in the mysteries of the faith, and confession of the sins of their past lives. They had to be convinced of the great dignity and excellence of the profession of the faith and of the precepts of Christianity; that their request, if it should be granted, would mean incorporation into a religious fellowship with God, once and for all; and that they would be required to show evident signs of a true conversion of the heart and an earnest desire for baptism.

When all these signs could be seen in them and were known to the whole Church, the public rite of baptism, the sacrament by which they were regenerated, incorporated them into the Church, so that they became members of it.

But the sacrament of baptism is nowadays conferred upon infants—for very important reasons, certainly, but before they attain the use of reason; so that where parents are negligent, Christians may now grow up to manhood and reach old age, without acquiring any knowledge of the dignity of our religion.

8. When instruction preceded baptism, all were instructed. Now, baptism is administered before instruction can be given, with the result that teaching formerly regarded as essential became first voluntary, then was neglected, and now has practically been abolished.

The real reason for this relaxation is that we are convinced of the necessity of baptism, but not of the need for instruction. Thus it was that in the days when instruction was given before baptism, the absolute necessity of the latter guaranteed the former.

Today, however, baptism comes before instruction, and since the child has been made a Christian without having been taught the faith, he thinks he can go on being a Christian without ever seeking to be taught anything. . . .

5. This was how it came about in former times, that there was never found anyone in the Christian community who was not very well instructed as to the faith.

Whereas the Christians of today live in such a condition of ignorance as to fill non-Christians with horror.

9. Whereas in the primitive Church, Christians displayed great gratitude for the grace of baptism, which was bestowed only after repeated requests and great constancy, today they are ungrateful for that same grace, to which the same mother, grown more indulgent, admits them even before they are ready for it.

And if in her early days that mother saw with such strong detestation the lapse of even one of her children, rare though such a fall might be; with what sorrow and loathing ought she to behold the lapses from the faith and the repeated falls of the faithful, so commonly seen in these days? Those who desert her now should indeed be the very ones to cling to her with the greater fidelity, since she has intervened so much the more promptly to save them—and on so much easier terms—from the damnation to which their conditon of Original Sin had rendered them liable.

10. The Church cannot but contemplate with grief the general abuse of the greatest of her graces; nor see that instrument (which she had provided to ensure their salvation), become the almost certain means of their eternal loss. For although the Church has made a change in her discipline, she has not altered her intention.

11. Baptism is however now received in a spirit so contrary to the mind of the Church that the situation can only be viewed with dismay. Nobody now meditates upon the glories and the effects of this great sacrament, because it is received without earnest desire and lively hope, because it was never asked for, because we do not even remember that we ever received it. (We never remind ourselves that we are living under a vow.)

12. Hence it was that in former days, those who had been

regenerated in baptism and had abandoned the vicious ways of the world to enter upon a life of holiness in the Church, so rarely fell away again and left the Church for the world; whereas today, nothing is so common as to see the vices of the world in the hearts of Christians.

This is how it has come about that in our day the Church of the saints is seen to be polluted by the presence in her midst of many wicked persons; and it is her own children, whom she herself conceived, bore and fed from infancy, who have introduced those people (the most cruel of her enemies) into her midst, even to allowing them to participate in her most august mysteries. [We now see in the Church] the spirit of the world and the flesh, the spirit of ambition and of vengeance, the spirit of impurity, so that her love for her own children has obliged her also to admit to the very sanctuary the most cruel of her persecutors. . . .[2]

13. But the disasters which have followed upon the relaxation of a discipline so salutary should not be imputed to the Church; for although she has modified her discipline, her general intention remains unaltered. For she had observed that the postponement of baptism exposed great numbers of infants to the consequences of the Fall, and she desired to save them from being the bond servants of sin unto (their) death—from being numbered with those who remained outside the Church. She was willing to accelerate the help she was able to give them, and it is only with deep sorrow that this provident mother sees how her provision for the salvation of children has been made an occasion for the damnation of adults.

Her true mind is that those whom she withdraws at so tender an age from the contagions of the world, should imbibe and grow up in ideas that are completely opposed to those of this earth. Thus she anticipates the use of reason by forewarning her children against those vices, into which an uncontrolled use of that reason, corrupted as it is, would certainly lead them. And even before they have acquired the use of reason, she fills that reason with her own mind and teaching, in order that those children of hers may live in a great

[2] This essay was probably written shortly before the *Provincial Letters* began to appear, and it forms a natural introduction to them. "The most cruel of her persecutors" are the ever-fashionable mortal sins, which according to the Jansenists, had been "admitted to the sanctuary" by the relaxed moral teaching of the Church.

innocence with respect to the world, and in a condition more distantly removed from vice than they would ever otherwise have known.

14. This is clear from the formalities surrounding baptism; for the Church does not confer the sacrament upon an infant until, by the voice of the sponsors, the child has declared its desire to be baptized, made its act of faith, and renounced the world and the devil. She desires them to persevere in these dispositions until death, and to keep the commandments inviolate; and she lays upon the sponsors a binding obligation to instruct the children concerning these things. For it is no part of her purpose that her children of today, whom she now nourishes in her bosom from infancy, should be less well instructed than the faithful of former times, who were not admitted to baptism until they had reached mature age. She does not expect those whom she receives today to be less perfect than those of old.

15. But it is obvious that the Church would not be satisfied with a lower standard, a less generous spirit, in those born as members of the household of the faith, than in those who aspire to baptism. We must therefore always have in mind the example set by catechumens: we must consider their zeal and their devotion, their horror of sin, their generous renunciation of the world. And if they be judged unworthy of baptism because they lack these dispositions, what shall be said of those [who pronounce such a judgment?]

16. The Christians of today, therefore, must show themselves willing to receive the kind of instruction they would would have been given [in former times, if they had offered themselves] as candidates of baptism. [Also, they must show themselves willing to accept penance of such a nature that it will never occur to them to fall away from the faith; moreover, they must show less aversion to the austerity of their mortification than to the deceptive charms and seductions of vicious habits.]

To dispose them to receive intruction, they must be given some knowledge of the various customs in relation to penance that have been known in the Church at different times.

They must have before their eyes the example of the

catechumens of old, and consider their ardor, their devotion, their horror of the world, their general renunciation of its vanities. For if in former times even these were not deemed worthy to receive baptism unless they had the right dispositions, is it not just that those who do not show the dispositions after they have received baptism, should make every effort to develop and practice a generosity of the mind, and should pass the rest of their days in salutary penitence; and that they should exhibit less aversion to a life that is crucified to the world, and find less to charm them in the habitual enjoyment of the poisoned delights of sin.

Prayer to Ask of God the Good Use of Sickness

Pascal had never enjoyed good health. Some authorities have felt that he was neurasthenic. He himself stated that he had never passed a day without suffering. Some have spoken of a brain tumor, or of tuberculosis with complications. In Pascal's case his illness softened his spirit, tamed his pride, and assimilated him more closely to the suffering Christ upon whom he had so often meditated. His sufferings were very great and in the Prayer for the Good Use of Illness he begs God's redeeming grace, cries out in contrition for past faults, and pleads for strength to endure his sufferings in union with the Passion of Christ. This prayer probably belongs to the latter part of Pascal's life, for it expresses a spiritual maturity, a depth of faith that ranks it with the greatest writings of Saint Augustine or Saint Teresa.

1. Lord, Thou art good and gentle in all Thy ways, and Thy mercy is such that not only the blessings but also the misfortunes of Thine elect are but dispositions of Thy compassionate will. Grant me then that I may not behave like a heathen in the condition to which Thy justice has reduced me. Grant that I may still recognize Thee as my Father and my

God—as a Christian ought to do—in whatever condition I may find myself placed, since the change in my own state can bring none to Thine. For Thou art ever the same, though I may be subject to change: and Thou art not less God when Thou dost afflict and punish, than when Thou dost visit with consolations and indulge with favor.

2. Thou gavest me health that I might serve Thee—and all that I did with Thy gift was to abuse it.[3] Now, therefore, Thou sendest me ill-health for my correction: suffer me not, then, to misuse even that correction, so that I offend Thee by my own impatience. I made a bad use of my health, and with justice dost Thou punish me for it: let me not make a bad use of Thy punishment. And since the corruption of my nature is such that it renders even Thy favors harmful to me, do Thou grant, O my God, that Thine all-powerful grace may convert Thy punishments into healing. Since my heart, while it had its strength, was full of the love of the world, do Thou destroy that strength for my sanctification: do Thou employ weakness of the body, or else the zeal of charity, to render me incapable of the enjoyment of the world, that I may at last find all my joy in thee alone.

3. O God, before whom I must render an exact account of all my actions at the end of my life and at the end of the world! [4]

O God, who does maintain the world and all earthly things in being, only to try thy people for their good, or to punish sinners!

[3] This marvelous canticle, blended of David's music and the fidelity of Job, defies the translator. It exults in the victories of divine grace, in terms of unforgettable melody, and in a secure and enduring hope. This paragraph, with others such as paragraph 13 below, has often been alleged to indicate a dissolute past. All the weightiest evidence is against such a supposition. Here, as elsewhere throughout his writings, Pascal "sees in the things that happen, the hand of God." Like other mortals, he was fallible, and he made mistakes in the details of his theology of grace. But he was not in error when he was at prayer: he does not ask to be exempt from suffering, but only for grace to accept and bear it. We observe that the canticle falls naturally into the style of a litany.

[4] Thought crowds upon thought as Pascal meditates upon the Last Things, the particular and general Judgment. Well versed in the forms and language of the law, this cultivated gentleman, friend and employee of Richelieu, and the nobility of France, uses impassioned language to draw the spirit upward into those "infinite spaces" in which he had begun to dwell.

O God, who dost abandon sinners that are hardened to their own sensual and vicious ways, for as long as they shall live upon earth!

O God, who dost cause our bodies to die, and who at the hour of death dost separate our souls from all that they have loved in this world!

O God, who at that last moment of my life, wilt snatch me away from all the things to which I have attached myself, and upon which I have set my heart!

O God, who at the last day wilt consume the heavens and the earth and all the creatures they contain, to show all mankind that nothing subsists but Thou, and that nothing therefore is worthy of love but Thou, for nothing endures but thou alone!

O God, who shall destroy every vain idol and every fatal object of our passions!

I praise Thee, O God, and all the days of my life will I bless Thee, because it has pleased Thee to anticipate in my favor that day of dread, when Thou didst choose to reduce me to weakness, and so to destroy the power over me of the things of earth!

I praise Thee, O God, and all the days of my life will I bless Thee, that it has pleased Thee to bring me low, to place me in a condition where I am incapable of enjoying the mild and easy conditions of good health, and the pleasant things of the world; and that Thou hast in a measure destroyed in me, and for my good, those deceitful idols that in the day of Thy wrath Thou will destroy utterly, that the wicked may be confounded.

Grant then, O Lord, that I may judge myself in accordance with that measure of destruction that Thou has wrought in me, that thou mayest not judge me Thyself hereafter according to that utter destruction Thou wouldest have me make, of my own pride of life and the delights of this world. For at the instant of my death, O Lord, I shall know myself to be separated from the world and stripped of all things, alone before Thy face, there to make answer to thy justice for all the seditions, all the perturbations of my heart. Grant therefore that in this condition of sickness I may consider myself as in a kind of death, separated from the world, stripped of all those things to which I am attached, alone in thy presence, there to implore of Thy mercy the conversion of my heart. And do Thou grant, that thus I may have that greatest of consolations—the knowledge that Thou sendest me now a kind of death, that Thou mayest therein apply to me Thy mercy, before thou sendest me death itself, whereat I must face thy examination, and hear thy sentence. Grant me then, O my God, that as thou has intervened for me before my death, so I may make atonement before I meet the severity of thy judgment;

That so I may find mercy in Thy presence.

4. Grant, O my God, that I may adore in silence the dispositions of Thine adorable Providence in the ordering of my life; that this scourge may be a consolation to me. While all was tranquil, I lived with the bitterness of my sins; now that Thou dost afflict me with salutary sufferings, do Thou grant me to taste the heavenly sweetness of Thy grace.

Yet do I know and acknowledge, O my God, that my heart is very obdurate, and so full of the fancies and opinions of this world, its cares, anxieties and attachments, that

Neither sickness nor health,
Nor the exhortations of thy clergy,
Nor any reading of books—
Not even thy holy Scriptures and the Gospels—
Nor thy most holy mysteries,
Nor almsgiving, nor fasting, nor mortifications,
Nor miracles,
Nor the use of the sacraments,
Nor the Sacrifice of Thy body.
Nor any effort of my own, nor those of all the world together, can do anything at all, even to begin the work of my conversion,
If Thou go not before all these things and follow after them with the very special aid of Thine efficacious grace.[5]

Therefore do I cry to thee, O my God, the Almighty, to beg of Thee a gift that all created Nature cannot bestow. Nor would I be so bold as to direct my cry to Thee, if any other were able to grant my petition. But since this conversion of the heart that I ask of Thee, O God, is a work that exceeds the capacity of Nature, I can but make my supplication to

[5] This passage summarizes the formal effects of actual grace. It falls naturally into the rhythms and ideas of I. Cor. 13, and prepares the mind for the rapturous utterances of the next paragraph. Pascal made frequent use of the euphony of his native tongue, to appeal to the imagination and touch the hearts of his readers, the sophisticated society of his day.

Nature's Almighty author and to the master of my heart. To whom shall I cry, O Lord, to whom shall I have recourse, if not to Thee? Not all of that which is less than God Himself can fill up my expectation. It is God Himself that I require and seek; and to Thee only, O God, do I turn, that I may obtain Thee. Open Thou my heart, O Lord, and come Thou into that place of insurrection, which is in the occupation of vices which keep it in subjection. Do Thou, then, enter there, as into the house of the strong. But do Thou first bind the strong man, the powerful enemy who has dominion there, and then do Thou take the treasure that is in it. Take, O Lord, my affection, which the world had stolen away: take this treasure for Thyself—recover it, rather, for it belongs to Thee of right, a tribute due,[6] having Thine own image stamped upon it. Thou Thyself didst stamp that character upon me at the moment of my baptism, the moment of my second birth; but it has so been defaced by the superscription of the world, that Thine own image can scarcely any longer be seen. Thou alone hadst the power to call my soul into being; Thou alone canst create it anew. Thou alone couldst stamp the piece with Thine own image: Thou alone canst recast it, and restore to it Thy likeness that had been defaced, the resemblance to Jesus Christ my Redeemer, who is Thine own image, being Himself the character of Thine own substance.

5. How happy is the heart, O my God, that can love an object so pleasing as thyself, an object that will never do it the least dishonor; the heart that is able to find its rest in an object so wholesome to itself! I well know that I cannot love the world without displeasing Thee, without doing harm and dishonor to myself: and yet the world is still the object of my delight. How happy, O my God, is the soul whose delight is in Thee, since it is able to give itself up to the love of Thee, not only without the least scruple, but even with merit. How secure and durable shall its happiness be, therefore, since its confidence shall never be in vain. For Thou, O Lord, endurest forever, and neither life nor death shall ever separate the heart that loves thee from the object of its desires; and in that very moment when the wicked and their idols shall be

[6] Matt. 22:15–22. Pascal's reference is to the debasing of the coinage by traders, who converted it into tokens for the purposes of commerce.

swallowed up in one common ruin, the just shall be united to thee in a common glory. The wicked shall perish, together with the perishable objects to which they have been attached; and the just shall subsist eternally with that eternal and self-subsistent object to which they have become so closely bound. O how happy are they who, with an entire liberty, yet by an inflexible resolution of the will, love with a perfect freedom that which of necessity they are bound to love!

6. Do Thou bring to perfection, O my God, the good dispositions Thou hast inspired in me. Be Thou their end, as Thou has been their cause and motive. Do Thou crown Thine own gifts—for I acknowledge that they are from Thee. Yes, my God; and I am very far from claiming that my prayers have any merit that could compel Thee to answer them of any necessity. With great humility do I acknowledge that I have given to creatures a heart that Thou formedst only for Thine own, and by no means for the world nor for myself. Therefore can I hope for no grace except Thou bestow it of Thy mere mercy, for there is in me nothing that could bind Thee to bestow Thy grace upon me. All the natural impulses of my heart can but offend Thee, whether they tend toward creatures or to myself. I therefore thank Thee, O my God, for all those good impulses Thou hast inspired in me, and for that impulse especially that causes me to thank Thee for them.

7. Move Thou my heart, O Lord, to repentance for my faults; for without such interior sorrow, the ills with which Thou chastenest my body will only be to me a new occasion of sin. Make me truly to know that bodily ills are but the signs of disorders of the soul, and punishments for them. But grant, O Lord, that they may also be a remedy, if they bring me, by means of bodily pains which I certainly feel, to a consideration of that sickness which I was never able to feel in my own soul, although it was all ulcerated and covered with sores. For the greatest of all my soul's disorders, O Lord, is that very insensibility, and the extreme lassitude which deprived it of any feeling for its own misery. Make me to feel it sharply, and do thou grant that what of life remains to me may be an unbroken condition of penitence, that shall

wash away all the offenses of which I have been the cause.

8. O Lord, although my life has been free from grave offenses, because Thou has removed far from me the occasions of sin, it has nonetheless been made hateful to Thee.

By reason of its habitual negligence;

By the misuse of Thy most august sacraments;

By contempt of Thy word and of Thine inspirations;

By my sloth;

By the unprofitable frivolity of all my actions and all my thinking;

By the entire waste of the time that Thou gavest me—and Thou didst give it only that I might worship Thee,

That I might in all my occupations seek ways of pleasing Thee;

And that penance might thus be done for the sins that are committed every day, and which are so commonly found even among the just, that their lives also ought to be passed in a condition of perpetual penance, if they are not to [put their souls in hazard by their mere temerity, and so] fall away from their condition of justice. For all these reasons, O my God, have I always been found opposed to Thee.

9. Yes, Lord: until this day I have always been deaf to Thine inspirations: I have despised Thine oracles;

My judgments have been opposed to Thine.

I have raised objections to the holy maxims which Thou didst bring into the world from the bosom of Thine eternal Father, according to which Thou shalt judge the world;

Thou hast said: Blessed are those who mourn, and woe to those who are comforted!

And I have said: Woe to those who mourn, and blessed are those who are comforted!

I have said:

Blessed are those who enjoy an ample fortune, a glorious reputation, and robust health!

And why have I thought them blessed, if not because I saw that their advantages gave them a very ample liberty to enjoy the things of this world, liberty, that is, to offend Thee? Yes, Lord, I confess that I have esteemed health a blessing, not because it makes Thy service easy, since a man in health can carry out more duties and do them more easily, keep a stricter vigil before Thee, and do more for his neighbor; but because with health in my favor I could let myself go, and with ever less restraint, in the love of the abundant delights of life, and the more wholehearted enjoyment of harmful pleasures.

Grant, O Lord, that I may by Thy grace reform my corrupted mind, and bring my modes of thought into conformity with Thine. Teach me to call myself happy that I am afflicted, and grant that, since all power of ordinary activity is taken from me, my interior desires may be purified, so that they are no longer in conflict with Thy will. So let me find Thee within when I seek Thee there, since in my state of weakness I cannot go abroad in search of Thee. For Thy Kingdom, O Lord, is within Thy faithful, and I shall find it within myself, if I find there Thine own spirit, and the ways of God.

10. But what can I do, O Lord, that can persuade Thee to shed forth thy spirit over this sorrowful and wicked world?

All that I am is obvious to Thee, and I find nothing in myself that can be pleasing to Thee.

I can see in myself, Lord, nothing but my sufferings—but these bear some resemblance to Thine own.

Do Thou look then O Lord upon the pains that I suffer, and on those that are to come upon me.

Look Thou with eyes of mercy, O my Saviour, upon the wounds that were made by Thine own hand.

O Thou who didst love Thine own suffereings, though they were unto death—

O my God, who didst become man that Thou mightest suffer more than ever any man did, and only for the salvation of men—

O my God, who when men had sinned didst become incarnate, and who didst take upon Thyself a body, only that Thou Thyself mightest suffer in that body all those afflictions that our sins had merited for ourselves—

O my God, who didst so love these our bodies that suffer, that thou didst take upon Thyself a body that should be more overwhelmed with suffering than any other body that ever underwent the woes of this world—

Be pleased to look with favor upon my body, not for itself nor for what it contains (for all that is in it is deserving of Thine anger), but for the pains it endures, which alone can merit Thy love.

Do Thou love my sufferings, O Lord, and may my sorrows invite Thee to visit me. But so that the place of Thine abode may be perfectly prepared and ready for Thee, do Thou grant, O my Redeemer, that if my body has this in common with Thine

—That is suffers because of my offenses,

My soul may also have this in common with Thine

—That it suffer afflictions for those same offenses;

So that thus I too may suffer, with Thee and like Thee, in body and in soul,

For the sins that I have committed.

11. Grant me the grace, Lord, to unite Thy consolations with my sufferings,

That I may suffer with a Christian patience.

I do not ask to be exempt from sorrows,

For that is the recompense of the saints;

But I earnestly entreat that I be not abandoned to the sorrows of our human nature

Without the consolations of Thy spirit:

For that is the curse of the Jews and the heathen.

I do not ask for fullness of consolations without any suffering,

For that is the life of glory.

Neither do I ask, Lord, for the fullness of misfortune without any consolation,

For that is the condition of the Jews.

But I ask, O Lord, that I may be given to feel the full burden of the pains of our nature for my sins.

And the consolations of Thy spirit through Thy grace,

For that is the true condition of Christianity.

Let me not feel the pains without the consolations,

But grant that I may feel the pains and experience the consolations together,

And come at last to the knowledge of thy consolations without any sorrow.

For Thou didst leave the world to languish in its natural sufferings,

O Lord, without any consolation,

Before the appearing to us of Thine only Son.

But now Thou dost console us in our sufferings, Thou lightenest the burdens of Thy faithful,

By the grace that is bestowed on them by Thine only Son.

And Thou dost refresh beyond all measure Thy saints in Heaven,
With the vision of the glory of Thine only Son.
Such are the steps and stages by which Thy work is done:
Thou hast drawn me out of the world that languishes;
Help me so to pass through the world that is suffering,
That I may come to that realm of glory.
This is the grace that I ask of Thee.

12. Suffer me never to be so far removed from Thee, that I could ever contemplate Thy soul, sorrowful unto death, and Thy body, stricken and slain for my sins, without being able to rejoice that I also am called upon to suffer both in my body and my soul. For what can be more shameful—yet what is more commonly found among Christians, and in myself—than that men should live at ease while Thou dost sweat blood for the expiation of their sins? that

Souls who profess to be Thine;
Souls who by their baptismal vows have abandoned the world to follow Thee;
Souls who have solemnly promised in the face of all the Church that they would live for Thee and die in Thee;
Souls who profess to believe that it was the spirit of this world that pursued Thee to the death and crucified Thee;
Souls who believe that Thou didst offer Thyself to the wrath of God and the cruelty of men to pay the ransom for their sins;
All those souls, I say, who believe these things to be true—
For whom Thy body is indeed the victim that was offered once for
Their own salvation;
That the pleasures of the world were the sole reason and ground of Thy sufferings;
That the world was itself, as it were, Thy executioner;
Then that these very men should nevertheless choose to pander to their own bodies by indulging in those very pleasures, and in that same world that sought to destroy Thee?

Suppose a man to have murdered his own father—a father who would have given his life for the life of that son. And suppose such a murderer to be rewarded with flattery and public honors: no man of principle could behold such wickedness without a shudder of horror. Yet

that man can be content to live in perfect happiness
—as I myself have done—
in a world which he knows to have been
guilty of the murder of his God and Father,
who gave Himself for his salvation.
and who bore in His own body the penalty of His sins,
It was but justice, Lord, that Thou didst interrupt so sinful a joy as that in which I was reposing, and in the very shadow of death.

13. Uproot in me then O Lord, the self-pity on which self-love would feed, if I were to dwell upon my sufferings.

The longing for the things of earth, for the satisfactions that can never fully please my heart, since they are not directed to Thy glory; but do Thou clothe me in a sorrow more in conformity with Thine own.

May my sufferings serve to appease Thy wrath. May they be made to me occasions of grace and means to my conversion.

Let me henceforward ask for neither health nor life, except that I may spend the one, and end the other, for Thee, with Thee, and in Thee. I ask Thee not for health or sickness, life or death: do Thou dispose for me of health and sickness, death and life, for Thine own glory, for my salvation, for the service of the Church and of Thy saints—into whose company may Thy grace admit me. Thou alone knowest what is expedient for me; Thou art my sovereign Lord; do with me as Thou wilt. Do Thou give, or take away. Only do Thou conform my will to Thine. And do Thou grant that with a humble and perfect submission and a holy confidence, I may dispose myself to accept the decrees of Thine eternal Providence, and that I may receive with equal reverence all things whatsoever that Thy hand awards.

14. Grant, O my God, that with an ever steadfast mind I may accept whatever shall befall me, since we know not what to pray for as we ought, and I dare not without presumption hope for one thing rather than another, nor seek to make myself the arbiter of my own destiny, the author of effects which are reserved to Thine own wisdom, and the knowledge of which Thou art pleased to withhold from me. One thing only do I know, O Lord: that to follow Thee is good, and to offend Thee is sin. Apart from this I cannot know what is the worse or better part in anything

that can befall me: I know not what, of all the things of earth, is for my good—whether health or sickness, riches or poverty. That is a degree of discernment which passes the power of men and angels; a mystery hidden in the secrets of thy Providence, which I adore, and the depths of which I do not seek to plumb.

15. Do Thou grant, O Lord, that, such as I am, I may conform myself to Thy will:

That in the midst of suffering I may glorify Thee.

Without those sufferings I cannot attain to Thy glory: and Thou Thyself, who art my Saviour, hadst no desire to go to Thy Father by any other way than this.

By the print of the nails did Thy disciples know Thee;

And by the marks of suffering shalt Thou know who are Thy disciples.

Do Thou own me for Thine by the pains I endure in my body, in my mind, by reason of the sins I have committed against Thee.

And since nothing is acceptable to God unless it be offered in Thy name, do Thou unite my will to Thine, and my sufferings to those that Thou didst undergo: may my sufferings be lost in Thine.

Unite me to Thyself.

Fill me with Thyself and with Thy Holy Spirit.

Come Thou into my heart and my soul

That there Thou mayest bear for me my sufferings.

That there Thou mayest in a measure make up whatever remains for Thee to suffer of Thy passion,

That passion that Thou endurest in all Thy members until the number of Thine elect shall be complete in the fullness of Thy mystical body; so that when my being is filled with Thee, it shall no longer be I that live and suffer, but Thou that livest and sufferest in me,

O my Saviour;

And that since I thus have some small part in Thy sufferings, Thou shalt fill me entirely with that glory that Thy sufferings won for Thee, that glory in which Thou livest with the Father and the Holy Ghost, forever and ever. Amen.

On the Conversion of the Sinner

This fragment of Pascal, deeply biblical, really needs no commentary. Probably dated in November or December of 1654, it should be read in conjunction with the Memorial.

When God is pleased to enter into intimate converse with the soul, His first action is to bestow an extraordinary knowledge and insight, by means of which the soul is brought to reflect upon itself and upon things in general, in a way that is altogether new.

This enlightenment instills a holy fear, which stirs up in the soul a certain condition of trouble by breaking in upon the heedlessness with which that soul had formerly indulged its pleasures.

Thus it is that she can no longer quietly enjoy the things in which she used to take delight. A constant wakeful scruple nags at such indulgence, and she no longer finds the accustomed sweetness in those old pleasurable ways, although she had formerly indulged in them with the greatest freedom and with complete easing of the heart.

Yet she experiences an even greater aversion to the acquisition of good habits than she does to the vanities of the world. This is because, on the one hand, the things of earth are always before her eyes, and they stir her fancy more directly than any hope for things invisible can do; whereas on the other hand, the durable, substantial nature of the things that are not seen makes an infinitely more powerful appeal than the vanity of things seen could ever offer. Thus the mere presence of the one, and the commanding authority of the other compete for her allegiance; and triviality in the one, austerity in the other, exasperate her to aversion for them both, with the result that disorder exists where there was none before, and a condition of confusion is created within her.

She is now able to look upon perishable things as of no account, as mere trash. She sees quite clearly that all that she has loved will certainly perish forever; and the thought fills her with horror, because she also perceives that with each moment that passes, she is being drawn ever farther from finding enjoyment in what she has regarded as her good. She sees all that was dearest to her slipping out of her grasp, and that at the end a certain day will dawn in which she will find herself stripped of all those things in which she had set her hope. Thus she has attained to a clear understanding that those things to which her heart had become attached were merely brittle and vain, and that when the time should come for her to leave this life she would be alone and defenseless, since she had lacked the prudence to acquire solid and authentic treasure of another kind, which would be sufficient to sustain her not only in this world but in the life to come.

The soul therefore soon learns to regard as worthless trifles all those things that are destined to perish: Heaven and earth, mind and body; relatives, friends and enemies; possessions, poverty, misfortune, and disgrace; prosperity, honors, and shame; public esteem and scorn; authority; necessity; sickness and health, and even life itself; in a word, anything less immortal than her own soul is powerless to satisfy the desires of a soul in search of stability, of a condition of happiness as lasting as her own being.

The soul begins to be astonished that she should have been content to live in this condition of blindness. She considers, on the one hand the length of time she has been in this state, and the great number of souls there are who live in the same way; and she bears in mind, on the other hand, the stability of the principle, that an immortal soul cannot expect to find its happiness in perishable things which must in any event be taken away from her at death. Thus she enters into a condition of holy confusion and astonishment—a state of distress which may be said to do her a great deal of good. A certain argument begins to carry weight. However many there be that grow old in the ways of the world, and whatever authority may be conferred upon a way of life by the mere numbers of those who profess it, it is a constant testimony of experience that, whatever the soundness of the pleasures conferred by the things of this world—an opinion demonstrated to be false by an infinite amount of disastrous and repeated experience—a day will come when loss of them, or death itself, will deprive us of them forever.

Thus the soul may have gathered about herself a store of temporal treasure—wealth, knowledge, or fame. Yet she is confronted at every moment with the ineluctible fact that a day will come when she will be stripped of all these pleasurable things. They may have been good of their kind, they may have possessed some degree of power to confer a lawful satisfaction, but they cannot bestow a happiness that will endure forever. The soul is thus compelled to reflect that, though such earthly attainments may have given her a measure of genuine happiness, that happiness is not of an eternal order, but comes to an end with the end of earthly life.

By the acquisition and practice of a holy humility, which is raised by God above the level of spiritual pride, she begins to lift herself above the level of the common run of men. She condemns their behavior, hates their maxims, weeps for their inability to see. She turns all her powers to the search for the true good, and she understands very well that true good must possess certain necessary properties: it must be as durable as herself; it must be of such a quality that it cannot be lost or taken from her except by her own consent; and it must be of such a nature that there can be nothing more precious to her.

The soul now sees clearly that she has hitherto found this last requirement satisfied by the very condition of blindness in which she was content with the things of earth, than which she has reckoned nothing more to be desired. But since she failed to find in that love the quality of durability, it was obviously not the sovereign good. Therefore she seeks that sovereign good elsewhere; a shadowless light has healed her blindness, and she now seeks her good neither within herself, nor without in the things of earth, nor ahead of herself [in things that appeal to her sight], but in the things that are above.

This exaltation of the view is an activity so eminent, so transcendent, that it does not stop at Heaven, nor at the angels, nor at the most perfect of created beings. The soul passes by every creature, and the flight of the heart is only stopped by arriving at the very throne of God, where indeed she at last begins to find her happiness; and this is a good of such a nature that nothing can be more precious to her, neither can it be taken from her save by her own consent.

While she has not yet reached a state in which she can already feel those compensations with which God rewards the soul proficient in virtue, still she already understands that creatures are not to be preferred to the Creator. Her reason is now enlightened by grace, and it acknowledges that nothing is more worthy of love than God Himself—and that He can only be taken from those that reject Him: for to long for Him is to have Him in possession, and to refuse Him is to lose Him.

Thus the soul rejoices to have found a good that cannot be taken from her, because she so earnestly desires to have it, and nothing can be more noble than that good.

With these new thoughts she begins to contemplate the elevated ways of her Creator, in a state of profound humility and heartfelt adoration. She is conscious that in the presence of God she is as nothing, and she is unable to express in any adequate terms her realization of her own poverty. Nor can she form any sufficiently lofty idea of the sovereign good, and she makes new efforts to reduce herself to the ultimate levels of self-annihilation; as she contemplates God in His majesty, and seeks to discover ways of His being that are ever new. Such lofty meditations exhaust her powers, and she worships in silence. She now sees herself His creature, but defaced, deformed and unprofitable. She redoubles her devotion and thanksgiving, desiring only to thank Him and worship Him forevermore.

And finally she acknowledges the work of His mercy toward herself, that He has been pleased to appear in His infinite majesty to so mean and contemptible a worm of earth. She makes a firm resolution that she will be forever thankful, and she now finds herself perplexed that she could ever have preferred a multitude of vain things to this one divine master. In a spirit of compunction and penitence she pleads His mercy, pleads that His wrath be stayed, pleads that His fury consume her not, great though her wickedness may be in His sight. . . .

She earnestly prays that since God has been pleased to show Himself to her, He will Himself be her guide, and plant in her the graces that will at last bring her to Himself. For since it is to God Himself that she now aspires, she has no desire to come to Him by any other way than He has Himself decreed: He Himself is to be her way, her object, and her last end. Having offered those prayers, she begins to act, and to ask counsel [of those that can help her].

She begins to know God; she desires to come to Him. But since she as yet knows nothing of His ways she will, if her desire be firm and genuine, do as travelers do when they have missed the direct road to their destination: she will ask those who are familiar with the district.

She makes a firm resolve that she will live for the rest of her life in conformity with His will. But the weakness of her human nature, and her tendency to fall back into those sins in which she formerly lived, have debilitated her will and weakened her power to arrive at that condition of happiness. She therefore petitions that His mercy will provide her with the means to come to Him, to attach herself to Him, and to adhere to Him with fidelity forevermore.

In this way the soul acknowledges that it is but her duty to worship God, since she is His creation; to offer Him thanks, because her thanks are due; to make amends to Him because she has offended, and to beg His favors, since she has none of her own.

Letters

Letter to His Sister Gilberte, Madame Périer

This letter bears witness to Pascal's extraordinary delicacy of conscience, his constant search to find the ultimate motives that prompted his action, his concern for naked sincerity.

January 26, 1648

My dear Sister,

We[1] have received your letters. I intended to answer the first letter you wrote to me, more than four months ago, but I was not well, and some business matter or other prevented me from writing. Since that time, either because of my poor health,[2] or for lack of leisure, or for some other reason, I have been in no fit condition to write to you. I have but little to spare at present of either time or health. The latter however I am trying to attain, though without driving myself, and I cannot tell how long it is going to take. My principal reasons for writing this letter are, first, to give you a hint of how those visits are going that you know about, and concerning which I had hoped to have some news that would please you; and secondly, to answer the letters you have written meanwhile. As to these, I can only say that they have given me great pleasure: I have had from them so much solid satisfaction as can scarcely be described in speech. I beg you to believe me when I say that although I have written nothing to you, scarcely an hour has

[1] We: Blaise Pascal and Jacqueline, who was with her brother in Paris during the winter of 1647 (when the meetings took place with Descartes), to make a retreat with M. Singlin. Pascal hated correspondence, and the style of his letters is very often brusque.

[2] His family and friends were inclined to think that Pascal was neurotic. The sufferings that preceded his death at the early age of thirty-eight took them unawares.

passed in which you have not been present to me, and in which I have not made new petitions for your perseverance in the grand design that God has inspired in you. With every letter that brought me new evidence of your intention, I felt a new access of joy; and I have been quite carried away by seeing your perseverance in it, although you had received no news of what we were doing. All this made me consider that your resolution was sustained by something more than human, since that design of yours had no need of human resources to strengthen it. I might have cherished the hope, all the same, of making some contribution, but I have none of the resources necessary for the purpose. My weakness is such that if I were indeed to undertake it, my doing so would be an act of temerity rather than of charity, and I would rightly fear for both of us [3] the misfortune that threatens the blind leaders of the blind. I have been inexpressibly more conscious of my disability since the visits of which I speak; and so far am I from having drawn from them sufficient light for others, that I have derived from them nothing but confusion and trouble for myself. May God soothe me in my disturbed condition, and may He help me to work in spite of it, without haste or anxiety, for I well know that either of these would only carry me further away from Him. I tell you that God is indeed able to calm me, and that I shall be able to do that work,[4] because I am finding all things an occasion for bringing Him to another birth, another growth and increase,[5] in those persons in whom

[3] i.e., for Jacqueline and himself.

[4] The work of appealing through his writings to the freethinkers among his contemporaries, especially in the projected *Apology*, which was already taking shape in his notes, the fragments of the *Pensées*.

[5] Cf., G. Manley Hopkins:

> . . . And makes, O marvelous!
> New Nazareths in us, . . .
> New Bethlems, and he born
> There, evening, noon, and morn—
> Bethlem or Nazareth,
> Men here may draw like breath
> More Christ and baffle death;
> Who, born so, comes to be
> New self, and nobler me,
> In each one and each one
> More makes, when all is done,
> Both God's and Mary's Son. . . .

"The Blessed Virgin Compared to the Air We Breathe."

I had expected to find nothing but dissipation: so that, seeing myself stripped down to my own resources, nothing remains to me but the entreaty that God will bless my efforts with success. If I am to succeed, I shall need to discuss the project with two classes of persons: those having the requisite knowledge; and those who are disinterested. Now the first class will give me no help: henceforward, therefore I am looking only for the second. This is why I am so very anxious to see you, for letter writing is a time consuming business, and practically useless for the present purpose. All the same, I will write to you a few words on the subject now and then.

The first time I saw M. Rebours [6] I made myself known to him, and he received me with about as much civility as I could perhaps expect: even so, his compliments were paid to me as my father's son—and I had to accept them as such. When the first civilities had been exchanged, I asked his leave to see him again from time to time, which he said I might do. I now therefore have access to him, and I do not count this first interview as a visit: it simply secured me permission to visit. I was there [7] again a little later, and while talking of other things I told him, with my usual openness and simplicity, that we had seen their books and those of their opponents. This was enough to convey to him that we held the same views as the Port-Royalists, and when he heard it he showed a certain pleasure. I then told him I thought it possible to demonstrate many things from the principles of common sense, that were said by his opponents to be contrary to it; and that a well-conducted argument would persuade belief in those things—although we are required to believe them without recourse to reasoning.

Such were the words I used, and I cannot think that there was anything in them that could be called contrary to personal modesty, even of the strictest kind. But you are well aware that every human act may spring from two sources, and that those words of mine may have come from a root of vanity and from too much confidence in my own

[6] Antoine de Rebours (1596–1661) became a Solitary of Port Royal in 1640. He was confessor to the nuns until 1661, when he was relieved of the post. Pascal seems to have had several conversations with him, and on the whole to have made a poor impression.

[7] i.e., at Port Royal.

powers of reasoning. Such a suspicion may have been present to his mind, and it may have been fortified by his knowledge of my studies in geometry. This would be quite enough to make him think my remarks a little strange. He gave me a hint of this, in a rejoinder so very modest and so humble, that it ought without doubt to have abashed the pride that he wished to rebuke. But I persisted in explanations, and tried to bring him to understand my motive; my self-justification only increased his suspicions, and he took my excuses for mere obstinacy. I acknowledge that what he said was so persuasive that had I actually been in the condition he assumed, he would certainly have talked me out of it. But as I had no reason to think that I suffered from the disorder to which he referred, I put up some resistance to the medicine he offered. The more violently I resisted it, however, the stronger did he make it, for he regarded my resistance as mere stubbornness. The more he urged me, the more did my polite evasions show him that I did not judge the remedy to be necessary. Thus the whole of that first interview passed in an atmosphere of misunderstanding and embarrassment—a condition which has continued through all our subsequent meetings, and has not even yet been altogether dissipated. I shall not describe our later encounters in detail, for that would be neither necessary nor proper. I shall simply tell you the substance of what is said, or rather, the ground covered in our talks.

But I beg you above all things not to draw hasty conclusions from the news I sent you, for it may well be that my account of things is lacking in precision, and that might cause you yourself to entertain some suspicion or other, as much to my discredit as it is unjust. Because, to put it plainly, I have thought the thing over very carefully, and I find nothing but perplexity; in this condition it would be difficult and even dangerous to come to a decision. I have decided to suspend judgment entirely, as much on account of the weakness of my position as my lack of knowledge.

Letter of Pascal and His Sister Jacqueline to Their Sister Gilberte, Madame Périer

Pascal here comments upon the concrete ways in which God deals with men. It is in the living out of this particular friendship or love, this particular family relationship, that the invitation of God is felt and the gesture of man's free "yes" to God is made.

April 1, 1648

We cannot say whether this letter will be as interminable as the others were, but we do know that we would certainly like to go on writing forever. We have with us here the letter of M. de Saint-Cyran, *De la vocation,* printed not long since without any approbation or privilege.[8] A good many people have been scandalized by it. We are reading it now, and when we have finished it we will send it to you. We shall be very interested to know your opinion, and also what my father thinks of it.[9] It is sublime writing.

I have more than once begun a letter to you, but was a little damped by yours to me, and I was also delayed by the conversations, or (if you prefer), the *cool receptions,* of which I have told you. But when we have done all we can to obtain information,[10] and provided we can bring ourselves to be a little circumspect, bearing in mind that there may well be "a time to refrain from speaking" on certain subjects, then I believe we may hope for the dispensation. For since we are not in doubt on either the one point or the

[8] Under Louis XIII and XIV, control of the French press was extremely strict, so that this unauthorized publication rendered its author liable to very harsh penalties.

[9] Because a dispute was in progress with Pascal *père,* who was opposed to Jacqueline's entry into Port Royal.

[10] i.e., of all that was involved if his sister should enter Port Royal.

other; and since we are assured on both sides that in all these discussions we seek nothing but the glory of God; and since scarcely anybody outside our own small circle is involved, I do not see the slightest reason why we should have scruples, so long as our intention remains as at present. If we add to these considerations the fact of our blood relationship, and to this again, the additional bond effected by a precisely similar operation of grace, I believe that we are far from having to defend our action, and are indeed obliged to act. For it seems to me that our happiness in that experience shared [11] has been so great, that we ought to be united also in remembering it and rejoicing in it. For we must admit that it is only from that time (which M. de Saint-Cyran wants people to call the beginning of life), that we can regard ourselves as truly related to one another; and that it has pleased God to unite us as closely in His new creation according to His spirit, as He has done in the earthly sense by relating us in the flesh.

We beg you, do not let a day pass without calling these things to mind, and often refreshing your memory as to the ways of God in this matter: the way in which He has been pleased to bring us together, not only as brother and sister, but also as children of the same father: for you know that my father forestalled us all, and that it was really his doing that we have been drawn into this project.[12] For these reasons we ought to marvel that God should have bestowed on us so close a relationship: and that a dual one, according to symbol and according to nature. For we have often said to one another that material things are but images of spiritual things, and God has shown . . . His invisible nature . . . the invisible things are clearly . . . perceived through the things that are made (Rom. 1:20). This thought is of such general application and so profitable, that nobody should allow any great while to pass without reflecting upon it. We have discussed the relation of these two classes of things in sufficient detail, so that I need not speak of them here. To write of them would take too long, and the subject is of such sublimity that it cannot but have remained in

[11] i.e., the experience of conversion.

[12] That his daughter should become a nun was an unforeseen consequence of the conversion of Pascal *père*.

your memory. In my opinion moreover, this particular article is an essential part of our belief. For our sins detain us in the grip of corporeal, earthly things, and these material burdens are not only a punishment for sin but also the occasions of new sins and the cause of the first sin we commit; therefore we have to make use of this same earth in which our Fall occurred, to recover from that Fall. This is why we must make good use of the advantage that the goodness of God has given us in holding always before our eyes the image of the good things we have lost; and in ringing us round, even in this state of captivity in which His justice has confined us, with so many objects that are constant reminders of that loss. Thus we ought to regard ourselves as malefactors thrown into a prison which happens to be full of likenesses of their liberator, and of instructive notices telling them how they can get out of the place. But it has to be admitted that those holy writings cannot be read without supernatural light: for just as all things speak of God—to those that know Him; and all things reveal Him, to those that love Him; so those same things hide Him from those that know Him not.[13] We also perceive that while we walk among the shadows of this world we are deluded by them, and we follow them out of a kind of perverse and debased blindness: we attach ourselves to shadows, and make them the last end of our desires. And this cannot be done without sacrilege, for God alone should be our last end, since He is our beginning and our true principle. For whatever resemblance created Nature may have to its Creator, and though it may be true that the most trifling things, the smallest and even the most disgusting things of earth, display by their very unity some measure of that perfection of unity which is only to be found in God; yet we may not lawfully pay to creatures the tribute of sovereign respect, because in the view of both God and man there is nothing more abominable than idolatry, the rendering to creatures the honor due only to the Creator. Scripture is full of the wrath of God poured out upon those that are guilty of this sin. The first commandment of the Decalogue forbids the worship of images of the Deity, and that commandment may

[13] Pascal's characteristic theme of the hidden God, derived in part from his wide reading in the Jewish mystics and also in the Torah and Midrasch.

be said to include all the others. But since He is clearly more jealous of our love than of our mere respect, it is clear that we can do Him no greater wrong than to give our preference to creatures, however closely they may resemble Him.

For these reasons, those to whom God has given an understanding of these great truths should make use of imagery of this kind, that they may enjoy Him whom the imagery represents, and that they may not remain for eternity in a condition of carnal blindness like that of the Jews, and be like them deluded into mistaking types for the reality. [Those are Christians] whom God, of His mere goodness, has withdrawn by the grace of baptism from a life of sin (for sin is the true nothingness, since it is opposed to God, who is true being). To these He has given a place in His true temple, which is the Church. At the moment of their creation to newness of life, He of His mere mercy withdrew them from the void, that He might give them a place in His Creation. These, then, have a double obligation to serve and honor Him, because as creatures they ought to remain in that subordinate order, and not profane the place they occupy; and as Christians they should unceasingly aspire to make themselves worthy to be members of the body of Christ. But whereas creatures of earth are content merely to discharge their obligations, and are satisfied with a limited perfection, because for them the perfection attainable on earth is of its nature limited; the children of God should set no limits to their purity and perfection, for they are members of a body all divine, of infinite perfection. For we see that Jesus Christ did not set any kind of limit to his commandment that we be perfect, but proposes to use a pattern of which the perfection is infinite, when He says, "You, therefore, must be perfect, as your heavenly Father is perfect," Matt. 5:48. Thus it is a very harmful error, but one very common among Christians, even those who aspire to holiness, to be persuaded that there is a certain state of perfection in which we may rest with security and beyond which it is not necessary to go; since there is no state of perfection which does not become an imperfection if we rest in it; a condition into which we can only avoid falling by climbing ever higher . . .

Letter of Pascal and His Sister Jacqueline to Their Sister Gilberte, Madame Périer

"We must be vigilant, and we must constantly purify the inner self, which is always acquiring new stains before it is rid of the old ones. Without this assiduous wish of renewal one is not capable of carrying the new wine—which must never be put in old bottles." Pascal here anticipates many of the emphases of modern depth-psychology with its accent on purity of motivation.

Paris, November 5,
afternoon, 1648

My dear Sister,

Your letter reminded us of a quarrel that we had forgotten, so far had it receded into the past.[14] We had made it our business to procure a good deal of information about all that would be involved, and this put the matter of our old and general complaint in a new light. The understanding to which we came did something to soothe my father's hostility to the project. We said what you had already said, though we did not then know that you had said it; and then we made our own defense by word of mouth, just as you had already done in writing, and again we did not know that you had done so until after we had spoken. For just as we had concealed nothing from my father, so he hid nothing from us: he told us everything, and so our suspicions were set at rest. You know how these perplexities are troubling the peace of the home in public as well as in private, and how much we need to be prepared for such

[14] Pascal *père* had not only refused to allow Jacqueline to enter Port Royal, but had taken steps to prevent her from communicating with the nuns. Gilberte's letter had probably made some reference to this old dispute. Her father died a month later.

incidents by the kind of advice which (too late) you have given us.

We have some advice to give you ourselves, about your own affairs. Our first point is in answer to your remark, that it was we who gave you the information you mention. 1° I have not the slightest recollection that I ever spoke to you on the subject, and this is the first I have heard of it. Moreover, if it should be true, I fear you could scarcely preserve the memory of it without also remembering who it was that told you—unless you deliberately put that person out of mind, so that you could refer back to God alone as the true source of the information. If you preserve this recollection as of something good in itself, you surely cannot believe that you had it from any other [than God], since neither you nor any other person could have learned of it from any source other than God. For although where knowledge of this order is concerned one does not limit oneself to thanking the person addressed (as though he were the sole author of the good one has received through him), there is all the same a danger of a certain opposition to the will of God, especially in persons not yet entirely purified of carnal notions, which makes them regard as the source of the good the mere channel that communicates it.[15]

Not that we should not express gratitude to people from whom we receive useful advice, and remember them and their counsel—provided they are persons who have the right to give it: our fathers, our Bishops, our directors; because these are masters, where other men are only disciples. But as to you and ourselves, the situation is not quite the same. For just as the angel forebade the worship offered by another holy servant of God, so I also must request you not to use these expressions of human gratitude any more; I beg you to be careful not to pay me such compliments, because I, like yourself, am but a disciple.

My second point is to answer your remark that you need not repeat such things because we know them already. This

[15] Pascal had throughout his life a scruple that he might be respected as the author of any work of charity he might perform, and that thus he might be exposed to a double temptation: to a sin of pride if he gloried in any act as though it were his own; and to a sin of vanity if he should seem to attract to himself a respect which ought to be given only to God.

causes me to fear that you do not make a sufficiently clear distinction between the matters of which you speak, and those that are talked of in the world. For it cannot be doubted that it is sufficient to have learned about worldly things once and for all, and to keep the lesson well in mind, so that there is no need for a repetition of it; but where the knowledge is of the heavenly kind, one lesson is not enough, even though it is given by an interior inspiration of God, if we are to preserve a similarly enlightened understanding of it, although our recollection of it may be clear enough. It is not that we are unable to remember it, for an Epistle written by Saint Paul is just as easily remembered as one of the books of Virgil; but knowledge thus acquired and added to, is nothing but an effort of the memory. The strange and secret language of Heaven, however, is not understood by those who are strangers there; and that same grace which alone can give us our first understanding of it is also essential for its increase. Grace deepens that knowledge, and ensures its constant renewal by engraving it again and again upon the hearts of the faithful. Grace makes that knowledge an ever-present fact, just as God is always renewing the Beatitude of the blessed, which is itself an effect and consequence of grace. Another example of the same kind is the eternal generation of the Son: the Church teaches that His being is maintained eternally by an eternal effusion of His substance, uninterrupted and without end.

Thus the continuance of the faithful in a state of justice is nothing other than the continued infusion of grace. It is not a grace bestowed once only and then subsisting forevermore. It is precisely this fact that provides us with a perfect instruction as to our condition, which is one of permanent dependence on the divine mercy. For if the flow of grace be ever so briefly interrupted, dryness inevitably supervenes. It is easy to see that in this condition of necessity we must always be making new efforts to acquire this constant renewal of the spirit, since the original grace is not preserved unless new grace be acquired, and we are likely to lose what we thought we could keep: like those who thought they could imprison light, and succeeded only in filling the prison with new shadows. We must be vigilant, and we must constantly purify the inner self, which is always acquiring new stains before it is rid of the old ones. Without this assiduous work of renewal one is not capable of carrying the new wine—which must never be put in old bottles.

Therefore you need have no hesitation about recalling to our minds the things that are stored in our memories and which need to be recalled to our hearts; for there is no doubt that your own words will be a more effective instrument of grace than any idea that the mind retains. Grace is given in answer to prayer, and the charity you have always shown in our regard is itself a prayer, belonging to that class of intercession which ought never to be interrupted. We should never be unwilling to read about holy things or to hear about them, however familiar to ourselves or generally well known; for our memory, and all the knowledge it retains, is after all no more than a thing inanimate and Judaic,[16] lacking a vitalizing spirit. It very often happens that God makes use of such external means to make His holy mysteries understood, and to leave men with less reason for vanity and self-satisfaction once they have submitted to His grace. Thus a book or a sermon of a very simple kind will do much more for a person who brings to them the right disposition than a more refined and elevated discourse, which normally conveys more of pleasure than instruction. We occasionally notice that those who listen to them as they should, though they may be unlettered folk, and indeed practically peasants, are touched at the mere mention of the name of God, or at the first utterance of a threat of Hell, though these may be the only parts of the sermon they understand, and although they may already have been perfectly familiar.

I come to your third point, which is that you write these things only to let us know your opinion on the subject. We commend your opinion, we praise your perseverance, and we thank you for communicating to us your view of the matter. We had already drawn a similar admission out of M. Périer, and the remarks we had induced him to make on the subject had reassured us. We cannot convey to you our pleasure in any better way, than to say that you would be equally joyful if *we* told *you* the same news.

There is nothing more of consequence, except on the

[16] Pascal does not use this word in any derogatory sense, as is proved by the many passages in his writings which extol Judaism. The word seems to have signified to him the literal interpretation, the earthly preoccupations of materialism, the "dead works" done by those who lack purity of heart.

subject of your plans for the house.[17] We know M. Périer is too deeply absorbed in his project to be able to think of two things at once, and that the plan is on such a scale that if it is ever to be finished he will have to give his whole mind to it for some time to come. We are also aware that the plan relates to one part of the building only. But apart from the fact that the project will in itself take too long, it will eventually (as soon as the first part is finished), require the inclusion of the remainder of the house; however firmly he makes up his mind not to include the whole house, and especially if he devotes to building, time which would be better employed in simply stripping away the meretricious details of the structure. We therefore advised him to do much less building than he contemplates, and to limit himself to what is strictly necessary, but using the same plan, so that he does not need to run into debt to complete the work, nor to run out of the necessary funds. We beg you to think over this matter very seriously, to make up your mind, and then to advise him; or else it may happen that he bestows more of prudence, care, and trouble on the building of a house that he is not obliged to build, than on the erecting of that mystic tower, of which as you know Saint Augustine speaks in one of his letters, and which he undertook to enlarge upon in his sermons.

Postscript by Jacqueline: I hope to write to you in my own name about my affair, of which I will send you all the particulars. But please pray for a happy ending.

If you know any good souls that will do it, please ask them to pray for me, too.

[17] The reference is to a property owned by Florin Périer at Clermont, to which he was making extensive alterations.

Letter to Monsieur and Madame Gilberte Périer at Clermont, on the Death of Their Father, Etienne Pascal, in Paris, 24 September, 1651

In this letter Pascal reflects upon the mystery of human suffering and its meaning in the divine plan. Its classic sincerity, the rejection of all spurious solutions, reminds us of the book of Job.

Paris, October 17, 1651

You have both received news by now of the misfortune that has befallen us all, and the unfinished letter we sent you described some of the happier circumstances which marked that time of grief, and must have afforded you some consolation. I can no longer withhold from you certain memories which my mind still treasures from that time. I pray that God may grant me renewal and increase of all those blessings that we formerly received through His grace,[18] and all that has lately been bestowed upon us through the good offices of our friends on this occasion.

I cannot remember where that first letter ended. My sister sent it off without noticing that it was not finished. But I seem to remember that it contained, if only in substance, some particular remarks on the ways of God in relation to our life on earth and to sickness; and it is to these topics, which I have very much at heart, that I wish once more to refer, because they contain a great deal that is very consoling. The bearing of what I said may not have been clear to you at the first reading, and my sister may not, at that first opportunity, have given you a very correct summary of my remarks. I shall therefore only speak in this letter of the conclusion to which those earlier remarks of mine were intended to lead—a conclusion so closely in con-

[18] Pascal's father had been instrumental in the conversion of all the members of his family.

formity with Christian teaching, so holy, so happy, so much to be desired, that every Christian (and not only those directly concerned because they were related to him), ought to find matter for rejoicing in it.

With so much by way of introduction, I begin what I have to say with words very consoling to any who, despite the heavy burden of this sorrow, are sufficiently quiet in mind to follow the argument. My view of the matter is that we ought to seek consolation in our sorrows, not in ourselves, nor in other men, nor in any created thing, but in God. And the reason for this is, that not even the whole of created Nature can be called the "first cause" of those accidents that we call evils; the one true cause of such things, their arbiter and sovereign ruler, is God alone. Therefore it cannot be doubted that we ought to go direct to the source, go back to the origin of these things, to find the surest easing of our grief. If we follow this precept, and if we consider our recent loss, not as an effect of chance, not as an inevitable development, the falling asleep of an exhausted nature, nor even as an accident that has happened to a toy, a plaything of the elements—a dispersing of the parts that were put together to make a man (for God has not abandoned His elect to caprice and chance); but as a sequel and consequence, indispensable, inevitable, just, holy, useful for the good of the Church, contributing to the glory of God and the greatness of His name; as a decree of His Providence ordained from all eternity, to be executed in the fullness of time, in such a year, on such a day, at such a time, in such a place, and in such manner; so that all that has happened was foreknown from the beginning, and was foreordained of God. If, I say, by a vigorous collaboration with the grace given, we can bring ourselves to regard this event, not in itself as a thing apart from God, but in detachment, as part of the intimate working of the will of God, according to the justice of His own decree, part of the ordering of His Providence, which is the true cause of it, and without which it could not have happened, by which it has in fact happened; and the manner in which it has happened was also directed by His will. Let us then adore in humility and silence the impenetrable majesty of His secrets. Let us venerate the holiness of His decree. Let us bless the controlling hand of His Providence. And as we unite our will with the very will of God, we shall desire, with Him, in

Him, and for Him, the thing that He has willed in us and for us from all eternity.

Let us then make our meditations along these lines, and learn a lesson that was taught me by a great man at that time of our greatest affliction: that there is no consolation anywhere but in the truth. It cannot be doubted that neither Seneca nor Socrates have anything very convincing to say at such a time. They were in that state of error which blinded all men in that first era of the world. They all held that death is natural to man, and all those discourses which they grounded in that false principle are so futile that the only purpose they serve is negative, for they show by that very futility how weak are the majority of men, since the noblest writings of the greatest among them are so mean and so puerile.

But with Jesus Christ it is not so, nor with the canonical books of the Scriptures. There the truth is to be found, and it is as certain that consolation may be drawn from the Scriptures as it is that they are infallibly free from error. Let us then meditate upon death in the light of the truth, as taught by the Holy Spirit in the Scriptures. We have the great advantage of knowing that death is, in fact and in intention, a punishment of sin, imposed upon man for the expiation of offenses, and necessary if man is to be rid of sin. We know that only by death can the soul be delivered from that fleshly concupiscence which is the burden even of the saints in this world. We know that the whole of life, and especially of the Christian life, is an unceasing oblation made to God, since it is an uninterrupted act of sacrifice terminated only by death—for just men as for our Lord. We know that when Jesus Christ came into the world He regarded Himself as a sacrifice, an actual victim offered to God for mankind (Hebr. 1:3, 5, 7:27). We know that His birth, life, and death, His resurrection and ascension, His presence in the Eucharist, and His sitting forever at the right hand of God, are but so many parts of a single and unique act of sacrifice. And we know that all the things that happened to Jesus Christ ought to happen to all His members. Let us then consider this life as a sacrifice, and let the misfortunes of life affect the spirits of Christians only in so far as they serve to diminish or to complete that sacrifice. Let only that chance be called evil which delivers to the devil the man who ought to be wholly given to God; but where a man who was in bondage to the devil through the sin of Adam is made into a child of God, let the event that makes him such be called nothing but good. And by this rule let us examine the nature of death.

If we are to meditate usefully on this subject, we must have recourse to the person of Jesus Christ: for all that is in man is an abomination; and God only accepts men through Jesus Christ as mediator. If we go not in by this door, we shall find within ourselves nothing but real evils or abominable pleasures; but if we see all things as they are in Jesus Christ, we shall find them all consolation, all satisfaction, all edification.

Let us then meditate upon death in Jesus Christ, and not without Him. Without Jesus Christ, death is fearful, detestable, a horror of Nature. *In* Jesus Christ, death is something very different, something to be accepted with love, a holy thing, the joy of the faithful. All things are sweet in Jesus Christ, even death. This is why He Himself suffered and died, that He might sanctify death and suffering. As God and yet man, He was all that was noble, yet He was also all that was outcast and despised, so that all things except sin might be made holy in Him: that He might be the pattern and exemplar for men of all conditions.

As we meditate upon what death is, and upon the death of Jesus Christ, we must look at the place occupied by death in His continual and uninterrupted oblation. For this purpose we must observe that in any sacrificial act the principal feature is the death of the victim. The offering and consecration of the victim are anterior dispositions of the will; but the crowning moment of the sacrifice is the moment of death, in which life is extinguished, and the creature renders to God the sum total of homage of which it is capable by an act of self-annihilation before the eyes of His majesty, and by adoring His sovereign being, which alone has real existence. It is true that there is another element in the sacrifice which is still present after the death of the victim, and without which that death is of no avail: this element is the acceptance by God of the oblation made to Him. As the Scriptures say "The Lord smelled the pleasing odour," Gen. 8:21. It is this acceptance that crowns the oblation; and yet it must be regarded as an act of condescension made by God to man, rather than in any way meritorious in man; and it remains true that the last act of man is his act of dying.

All these things were accomplished in Jesus Christ. When He came into the world, He offered Himself: "Christ, who through the eternal Spirit offered himself without blemish to God . . . when He came into the world He said, Sacrifices and offerings thou hast not desired, but a body hast thou prepared for me. . . . Then I said, Lo, I have come to do thy will, O God, as it is written of me in the roll of the book," Hebr. 9:14, 10:5. That was His oblation. His sanctification followed immediately upon His oblation. His sacrifice endured throughout His life and was consummated by His death. "Was it not necessary that the Christ should suffer these things, and enter into His glory?," Luke 24:26. And although He was the Son of God, He had to learn obedience. "In the days of his flesh, Jesus offered up prayers and supplications, with loud cries and tears, to Him who was able to save Him from death, and He was heard for His godly fear," Hebr. 5:7. And God raised Him up, and sent His glory (which had been prefigured in former times by the fire from Heaven, which fell upon the sacrificial victims, to burn and consume the bodies [I. Kings 18:37–39]), that His life might be spiritual, the life that is lived in glory. This is what Jesus Christ obtained, this is what was accomplished by His resurrection.

It was by the death of Jesus Christ that His sacrifice was made perfect. That sacrifice was consummated, even in His body, by His resurrection, in which the image of sinful flesh was swallowed up in glory. Jesus Christ had now accomplished all that was required of Him. It remained only that His sacrifice should be accepted by God, and that, in the same way as the smoke of the burnt offering rose to Heaven, and carried the odor of the sacrifice to the throne of God, so Jesus Christ might also be borne upward, offered, and received at the throne of God, in His risen and glorified condition, an offering made perfect. This is what was accomplished at His ascension, when He rose by His own power, and also was borne up by the Holy Spirit, who was about Him on all sides. He was lifted up like the smoke of those victims of sacrifice that prefigured Jesus Christ; He was carried up by the supporting atmosphere, a symbol of the Holy Spirit. The Acts of the Apostles expressly say (3:21, 7:56, etc.) that He was received into Heaven, and this is written in testimony that His holy sacrifice of Himself accomplished upon earth, had indeed been accepted by God and received by Him, to burn in glory forevermore.

This was the state of things with our sovereign Lord. Now let us consider how matters stand with ourselves. From the moment we enter the Church (which is the world of the faithful and especially of the elect, into which Jesus Christ also entered, by a special privilege of the only Son of God, at the moment of His Incarnation), we ourselves are offered and sanctified. Our sacrifice continues throughout life, and is completed at death, when the soul, leaving behind all the vices and love of the world which infect it so contagiously and continuously during its life on earth, completes its immolation and is received into the bosom of God.

Let us not then afflict ourselves, as do the heathen who have no hope. We did not lose my father at the moment of his death. We did, in a sense, lose him when he entered the Church at his baptism. From that moment he belonged to God. His life was dedicated to God, and all that he did was done for God: if it was done for the world at all, it was still done solely for the glory of God. At the moment of his death he was totally removed from bondage to sin, and in that moment he was received by God; his sacrifice was completed and received its crown. Thus he had done what he undertook to do: he completed the work that God gave him to do; he accomplished the one thing for which he was created. The will of God was accomplished in him, and his own will was absorbed in God. And may our own will, the will of man, never separate what God has united.[19] And may we learn to stifle, or at least to moderate by our understanding of the truth, the impulses of a corrupted human nature deceived by false images, which can only trouble with illusions those holy impulses which ought to be inspired in us by the spirit of truth and by the Gospels.

Let us then no longer look toward death as pagans do, but with Christian hope, as Saint Paul teaches (I Thess. 4:12), for the virtue of hope is the special privilege of Christians. Let us no longer regard the body of a deceased person as mere carrion, an infected carcass; although this is all that it appears to be—but here the appearances are deceptive. Let us rather see the body as a temple of the Holy Ghost, inviolable

[19] Do not let our united family be divided by quarrels over the inheritance.

and eternal, as our faith teaches. For we know that the bodies of the saints are indwelt by the Holy Spirit until the Resurrection, and that they will be raised at that day by the power of that spirit who dwells in them for that very purpose. This is the teaching of the Fathers. It is for this reason that we honor the remains of the dead, and this doctrine is the true origin of the custom in the primitive Church, of placing a consecrated Host in the mouth of the dead person: he was indeed the temple of the Holy Ghost, and therefore he merited to be intimately united in this way with the Blessed Sacrament. The Church has abandoned the custom: not that the dead are not numbered with the saints, but because the Eucharist is a sacrament of life and of the living, and ought not be given to the dead.

Let us no longer consider a dead man as one that has ceased to live, whatever Nature may suggest; but as one who has begun to live—as the truth assures us. Let us no longer say that his soul has perished, and is reduced to nothing; but that it is quickened and united to God, the living and the true. If we attend to these truths we shall be able to correct erroneous notions which have become part of our thinking, and also those impulses of horror which are so natural to man.

If we are to suppress effectively those instinctive reactions of horror, we must clearly understand how they originate. If I am to outline the subject for you in a few words, it is necessary to state in general terms what is the source of all our vices and all our sins. This is what I have learned from two very great and singularly holy persons. The truth that provides the key to the mystery is this, that God created man with two loves: the love of God, and the love of self. These two loves were however subject to a law, that man's love of God should be infinite, having no other object than God only; and that man's love of himself should be finite, and in all things subordinated to the will of God.

Governed by such a law, man could love himself without sin; and he would indeed have sinned if he had failed to love himself.

Later, man fell into sin, and simultaneously lost the first of these loves. The love of himself was now in solitary possession of a great soul capable of infinite love; and self-love expanded therein, overflowing and filling the void that was left there when God withdrew Himself. Man now loved himself alone, loved himself infinitely, and loved all things for himself and with the whole of his being, that is, infinitely.

That was the origin of self-love, which in Adam was according to his nature and, in his condition of innocence, was in conformity with justice. But when he sinned, and because he sinned, Adam became both guilty and disordered.

Such was the origin of his self-love, the cause of its defect and excess. From the same cause sprang the love of power, the love of idleness, and other defects. It is easy to demonstrate the fact, so let us address ourselves to our one topic. The horror of death was natural to Adam in his state of innocence, because his life was very pleasing to God, and was destined to be attractive to his fellowmen: and death was to be dreaded because it would terminate a life that was being lived in conformity with the will of God. Once man had sinned his life became corrupt, his body was at odds with his spirit, and both were at enmity with God.

Although a change so dreadful as this had infected a life formerly so holy, the love of that life nevertheless remained; and with it, the equally powerful dread of death; so that an attitude which in Adam was a state of justice, has become unjust and guilty in ourselves.

Such was the origin of the fear of death, and the reason why it is an imperfection.

Let us now explain this aberration of Nature by the light of faith.

In a state of innocence the fear of death is natural: death does indeed inspire horror when it puts an end to a life that was all purity. It was right to hate a death that separated a holy soul from a pure body. But it is right to welcome it, where it separates a holy soul from a disordered body. It was right to flee from death, to postpone it, when it destroyed the peaceful union of body and soul; but not when death brings peace, when it soothes at last a strife that in life could never be composed. And finally, when death advanced upon a body that was innocent, when death robbed that body of its freedom to worship God, when death separated from a soul a body that had been all submission, and totally compliant with the controlling will, when death puts an end to all the good works that a man can do—then it is but right to hate it. But where death terminates a life that was impure, and takes from a body the liberty to sin, when she deprives of his soul a mighty rebel, who opposes all the motives of his own salvation, it would be very improper to look at it in the same light.

Let us then not abandon that love of life that was planted in us with our human nature, for it was something that we received from God; but let our love be for that life which God intended we should love, and let it not be bestowed on any object alien to Him.

And when we endeavor to conform ourselves to the love that Adam had for his life of innocence, and to that which our Lord Himself had for His own life of holiness (as appeared in his utterances and in His Passion, when He expressed horror at the approach of His death), we must also teach ourselves to hate any way of life that is contrary to the life that Jesus Christ loved; and to fear death only as He feared it, that is, as an event befalling a body acceptable to God; but we are also to see to it that we have no reason to dread for ourselves the death of the wicked, which punishes the guilty body, cleanses the vicious one, and if we attend to that, our attitude to death will be very different, provided also we have a little of faith, hope, and charity.

It is one of the great principles of the Christian religion, that all that happened to Jesus Christ must happen in the body and soul of every Christian. Jesus Christ suffered during his life on earth, He died to this mortal life, He rose to newness of life, He ascended into Heaven, and sits at the right hand of the Father. In the same way, the Christian's body and soul must endure suffering, die, and rise again, and sit in Heaven at the right hand of the Father.

All these things are accomplished in this life in the soul of the Christian, but not in his body.

It is the Christian soul that suffers, and that dies to sin in penance and baptism. It is the soul that rises to a new life in that same baptism. It is the soul that leaves the body and ascends to Heaven at the moment of death, and is seated at the right hand of the Father at a time that God ordains.

None of these things happens in the body during its life on earth; they all take place in it afterward.

For at the moment of death the body dies of its earthly life, at the general judgment it will rise to a new life, after the judgment it will ascend into Heaven, and there it will sit at the right hand of the Father.

Thus the same things happen to body and soul, but at different times; and the changes that take place in the body, only do so when the developments in the soul have completed their course, that is, at the moment of death; so that death is the culmination of the bliss of the soul, but for the body it is only the beginning of the blessed state.

We see then by what admirable ways the wisdom of God provides for the salvation of His saints; and Saint Augustine teaches that God has ordered the lives of men in this way, because if a human body were to die and rise again to eternal life in the one act of baptism, obedience would never be learned except through the love of this earthly life. Whereas the greatness of faith is more clearly and strikingly seen, when immortality has to be attained by passing through the valley of the shadow of death.

This certainly is what we believe, this is the faith that we profess. And I believe we already have in this letter more matter than the minimum required for my own poor efforts to console you in your sorrow. I would not have ventured to offer you such comfort from my own ideas; what I have written is mere repetition and summary of what I have learned from others. I can therefore send it to you with a certain security, praying that God may bless the seed and give it increase, since without Him, as He Himself said, we can do nothing, and His most holy Words can, without Him, take no root in us (Mark 4: 13–20).

Not that I would wish you to be lacking in natural feeling; the blow is too heavy, it would in itself be quite insupportable without supernatural assistance. It would scarcely be reasonable, moreover, that we should expect one another to be without all sorrow, as though we were angelic beings, who have no natural faculties [but only intellect and will].[20] Neither would it be just that we should be left without consolation, like noble savages who know nothing of grace. But it is certainly just that since we are Christians, we should know what it is to be afflicted, and what it means to be comforted; and that we should value the operations of grace above our personal feelings, saying with the Apostle, "When reviled, we bless; when persecuted, we endure," I Cor. 4:12; so that grace be not only present in us, but gains the vic-

20 Pascal's writings provide cumulative evidence that he was very well read in the Scriptures and in theology. His remarks on the angels are in conformity with the teaching of Saint Thomas (S. Theol. I.q. 62, 8. ad 2; II–II, q. 83, 10, ad 2.)

tory in us; that in the very act of hallowing His name, His will should be made our own; that His grace reigns on earth and subdues our human nature; and that our afflictions be as it were matter for oblation, consumed and annihilated by His grace, and for His glory; and that these personal sacrifices be taken to signify and foreshow that universal oblation in which the whole of created Nature is to be brought to fruition by the power of Jesus Christ.

Thus may we derive merit from our imperfections, since these will be the matter of our sacrifice; for it is the aim of true Christians to gain spiritual advantage even from their imperfections, since all things work together for good to the elect.

If we examine this question carefully, we shall find much to edify us, in considering the truth of the matter as we said just now. For since it is true that the death of the body is but a type of the death of the soul, we have to proceed from the principle that in the crisis of death we have many resources and aids, which justify us in hoping for salvation of our souls. It is therefore certain that though we may not be able to prevent the feeling of grief, we may yet learn a certain useful lesson from it, which is this: If the death of the body is so dreadful a thing that it can cause so much sorrow, the prospect of the death of a soul would cause grief that could not by any means be comforted. Now, God has sent us the first of these afflictions, but He has turned away the second. Let us then consider the greatness of our blessings in the greatness of our sorrows, and realize that the very heavy load of our sorrow is only in proportion to the greatness of our joy.

One thing only may moderate that joy, and that is the fear that our father may be required to languish for some time in those pains that are intended to cleanse the stains of sins committed during his life on earth. And we ought now to direct our minds very seriously to actions that shall turn away from him the wrath of God.

Prayer and sacrifice are sovereign remedies for his pains. But during this time of mourning I have learned from a holy man, that one of the most lasting and beneficial charities to the dead is to do with the most careful attention the things they would wish us to do if they were still with us on earth: to follow the sanctified teaching that they gave us; and to attain for their sake to that moral perfection which they now expect of us.

If we do this, we make them in a certain sense live on in ourselves, for the precepts which continue to direct and control us were their very own. And just as the heresiarchs will be punished in the next life for the sins into which they drew their followers, and in which their own malice continues to be active, similarly the just will be rewarded, over and above what they have deserved for themselves, for those meritorious acts performed by others but due to their own counsel and example.

Let us then do all in our power to live so that our lives may be but a continuation on earth of his life, which now is passed in the presence of God. And we may take comfort that in heart we are united, for it seems to me that in that unity his life also is continued. And when we meet, may our being together restore him in a sense to our midst, in the same way as Jesus Christ is present in the assemblies of the faithful.

I pray God to form these feelings in us and to sustain them; and to increase in me those that he seems to plant in me, of loving you and my sister more tenderly than ever before. For it seems to me that the love we had for my father ought not to be lost to us, but that we should bestow it now upon one another; and also that we should, above all things, make his love for us increase, if that were possible, by loving one another more than ever we did.

I pray God to strengthen us in these resolutions, and in this hope I beg you will allow me to give you a word of advice, which perhaps you do not need from me; but I will give it just the same: once we have found ourselves a few memorials of a personal nature to remind us of him, we should by no means miss the opportunity to provide for practical needs with something which, while useful, will also be something that he himself used.

I am the person most closely concerned in this matter. If he had died six years ago I should have been lost; and although I may well believe that my present need of him is less compelling. I know that he would have been necessary to me for ten years more, and useful to me all my life. We may, however, hope that since God has ordained the matter at this time, in this place, and in this manner, no doubt it is what is most expedient for His own glory and for our salvation.

The idea may appear strange, but I think all that happens ought to be seen in this light, and however sinister events may appear to us, we may hope that God will bring out of our very grief the springs of joy for us, if we leave the control of those events to Him.

We know of persons of rank who, upon hearing that an important member of the family was in danger of death, have offered prayers for the life of the dying man. The man was spared—and he was from that moment the cause or occasion of so much strife in the family, that it would clearly have been better if the prayers of the family had not been heard.[21]

It is certain that man is a poor creature, ill-equipped to form a balanced judgment about the course of events that are still in the future. Let us then hope in God, and let us not weary ourselves and one another by indiscreet and rash prophecies. Let us commend to God the ordering of our lives on earth, and let us pray that no disagreements may have dominion over us.[22]

Saint Augustine says that in every man there is a serpent, an Adam and an Eve. The serpent is unregenerate human nature, the unfettered senses, Eve is concupiscence, Adam is reason.[23] The serpent, nature, tempts us continually; concupiscence keeps our desires awake; but no sin is committed if the reason does not consent. Let Eve and the serpent do what they will, if they cannot be prevented; but let us beg of God that Adam be so strengthened by His grace that he may always carry off the victory, and that Jesus Christ may in turn triumph over him, and reign over us all forever. Amen.

[21] The attempt to alter the course of the Divine will led to increased bitterness over the eventual division and administration of the family property.

[22] Pascal here lapses into concern about earthly contingencies. He had been very dependent upon his father, financially as well as personally, and he needed the proceeds from his father's estate for the continuance of his scientific work, so that he could launch his new "arithmetical machine" as a commercial enterprise.

[23] The effect of this application of the words of Saint Augustine upon his female correspondent may be judged from a comment made by Mère Agnès: "Mlle Pascal most humbly intercedes for the conversion of her brother."

Preface for a "Treatise on the Vacuum"

The "Treatise on the Vacuum," was completed in 1651 but was lost soon after Pascal's death. The work is known only from a few fragments published by Florin Périer in 1663.

This remarkable fragment, probably written in 1647 was first published under the title of "Concerning Authority in Matters Philosophical." In it Pascal carefully distinguishes and limits the rôle of arguments from authority. He notes that in physics or mathematics it is useless to appeal to ancient or modern authorities; what we should do rather is to trust intelligence in these spheres and attempt to improve upon the solutions given by past authorities. Today, this principle seems self-evident but in Pascal's time it was a much needed and very valuable insight.

Respect for antiquity is nowadays carried to such extremes, even in relation to matters where opinions of the old philosophers ought to be given less weight, that every mental image of the ancients is venerated as an oracle, and even their dark sayings are elevated into mystic secrets; [1] so that it is impossible today to propose a new scientific hypothesis without offending somebody,[2] and a text cited from an old authority will suffice to destroy the strongest argument of a living one. It is no part of my present intention either to correct one excess by practicing another, or to refuse all recognition

[1] The condemnation of Galileo was still fresh in the minds of scientists, and the writings of the Cabalists were, in the time of Pascal, enjoying a new vogue.

[2] A reference to the abandonment by Descartes of his "World"—a projected treatise on the physical theory of the universe and on anatomy as the basis of medical science—when he heard of the condemnation of Galileo.

to the classical writers, simply on the grounds that people are quoting them too freely.

I do not claim that their authority should be rejected outright in favor of reasoning processes alone—even though the present tactic is to establish the authority of the Ancients as the only rule, to the prejudice of any reasoning process.

In order to make this important distinction accurately, we have to bear in mind that those who regard the Ancients as a final court of appeal rely in fact upon the power of memory and upon the mere testimony of history: they are only concerned to know what their authorities have written; while the other party relies solely upon the force of argument. These are the true dogmatists, for their object is to search for, and find, truths at present hidden.

Those in the first category are as restricted in outlook as the books to which they appeal. . . .

The force we allow to the respective arguments must be regulated according to this distinction. . . .

In all matters where we only seek to know what an author has written, as in history, geography, jurisprudence, languages, and (especially) theology, in any subject, in short, where what we seek is a matter of fact, or of an institution human or divine, we must of necessity refer to the appropriate books, since the sum of available knowledge is contained therein: whence it follows that the whole of available knowledge may be acquired in this way, and that nothing can possibly be added to it.

If it is a question of knowing who was the first king of the French; where geographers situate the first meridian; what is the ordinary vocabulary of a dead language; and other matters of a like nature, where can we find the answer except in books? And who could possibly add anything to what the books teach us—since we only need such information as they contain?

Authority alone is able to enlighten us concerning facts; and authority carries most weight in theology, because in this science authority is inseparable from truth, and we only know the truth from authority. Thus, to give complete certitude in those matters least comprehensible to reason, it is sufficient to show where they are discussed in the sacred books; (similarly, we may demonstrate that incertitude exists on some subjects which appear to be very probable, merely by showing that the Scriptures say nothing about them). Because first principles are not subject to either intellect or reason [but are known naturally by the mind]; and because the mind of man is too weak to attain to certitude by its own effort, and can only attain to this high level of understanding if it be lifted up to it by an Almighty and supernatural power.

But in matters that offer themselves to the senses or to the reasoning faculty, the situation is different; here, authority is useless; only reason is equipped to know them. Each of these spheres of knowledge has laws of its own. Whereas in the one field of knowledge the theologians formerly had all the advantage, here the scientist takes charge. The subjects with which he is concerned are in proportion to the range and power of the mind, and the mind has boundless liberty to extend the field of inquiry: the fertility of the human mind is inexhaustible, and it is perfectly capable of making new discoveries forevermore and without interruption. . . .[3]

Thus geometry, arithmetic, music, physics, medicine, architecture, and all other sciences dependent upon experiment and reasoning, have to grow by addition if they are to become perfect. When the Ancients came to them, they found no more than an outline, a sketch made by their predecessors; and we shall leave them to those that come after us, in a more finished state than we received them. The perfecting of any science requires time and trouble; and it is obvious that, although our own expenditure of trouble and time may have registered less actual progress than did theirs, yet the sum of both endeavors taken together must necessarily be greater than the separate achievement of either.

Recognition of the difference in the quality of the two achievements, the ancient and the modern, should make us deplore the blindness of those who claim that authority alone and not reasoning and not experiment may decide in matters of physical science, and it should fill us with hor-

[3] Many of his contemporaries thought this an extravagant claim by a vain man; but Pascal would have been a completely happy man in the midst of our own scientific revolution.

ror at the wickedness of those who appeal to reason alone in matters theological, rejecting the authority of Scripture and the Fathers. We ought to instill courage into those timid souls who dare not make advances in physics; and we should confound the insolence of those presumptuous persons who introduce novelties into theology. The wickedness of these times is however of such magnitude that we see many a novel opinion in theology that was unknown to the early Church, and yet is maintained with stubbornness and received with approval; whereas the advances made in physics, though these are not many, should, it appears, be denounced as false if they conflict in the slightest degree with received opinions: as though we were in duty bound to follow the old philosophers, but fidelity to even the earliest of the primitive Fathers were merely a matter of courtesy! I leave it to persons of sound judgment to note the gravity of this abuse, which inverts with such injustice the rank and dignity of the sciences. I believe that few will be found who will consent that such freedom be or ought to be used anywhere else, on the grounds, for example, that new discoveries are always errors when they concern matters which cannot be investigated without presumption; but are absolutely necessary for the completion of our knowledge of many subjects at a lower level, but which we ought, all the same, not to venture to touch.

Let us distribute with a more even hand our credulity and our unbelief, and let us set some limits to the awe in which we stand of the Ancients. If reason justifies that respect, she should also restrain it, and keep it within bounds; and let us reflect that, if the Ancients had taken the attitude that they dared not add anything to the system of knowledge they themselves had received; [or] if their own contemporaries had raised the same objection to receiving their new ideas, then they themselves and their posterity also would not have had the benefit of the discoveries which in fact they made.

Now, the Ancients made use of the knowledge they had inherited, only as a means whereby to add to it, and this fortunate boldness opened to them a way to great things; we also should accept in the same spirit the ideas that they mastered and handed on to us. We should follow their example, and make those ideas the instruments of our investigations, and not an end in themselves; so that while we certainly imitate them, we may also endeavor to surpass them.

For what could be more unjust than to take the ancient philosophers more seriously than they took their own forerunners, and to preserve toward them an inviolable respect, such as they have only merited from us precisely because they did not stand in awe of their own Primitives?

The secrets of Nature are hidden: though she is continually working, we do not always discover her effects. Time reveals them from age to age; and although the operations of Nature are uniform and indifferent, she is not understood to the same extent from one generation of scientists to another.

Experiments enable us to understand the secrets of Nature, and investigation is always going on. But experiment is the basis of physics; therefore the results established by experiment are being accumulated in proportion.

By reasoning in this way, we may nowadays accept new ideas and opinions, without in any way slighting [the ancient philosophers] or being guilty of ingratitude, since the elements of knowledge transmitted by them to ourselves have served as the staircase to our own [more advanced] knowledge; and since, in this advantageous situation, we are indebted to them for the advantages over them which we in fact enjoy: for they raised themselves to a certain level, and to that level by their aid we also were able to rise; the slightest effort now enables us to rise much higher than they, so that with less difficulty (and also with less glory), we find ourselves ahead of them. This is why we are able to discover things which it was impossible for them even to suspect. Our vision has a wider range, and although they understood as well as we, all in Nature that they were able to observe, yet there was for them less of Nature to be understood, and we can see more than they.

Yet it is marvelous to see how their ideas are venerated. It is made a crime to contradict them, an act of treason to add anything to them, as though they had left no more truths to be understood.

Is it not undignified to place the reasoning powers of men on a level with the instincts of animals? Since we eliminate the principal difference between them, which is that the results of reasoning processes increase without cessation, whereas instinct is stable, not subject to development. The cells of the honeycomb were as precisely measured a thousand years ago as they are today, and every bee constructed its first hexagon as accurately as it does its latest. It is the same with everything produced by this mysterious impulse. Nature instructs them in proportion as necessity impels them; but this fragile science is lost with the necessities which called it into being. As they received it without forethought, they take no pleasure in preserving it; and everytime the instruction is given them it is new to them. For Nature has no other object than the maintenance of the animal creation in a state of limited perfection, so that she instills into them this necessary knowledge, in which she allows of no variation, lest the stock should deteriorate; and to which she allows of no addition, lest the animals should advance in understanding beyond those limits which Nature has ordained for them. It is not the same with man, who was formed only for the infinite. In the first years of his life his condition is one of ignorance. But as he advances, he learns for himself, and without ceasing to do so: for he derives advantage not only from his own experience, but also from that of those who went before him. He retains forever in his memory all knowledge he himself ever acquired; and the knowledge of the Ancients is ever present to him, in the books in which it is prserved. And just as he can himself preserve that knowledge, so also he can add to it without difficulty. So that in a certain sense men may be said to be today in the condition in which those ancient philosophers would have been found, if they could have survived till this present time, always adding to the knowledge they formerly had that which their studies would have acquired for them in the course of so many centuries. Thus it is by a special prerogative that every man advances in knowledge from day to day, and also that all mankind progresses continually in knowledge as the world grows older, since the same process goes on from one generation to another, as in the life of the individual. Thus the succeeding ages of human life on earth may be likened to the life of one man subsisting forever, and forever acquiring new knowledge. Thus we see what an injustice it is to respect mere antiquity in philosophers. For old age is that time of life most distant from infancy:

who does not see therefore, that the "old age" of our universal man should be sought, not in those early times nearest his birth, but in those the most remote from it. Those whom we call "the Ancients" were in fact young in all things, and it was they who properly speaking constituted the "infancy" of mankind. To their knowledge we have added the experience of the intervening centuries, and so it is in ourselves that we ought to find the maturity that we so much reverence in those others.

They ought to be admired for the consequences which they knew so well how to derive from the very small number of premisses they possessed. And they should be excused for that conduct in which they failed more from lack of the advantages of experience than from any deficiency in reasoning powers. . . .

At a time when the weakness of human vision had not yet been assisted by artificial means, was it not pardonable that the ancient explanation of the Milky Way should have been based on a supposedly greater solidity of the heavens in that region, which had the effect of transmitting light with greater power?

Would it not, however, be inexcusable in ourselves, if we remained fixed in those primitive ideas, since we enjoy the advantages conferred by the telescope, and by its means have discovered a multitude of small stars, the great brilliance of which has led us to recognize the true cause of the whiteness of the Milky Way?

Had not the ancients some grounds for the belief that all corruptible life was to be found within the sphere of the heavens that received the light of the moon, since in the course of many centuries of observation no case of corruption or of generation had ever been recorded outside that sphere of light?

Ought we not rather to be sure of the contrary, since [every astronomer on earth] has actually seen the generation of comets, as well as their disappearance, at vast distances beyond the limits of that sphere of light of the moon?

Similarly, with respect to the vacuum, they had a right to say that Nature would in no case support a vacuum, because all their experiments had led them to observe that she abhors such a condition.

But if the new experiments could have been known to

the ancient philosophers, they might have been convinced thereby, and have cited them as proving what they themselves had formerly denied [4] on the grounds that such a phenomenon was hitherto quite unknown. Thus when they asserted that Nature abhors a vacuum, they must be understood to be speaking of Nature as at that time known to scientific observers. No generalization could at that time be made. For not even a hundred reported observations, nor a thousand, nor any other number however large, would have been sufficient to justify the theory: so long as there remained a single instance that was doubtful, it would be sufficient to prevent the formulation of a generalized law, and if that one instance conflicted with other evidence, that alone [would prove it false]. For in all matters which depend for proof upon the establishment of fact and not upon demonstration, however clear, general law can only be formulated on the basis of a generalized enumeration of all the parts of the argument or of all the exceptions to the proposed law. Thus, when we say that the diamond is the hardest of all substances, we understand, "of all *known* substances": we cannot and we must not extend the statement to cover substances unknown; and when we say of gold that it is the heaviest of all substances, it would be temerarious to apply this general statement to cover hypothetical substances as yet unknown to us which may possibly exist in Nature.

Thus when the ancient philosophers declared that "Nature can in no case support a vacuum," they meant to convey that no vacuum had in fact been created in any experiment they themselves had seen; and they could not without temerity have extended the proposition to cover cases that were not within their knowledge. If such cases had indeed been known to them, no doubt they would have drawn the same conclusions as we have done; and their recognition of observed facts would have carried authority in that ancient world which we of today are so eager to constitute the sole authority in matters scientific.

Thus it is that without contradicting the ancient philosophers, we are able to affirm the contrary of what they say. Indeed, whatever authority the Ancients may have, the truth must always possess still more, although such truth be new;

[4] The ancient atomic physicists held that a perceptible vacuum is unrealizable.

for truth is always older than all the opinions that have ever been held concerning her, and we should be showing ourselves ignorant of her nature if we supposed that she began to be, at the time she began to be known.

Reflections on Geometry and the Art of Persuading

When Pascal reflected upon the question of method in philosophy he first considered the geometric method. This is the perfect model of the art of defining, demonstrating, proving with cogency those truths which lie within its ambit. Its rules are clear and simple, it gives us an infallible way of distinguishing truth from falsehood in its own area. However, this model method does not really suffice in those questions which touch history, philosophy, or theological truth. Especially it does not suffice when there is question of persuading man to accept truths concerning himself, the world of values, or his ultimate meaning and role in life. Here we must appeal to another art—that of persuasion. More subtle and difficult than the method of geometry, this art aims at a real *assent, not merely a notional one, at knowledge which evaluates, in place of merely theoretic knowledge. Pascal here is a precursor of many modern philosophers and theologians, such as Laberthonnière and Marcel.*

The Geometric Mind

In any investigation of the truth, three controlling motives may be present: first, that the truth in question may be found; then, that being found, it may be demonstrated; and that, once demonstrated, it may provide a means to distinguish truth from error.

Of the first of these motives I shall say nothing. I shall discuss the second in detail, and it will be found to include the third. For the method of proving a truth also provides a means of dintinguishing it from error; because when we test the proposed truth by applying known rules, we know at once whether it has in fact been precisely demonstrated.

Geometry satisfies all three requirements in a high degree. It meets the first because it has elucidated the art of discovering truths hitherto unknown. This art is called *analysis*, and it is unnecessary to discuss it here, since so many excellent books have been written about it.

The requirement that a truth, when found, be capable of demonstration, and in such manner that the proof of it be acknowledged invincible, is the only one that I shall here discuss. And for this purpose I need do no more than explain the method used in geometry: for this is an art which teaches to perfection [by means of constructions, even though these are not accompanied by any explanatory discourse. The art comprises two main stages: first, the proof of each proposition in turn; and then, the arrangement of the propositions in the best order. I shall accordingly divide my discussion into two parts of which the first will state the rules for demonstrating things by drawing conclusions from principles, as in geometry—a mode of demonstration which is methodical and perfect; and the second will comprise the rules for mathematical demonstration, which is methodical and also defined. So that when the two methods are combined, they will contain all that is necessary to conduct an argument that will prove a truth and demonstrate it; and I shall give both of them in full.[1]

Section I

ON THE METHOD OF GEOMETRICAL DEMONSTRATION WHICH IS SYSTEMATIC AND CONCLUSIVE

If a demonstration is to carry conviction, each of the steps by which it proceeds must be fully understood; and I can

[1] Pascal intended this essay to form the preface to an "Elements of Geometry" for the *Petites Ecoles* at Port Royal. He never completed the work, but Arnauld published a book on the same plan in 1667. See: A. Arnauld, *Oeuvres*, t. XLII, Paris—Lausanne, 1776.

scarcely make this plainer than by describing the steps in a geometrical demonstration. If such a description of geometry is to be complete, I shall first have to give some idea of a method still more eminent and even more refined, but to which men are scarcely ever able to attain: for what is beyond the resources of geometry is beyond the reach of man. It is however necessary to say something of this more refined method, even though it be impossible to apply it; and although success is far more probable by the one method than by the other.

I have chosen geometry as the best method for my purpose, because it is the only art or science which applies the true rules of reasoning. It does not lose time on the rules of the syllogism, for these come so readily to mind that nobody can possibly be ignorant of them. Geometry is based upon and limited to the correct procedure in argument, whatever the subject. Most people are unaware of the method, but it is useful to know it, as we may learn from experience: where two persons of equal capacity are engaged in debate, the one who knows some geometry (other things being equal) will carry the day—and his skill in argument will moreover continue to grow.

I wish therefore to make clear what is meant by "demonstration," by showing what the expression means in geometry—almost the only science known to man which can produce a demonstration which is infallible. [This is because it is the only science to apply a valid method, whereas all the others are in a state of confusion such as only geometers are well equipped to recognize.] [2]

This true method, if it could be applied, would enable us to construct demonstrations of a very exceptional value, for it would in the main be governed by two rules; it would use no expression of which the sense had not been clearly explained in advance; and it would never offer a proposition which could not be demonstrated from truths already known; in a word, that is, all its terms would be defined, and all its propositions would be capable of proof. I must however proceed in the same order as the art I am explaining, and I must therefore declare what I mean by "definition."

Geometers recognize only the kind of definition they call "nominal": and names are only given to things clearly

[2] The long passage in brackets, though contained in Ms. Périer, was omitted by Desmolets and later editors.

defined in terms perfectly known. It is of these only that I speak.

The use and application of such terms is, to render discourse intelligible and concise, by allocating a single meaning to a thing, and so signifying something that could only otherwise be indicated by using a plurality of words. Our terminology must however be so explicit that the name imposed can have no other signification; or, if it had others, these will be discarded, and the name will henceforth retain only its own special meaning. For example, if we wish to distinguish the numbers divisible by two, i.e., into two equal parts, from those which are not, the frequent repetition of the condition is avoided by drawing up a definition, as follows: Any number divisible by two, i.e., into two equal parts, shall be called an "even number."

Here we have a geometrical definition: for we first clearly designate a thing, in this case any number divisible into two equal parts; and we then proceed to give it a name from which every other possible meaning, if there ever were any such, has been evacuated, so as to bestow on it that of the thing indicated.

Whence it appears that definitions of this type are entirely arbitrary and ought never to be called in question. For a speaker is perfectly free to give any name he chooses to a particular object that is clearly indicated. He has only to take care that his liberty to bestow the name is not abused by giving the same name to two different things.

And even such definition would be permissible, provided the significations of the things so defined be not confounded, or extended from the one to the other.

But if anyone should fall into this vice, a very reliable and quite infallible remedy may be applied: this is, the mental substitution of the definition for the thing defined, the definition itself being kept always in view; so that when a man speaks, for example, of an even number, he understands precisely such number as is divisible into two equal parts; and the two things, the definition and the thing defined, should be so inseparably associated in his thought, that whenever either is mentioned, the other immediately comes to mind.

For geometers, like all methodical workers, attach names to things only in order to simplify description, and not to reduce the content or to change the idea or the character of the things they discuss; and they claim that a definition should always be short, since the mind will always supply the complete definition [i.e., the attributes, the genus, and specific difference] of a short statement, which they use only to avoid the confusion that may arise from superfluous words.

Nothing more promptly, nor more effectively, disposes of the objections of the captious sophist, than this method of definition, which should always be present to the mind, and is of itself sufficient to dispose of all kinds of difficulties and equivocations.

These things being well understood, I return to the explanation of the true order, which is, as I have said, to define all the terms enumerated in each proposition, and then to prove each proposition in turn.

Such a procedure would undoubtedly be very fine, but it is absolutely impossible: for it is clear that the first terms to be defined would depend upon other terms essential to their explanation, and these upon yet others, until we arrive at first principles, which defy definition; and which are so clear that no other principle can be found which will add anything to our knowledge of them.

Whence it appears that men are by nature powerless, and unchangeably so, to deal with any of the sciences in a final and unchangeable order.

But it does not follow from this that all systems of order have to be abandoned.

For there is one such system which is less esteemed, not because it is less certain but because it is less convincing. This is the method of geometry. It neither defines nor proves all the things that are, and for this reason it fails to convince, and yields pride of place to other sciences; but it assumes nothing but what is clear and constant and according to the light of nature, and for this reason it is perfectly reliable.

Where learning is reduced to silence, Nature herself will lend support. This order is the most perfect known to man, and it does not consist in defining and demonstrating all things; still less, in defining and demonstrating nothing at all. It consists in keeping to a middle way, between those who refuse to define things that are clear, understandable by all men, yet proffer definitions of everything else; and those who offer no proofs of the things that all men know, but proceed to prove all the others [that they do not know]. They who undertake to define and prove all things, and they who shrink from doing so with regard to things not self-evident, are alike guilty of sinning against this method.

This is what geometry teaches to perfection. It does not define such things as space, time, movement, number, equality (or similar ideas, and they are many), because such terms indicate the things they signify in so very natural a manner to anybody who understands the language, that any explanation of them would result in obscurity rather than enlightenment.

For there is nothing more feeble than the language of those people who offer to define simple terms. What need is there, for example, to explain what one understands by the word *man*? Are we not well enough aware what we are to understand by this expression? What advantage did Plato think he gained for us, when he defined man as "a two-footed animal without feathers"? As if my own idea of him, which is innate and which I cannot express, were not more clear and more reliable than the one given me by Plato, in a description as useless as it is ridiculous: since a man does not forfeit his humanity if he loses both legs; and a cock does not become a man when stripped of its feathers.

There are people who go to extremes as absurd as this, when they include the thing defined in the definition. I do not know who defined light as "the luminous movement of luminous bodies," as though the term "luminous bodies" and "luminous movement" could be understood without the idea of "light."

It is impossible to attempt a definition of "being" without falling into this absurdity: for a word cannot be defined without beginning with the verb, "It is . . . ," whether expressed or understood. Therefore, in any definition of being we should have to begin with "It is . . . ," so that we use the word defined in the definition.

From what has been said, it is sufficiently clear that some words are not susceptible of definition; and if Nature had not supplied the deficiency by providing a parallel idea which she has made known to all men, all our expressions of that notion would be nothing but confusion; whereas we all of us do in fact use words with assurance and certitude, as though all our interpretations were perfectly free from equivocation; for Nature has herself given us without any use of words, an understanding of the meaning of them, more precise than anything our human arts have acquired for us, with all our "explanations."

It is not because all men already possess the same idea of the essences of things, that I say that definition is impossible and would be useless.

Because, for example, one such expression is "time." Who is able to define it? And why try to do so, since all men know what we mean when we speak of time, without any more precise definition? There is however considerable difference of opinion as to the essential nature of time. Some say that it is "the movement of a created thing"; others, that it is "the measure of movement," and so on. Therefore I do not say that the *nature* of these things is known to everybody; only that there is a certain appropriate relation of the name and the thing; so that when we hear the expression, "time," we all turn our thoughts to the same thing. This is enough, and it disposes of the need to find a definition for this word, although afterwards, when we want to investigate the nature of time, once we begin to think about it, differences of opinion will arise; for a [nominal] definition is only constructed to designate the thing named, and not to explain its nature.

This does not mean that we may not use the word "time" when we speak of "the movement of a created thing," for as I said above, nothing is more arbitrary than a definition.

But from this particular definition it would follow that the word "time" designates two different things: one is that which all the world understands by the expression, and which all who speak our language intend when they use it; and the other is "the movement of a created thing"; for this, according to the new definition, will be an alternative designation.

We must therefore avoid equivocation and not confound consequences: for it by no means follows from our definition that the thing understood by us when we use the word "time" is in fact "the movement of a created thing." We are perfectly free to name the two things; we are not free to say that they are as like in nature as they are in name.

Therefore, if we advance the proposition that "time is the movement of a created thing," we have to ask what is understood by this word, "time." Do we, that is to say, use the word in the ordinary sense, as understood by everybody, or do we prescind from that sense for a present purpose, in order to give it a special meaning, "the movement of a created thing"? For if we strip it of every other meaning we cannot be contradicted, and we have a free definition, in consequence of which, as I have said, we have two things bearing the same name. But if we leave the word its ordinary meaning, only declaring that it is to signify "the movement of a created thing," then anybody may contradict us. We no longer have a free definition, but a proposition which, unless it be self-evident, requires proof. We are left with a principle or an axiom, but certainly not with a definition; because our enumeration of the ideas contained in the word "time" does not require that the word signify what is understood by "the movement of a created thing." It conveys merely, that our own conception of the content of the word "time" is this supposed movement.

If I did not know how necessary it is to understand this perfectly, and how at any time, in speech either familiar or scientific, words may be used as I have described, I should not have paused to discuss the matter. But I have had some experience of this kind of confusion in argument, and it seems to me that we can scarcely have too much precision in the use of words. It is for this reason, rather than for the interest of the subject itself, that I am writing this treatise.

For how many people think they have defined "time" when they call it "the measure of movement," and yet leave it with its ordinary signification? Although in this form it is a proposition, and not a definition at all! How many, likewise, believe they have defined "movement," when they say, "movement is not simply act, nor merely potency, but the act of being in potency"? And yet if they reserve to the word "movement" its ordinary meaning (as they do), they have not offered a definition, but a proposition; and by thus confusing definitions which they call "normal" (the true, free, permissible definitions of the geometers), with those which they call "real," or of the thing (which are very strict and not free at all, but exposed to contradiction); they leave a liberty to construct this class of definition as well as the other. Thus each disputant is defining the same terms by his own method, with a freedom which is as unlawful in the one case as it is valid in the other. Thus everything is brought to a state of confusion, all order and all light are lost and the speakers lose themselves and go astray in perplexities without end.

Such a state of affairs can never occur if we follow the order of geometry. This is a formal and prudent science, and it is very careful not to offer definitions of such simple terms as space, time, movement, equality, majority, diminution, all, and some others, which everybody understands for himself. But apart from the terms mentioned, the words used are so precise and distinct, that nobody needs a dictionary for the understanding of any one of them: all its terms are perfectly intelligible, either by the light of nature or by definitions which the art of geometry itself provides.

Geometry thus avoids all those vices which may be met when using the first method [of nominal and arbitrary definition], which declares only the particular meanings required by the speaker for his immediate purpose. She follows the same principle with regard to the second method [of real definition], which defines all such propositions as are not self-evident.

When geometry encounters first principles she comes to a stand, and demands that they be accepted and agreed with, for she has nothing more clear than they, by which to prove them. Thus everything that geometry proposes is perfectly demonstrated, either by proofs or by the light of nature.

Hence, wherever this science neither defines nor demonstrates, the sole reason is that definition and demonstration are alike impossible. Nature furnishes whatever geometry does not give; and while the procedures of geometry do not provide a method which is above the ordinary reach of the human mind, yet it possesses all that men can normally need. I therefore thought it right to introduce my discourse with these explanatory remarks.

It may be thought strange that mathematics should not be able to define any of those things with which she is mainly concerned. She can offer no definition of movement, numbers, space; yet these three things are her particular study, and according to the preponderating importance of each, the inquiry takes the name of mechanics, arithmetic, or geometry, the last of these applying to either the genera or the species.

But nobody will be surprised if we remark that since this wonderful science is concerned only with the most simple ideas, the very quality which makes them suitable for study also makes them incapable of being defined; so that the absence of a definition is a perfection rather than a defect. This absence does not arise from obscurity, but on the contrary from their extreme obviousness, which is of such a nature that while geometry cannot carry conviction by demonstration, she has all the certitude that demonstration could produce. She therefore assumes that the inquirer knows what is signified by such words as movement, number, space, and without pausing for superfluous definition, she penetrates into their nature, and discovers their marvelous attributes.

These three things [movement, number, and space] comprise the whole of the universe, in accordance with what is said in Wisdom 11:20b, "But by measure and number and weight has God ordered all things"; and they have an inherent, reciprocal, and necessary relation. For we cannot imagine movement without something that moves; and this thing being one, this unit is the origin of all numbers; and since movement cannot take place without space, we see that these three things are included in the first.

Time itself is also comprised in it, for movement and time are relative to one another: speed and slowness describe different modes of movement, and they each have a necessary relation to time.

Thus there are certain properties common to all things, and the knowledge of these opens the mind to the greatest marvels in Nature.

The chief of these is a twofold infinity, comprising those two infinities which find in all created things a point of contact: the infinitely great, and the infinitely small.[3]

For however swift a movement may be, it is possible to imagine one yet faster, and then to make this faster movement faster still; and so on to infinity, without ever arriving at a speed so great that nothing faster could possibly be imagined. And on the other hand, however slow a movement may be, it may always be retarded a little, and then again a little, and so on, to infinity, without ever arriving at a rate of travel so slow, that one could not reduce it by an infinity of slower speeds [before] coming to rest.

[3] We now come to a meditation of closely reasoned and difficult complexity, in which Pascal enunciates one of the great central themes of the *Apology*. These ideas are basic to his beliefs as to the nature, dignity, and destiny of man.

Similarly, however large a number may be, it is possible to imagine a larger one, and yet another which is larger still; and so on, to infinity, without ever arriving at a number so large that nothing can be added to it. And on the other hand, however small a number may be, a hundredth, or a ten-thousandth part, it is possible to imagine one smaller still without arriving at zero or the void.

Again, however vast a space may be, it is possible to imagine one yet more vast, and others again that are vaster still; and so on, to infinity, without ever arriving at one to which nothing can be added. And on the other hand, however small a space may be, we may always envisage one smaller still, and so on, to infinity, and we shall never arrive at an "indivisible," at that which no longer possesses the attribute of extension.

Similarly, with the concept of time, it is always possible to imagine a period of time ever longer, without any stop, and an interval ever shorter, without ever arriving at the last single instant, or an absolute-zero duration.

This means, in one word, that however swift the movement, however great the conceivable number, space, or interval of time, there is always another that is yet greater and one still smaller, and all are sustained in the intermediate between the void and the infinite, and are at all times infinitely distant from both extremes.

Not all of these truths can be demonstrated, and yet they provide the basic principles in geometry. But the reason which makes it impossible to demonstrate them is not their obscurity: on the contrary, it is their extraordinary obviousness; so that the absence of proof, so far from being a defect, is actually a perfection.

Whence we see that geometry can neither define things or prove principles—for one reason only, and it is one which confers an advantage: that both are set by it in a natural light of extraordinary clarity, which convinces the reason more persuasively than argument.

For what can be more obvious than the truth that a given number may be increased, whatever its magnitude? Can we not double it? That the speed of a movement may be doubled, or that a space may similarly be doubled?

And who can doubt that any number whatsoever can be divided by two, and each of these two halves by two again? And would each half be zero, or the void? For how could two halves each be zero; and yet be added together to make a number?

In the same way, let a movement be never so slow, can it not be decelerated to half-speed, so that it takes twice the time to cover the same distance, how is it possible that two such half-speeds [when each is at last reduced to a state of rest], should add up to the original speed?

Similarly, a space may be as small as you will, but you can always divide it in two, and then divide each half again. How can we say that each such half could ever be indivisible and without extension—since the same parts, before they were divided, made up the original extension?

There is nothing whatever in the knowledge natural to man which anticipates these ideas, or which surpasses them in clarity. And yet there are some minds—excellent in other respects—who demand proofs for everything, and are shocked by this doctrine of infinities; they cannot bring themselves to consent to it on any condition.

I have never known anybody who believed that a space could not be further extended. But I have met a few—and very clever men they were, in other respects—who have assured me that a space could be divided into halves, each indivisible, and they were unable to see the absurdity of it.

I went to some trouble to find out what might be the cause of the "blind spot" in these men, and I discovered that the principal reason was that they were quite unable to conceive of an infinitely divisible continuum: whence they concluded that the continuum is not divisible at all!

It is a disorder natural to man, that he should believe himself capable of the direct apprehension of the truth; whence it arises that he always tends to deny anything that he himself finds incomprehensible; whereas the fact is, that all his direct apprehensions are falsifications, and he ought only to accept as true those things of which the contraries are evidently false.

This is why, whenever a proposition is inconceivable, judgment should be suspended: the thing ought not to be denied for the reason, and only for the reason, that it is inconceivable. Let the contrary be examined: if it be manifestly false, the original proposition may be boldly affirmed, incomprehensible though it be. Let us apply this rule to our present subject.

There is no geometer anywhere who does not believe that

space can be divided and subdivided an infinite number of times. Moreover, unless he holds this doctrine he cannot be a geometer, any more than a man can be a man without a soul.

And yet, not one of these geometers understands division to infinity. Indeed, we possess our assurance of this truth by reason of one argument only—but it is certainly sufficient: we perfectly comprehend the absurdity of maintaining that by division and subdivision of a space, we arrive at last at an "indivisible," that is, at that which has no extension in space.

For what can be more absurd than to maintain that by dividing and subdividing a space we may arrive at the finality of division, so that when we make this last division into two, each of the resulting halves is not further divisible, each is without extension; and further, that these two "nothings" can be added together to make a "something" which has extension? For I would like to ask those who hold this doctrine, whether they do indeed believe in contact between two indivisibles? If the contact is between surfaces, the two things make one whole, and taken together they make one indivisible; if not between surfaces, then at one point only. Therefore each half has parts, and neither is an indivisible.

But let them confess, as they do when you press them, that their own proposition is as inconceivable as the other; let them recognize that it is not by our own capacity for conceiving such things that we ought to judge of their truth, since these two contraries are alike inconceivable; it is nevertheless of necessity certain that one of them is true.

Now with these imaginary difficulties, which are no more than a consequence of the frailty of human nature, let them compare these lights of nature and these solid truths: if it were true that space were composed of a certain finite number of indivisibles, it would follow that of two such spaces, each being a square having its opposed sides equal and parallel and one twice the size of the other, the larger would contain twice as many indivisibles as the smaller. Let them bear this necessary consequence carefully in mind, and then let them arrange a number of points [indivisibles] into squares, until they have constructed two squares, of which one contains exactly twice as many points [indivisibles] as the other: I will then call upon all the other geometers in the world to declare them masters. But if the thing is of its nature impossible, if, that is, it is impossible to arrange points into squares in such a way that one square shall be twice the area of the other (as it is, and as I could demonstrate here and now if the demonstration were worth stopping for), let them draw the obvious consequences.

And by way of consolation for all the trouble they would be put to in certain challenges, such as the concept of a space having an infinity of divisibles, seeing that such spaces can be traversed in so short a time, during which time the said infinity of divisibles would have been traversed, we must point out to them that it is not permissible to compare things that are not comparable. They may not compare such heterogeneous things as an infinity of divisibles and the brief interval of time required to pass through them. Let them rather compare the whole of space with the whole of time, and the infinity of divisibles in that space with the infinite moments of that time, and then they will find that they pass through an infinity of divisibles in an infinity of moments, and a small space in a short time, and in this proposition there no longer exists the disproportion which formerly perplexed them.

Again, if they find it strange that a small space should have as many parts as a large one, let them also understand that they are smaller in proportion; and let them look at the heavens through a small lens, to make themselves familiar with the fact that a vast area of the skies can be seen through each sector of the lens.

But if they are still unable to comprehend the fact that bodies, so small as to be imperceptible to the eye, can be subdivided like the firmament, there is no better way to cure them than to show them such a body through the microscope, which will enlarge the delicate organism into a picture of some size; and then let them see that by adding another lens ground to another curvature, the specimen can be enlarged almost indefinitely, until it is equivalent to the very expanse of the firmament that stirred their wonder. They will now agree that those objects must be very easily divisible; and let them remember that Nature can do infinitely more than art.

For after all, who has guaranteed to them that the lenses changed the natural dimensions of the specimens? May they not have restored the actual size, which their own human eyes had altered and compressed, as reducing glasses do?

It is a nuisance to have to stop for such trifles; but "there is a time to cast away."

It is sufficient to tell people who understand such matters that with reference to space, for example, you may multiply two zeros as often as you please, but they will never make unity, or one space. But there are certain other folk who try to evade the light by a marvelous answer: it is as easy, they say, to combine two indivisible or zero spaces into one space, as it is to produce unity out of two other units, neither of these being a number. You have to answer such an objection by pointing out that they might as well call a mob of twenty thousand men an army, though not a man of them be armed; that a thousand houses make a city, though not one house is itself a city; that parts make a whole, though no part is the whole; or, to stick to the comparison of numbers, that two binaries make one quaternary, and ten tens a hundred—though neither is true.

But an exact mind will not use comparisons so inaccurate that they confuse the unchanging nature of a thing with its optional and arbitrary name, which depends upon the caprice of the man who invents and bestows it. It is clear that discourse is made easy by calling twenty thousand men "an army," and a number of houses "a town," and ten units, "half-a-score"; also that this freedom of nomenclature gave rise to such expressions as "unit," "two-figure number," "four-figure number," "tens," and "hundreds"; and that these terms will vary in content according to our imaginative use of them, although they are actually of the same genus and do not vary as to their nature, for they are all in proportion to one another, differing only more or less; and although (since the various terms have been given a meaning), a binary is not a quaternary, nor a house a city, nor a city a house. But although a house is not a city, it is all the same a kind of miniature of a city, and there is a vast difference between not being a thing and being a miniature thing.

If a thorough understanding of this subject is to be acquired, it is essential to bear in mind the reason for which unity is not ranked among the numbers. Euclid, and all the early writers on arithmetic, had to apportion certain properties which were appropriate to every number except unity; and it was desirable to avoid the tiresome repetition that such and such condition "is found in all the numbers with the exception of unity." They therefore excluded the unit from the connotation of the word "number," taking advantage of the liberty I have already mentioned, that a nominal definition is arbitrary, and is constructed for present purposes, to declare the special sense in which the writer proposes to use the word. Thus, had they so desired, they could have excluded from the signification of "number" the binaries and tertiaries also, along with any others they desired, entirely at will, as suited their purpose in writing. For such definition is a matter of choice, provided the writer declare his meaning and adhere to it. Observe that the unit itself, and even fractions, may at need be brought into the numerical series. Indeed, a general proposition requires this, for the avoiding of such prolixity as, "in any number, and also in the unit and in fractions, such as property . . . ." And it is in this indefinite generalized sense that I have used it in all that I have written on the subject.

Euclid deprived the unit of the name of "number." This was permissible. But the same writer sought to show that the unit is, all the same, not zero, but belongs to the same order as number; and he thus defines the homogeneous numbers: "Numbers are said to belong to the same order, where if one of them be several times multiplied, the total is in excess of the other number." Since the unit may be multiplied indefinitely, and may therefore yield a result in excess of any other number, it follows that the unit belongs to the order of number precisely because of its essential and unvarying nature. This agrees with the meaning intended by Euclid himself, the very authority who tried to avoid calling unity a number.

This argument does not apply, however, to the language used of indivisibles in the context of space. For it differs not only in name, which is arbitrary, but also in category by its very definition; for you may multiply an indivisible as many times as you will, and it will never be comparable with any space, for it can never amount to anything but a single isolated indivisible; which follows of necessity from its nature, as I have already shown. Since this final proof is based upon the definition of the two things, "indivisible" and "space," we proceed to complete and perfect our demonstration.

An indivisible is that which has no parts; a space is that which comprises various separated parts.

According to these definitions, I say that two indivisibles, though united, can never form a space.

For when they are united, the two indivisibles are in contact at one part only: therefore those parts at which they touch are not separated, for if they were so, they would not touch. Now, by definition they have no other parts; therefore they have no separated parts; therefore they do not make a space, which is by definition composed of separated parts.

We could proceed to demonstrate the same consequence in respect of all such indivisibles as might be added to the list, and by the same reasoning. An indivisible, though it be multiplied any number of times, can never form a space. For the two things belong by definition to different orders.

In this way we demonstrate that indivisibles are not in the same order as numbers. By the same argument, two units may certainly make one number, because the unit and the number belong to the same order, but two indivisibles cannot form a space, because indivisibles and space differ in kind.

We see therefore that it is not reasonable to compare the relation of unit and number with the relation of indivisibles and space.

But if we wish to select a standard of comparison for the order of number, which accurately corresponds with the relation of the indivisibles of space, this will have to be the relation of zero to number. Zero is not in the same order as number, because though it be multiplied, the product is not a larger number. Thus zero is a true indivisible of number, just as the indivisible is the true zero of extension. We shall find the same to be true of rest and motion, instants and time: all these pairs of things are heterogeneous as to their magnitudes, for you may multiply them to infinity, but they will never form anything but indivisibles, and for the same reason. We thus discover a perfection of correspondence between these things, for all these magnitudes are divisible to infinity, yet they never become indivisible; so that they all occupy all that is intermediate between the infinite and the void.

Observe then the admirable relation which Nature has established between these things, and the two marvelous infinites which she offers to men, not that they may be comprehended, but that they may be admired. And we conclude our consideration with one last remark, that these two infinites, though infinitely different, are none the less relative the one to the other, so that a knowledge of the one leads of necessity to a knowledge of the other.

For in the case of these numbers, from the fact that they can be augmented to infinity, it follows unconditionally that they can also be divided to infinity. This is perfectly clear. Because if, for example, we can multiply a number up to 100,000 times, it is just as easy to take the 100,000th part of it, dividing by the same number as we used to multiply; so that each term of multiplication will also become a term of division, changing the whole number into a fraction. Therefore multiplication to infinity necessarily involves division to infinity.

The same relation between these two opposed infinites is observed with respect to space: for if a space may be extended to infinity, it follows that it may also be diminished to infinity, as appears from the following example: If we look through a telescope at a ship which is moving away from us at a uniform speed, it is clear that the point on the lens at which we observe a given element of the ship will also rise at a uniform rate as the vessel recedes. Therefore, suppose the ship to pursue its course to infinity, the said point on the lens will also rise to infinity; yet it will never rise to such a point that the horizontal ray of light between the eye and the lens is interrupted so as never to reach the lens, penetrating forever the space below the line of vision, yet never seeing the thing at which it is looking. We see then the consequence which follows of necessity from the fact that the ship sails on to infinity: a finite space below the line of vision, an infinity of division, and an infinity of divisibles.

They who are not satisfied with this reasoning, and who persist in the belief that space cannot be infinitely divided, need not claim that they are capable of carrying out a geometrical demonstration; and although they may be enlightened about other matters, they know little enough about this one. For it is not difficult to be a man of considerable ability, and yet a very poor geometer.

Those who clearly perceive these truths will be able to marvel at the majesty and the power of Nature, as shown in this twofold infinity which surrounds us upon every side; and through contemplation of this wonder they will learn to know themselves, and see themselves placed between the infinite and the void in space and number, movement and time. The realization will teach them to estimate themselves at their true value, and will give rise to meditations worth more than the entire system of geometry.

I have thought myself obliged to make this lengthy disquisition, for the sake of those who, although they may not at first understand this doctrine of the two infinites, are capable of being persuaded of it. And although some few of them may already be sufficiently enlightened to do without it, it may well be found that this discourse is necessary to the one class, and not entirely without value to the other.

Section II

THE ART OF PERSUADING

The art of persuading, of making argument acceptable as well as convincing, has a necessary relation to the way in which men assent to propositions, and to such conditions as may be annexed to those things we would have them believe.

Everybody knows that an opinion may be received by the mind in one of two ways: by way of the understanding, and by way of the will; and that these are the principal faculties of the mind. The more natural of these ways is that of the understanding, for we ought never to assent to any but demonstrated truths. The more usual way, however, though contrary to nature, is that of the will; for most men are brought to believe, not because the thing is proved, but because it pleases.

This motive for belief is, however, commonly regarded as superficial, undignified, and strange; wherefore all the world disclaims it. Each of us professes that he will only believe what merits belief, and only love what deserves to be loved.

I am not now speaking of divine truths, which I take care not to classify with those of which men need to be persuaded; for they are infinitely beyond the reach of unassisted nature: God alone can plant these in the soul, and He does it by such means as are pleasing to Himself.

I know that God has seen fit to ordain that truths should pass into the mind from the heart, and not into the heart from the mind; and this He willed, first, to humble man's proud reason, which claims that it must be the judge of such things as his own will shall choose; and secondly, to heal the weakness of the human will, which is always corrupting itself by filthy attachments.

It is for these reasons that we who speak of the affairs of men, say that we have to know men before we can love them: and the saying has passed into a proverb; whereas persons who have some knowledge of holy things are accustomed to declare that supernatural truths can be understood only by those who love them, and that we do not enter into the truth save by charity. This is one of the most fruitful of all their judgments.

From this it is clear that there is supernatural order ordained by God with respect to the truths of the faith; and that this is directly contrary to the order which is to be observed by men with regard to the truths of science and the natural world. Men have, however, corrupted the order ordained by God by making holy things serve profane uses; since we in fact believe scarcely anything but what pleases us. This is why we withhold assent to the truths of the Christian religion, for these are in opposition to our pleasures. "Tell us the things that please us, and we will hear thee," said the Jews to Moses, as though it were the being pleased with it should determine belief! God punished such disorder by imposing order, in conformity with His own being; by the same argument, He does not shed light into rebellious minds until the rebel will has been subdued; and that stubborn will is brought into subjection by an infused sweetness which is entirely of Heaven, pleasing the will and attracting it to Himself.

I shall speak then only of such truths as are within our human reach. And concerning these I say that the mind and heart are as doors by which they are received into the soul; but that few enter by way of the mind, whereas they are admitted in crowds by the capricious temerity of the will whenever it acts without counsel from the reason.

Each of the powers [of the mind and will] has its principle, which is the prime mover of its acts.

The principles which move the mind are the first principles, and these are known to all; for example, that the whole is greater than its part, with a few other axioms which are accepted by some but not by all; but which once admitted may—although they may often be false—be as powerful persuaders of belief as the most profound truths.

The principles that move the will are certain natural desires which are common to all men, such as the desire for happiness, which is normal in us all; together with a number of particular objects of desire, pursued by men that they may achieve their personal aims. These objects are all of them pleasing to the will, despite the possibility that to attain them may actually be harmful, so that they are able to move the will as powerfully and as effectively as they could if they constituted its true happiness.

So much for the principles which induce the consent of the will.

But what of the qualities by which it ought to be persuaded? For these are of a very different kind.

Some are derived from first principles and accepted truths, following from them of necessity. First principles are infallibly persuasive; for we have only to show their relation with a truth that has been conceded, and it follows of necessity that our opponent will be convinced.

For once we have shown their connection with a truth already accepted, he can no longer refuse to receive such principles into his mind.

Some of the things that persuade us are closely connected with particular objects of desire; these also are accepted with certitude; for from the moment the mind perceives that a given thing will bring it to possession of an object supremely desired, it will inevitably advance toward that thing with joy.

But sometimes the things that persuade us do so by a twofold attraction: that they follow from an undoubted truth, and that they satisfy a supreme desire; and then their effect is the most certain thing in Nature.

On the other hand, whatever does not correspond with either our beliefs or our pleasures, is inopportune, false, and completely alien to us.

There is no room for doubt about any of the foregoing

arguments. But the case is very different where the things of which we seek to convince people, while they are unquestionably based upon accepted truths, are also opposed to those pleasures in which they are most willing to indulge. And it is only too common an experience, that this indulgence and these pleasures expose us to a great peril that, as I said at the beginning, this imperious soul, though it boasted of acting only according to reason, makes a rash and shameful choice, and follows the desires of a corrupt will, in defiance of the arguments opposed to that will by an enlightened mind.

At this point a precarious balance is struck between the truth and the indulgence: knowledge of the one, and an inclination toward the other precipitate a conflict of which the outcome is most uncertain; for the result could not be predicted without an intimate knowledge of all that passes in the secret places of the heart—and of these things the man himself is scarcely ever conscious.

From what has been said, it is probable that, whatever the truth may be of which we wish to persuade, we must observe the person we have in view; we must know his mind and heart, the principles he accepts, the things he loves; we must then inquire whether the truth in question has any affinity with those principles of his, or with those things that he naturally loves the more as they give him more pleasure. Thus the art of persuading consists as much in pleasing as in carrying conviction, so much are men inclined to be governed by caprice rather than by reason.

Now of these two methods, the one of convincing, the other of pleasing, I shall here give the rules only of the first, on the assumption that we have accepted the principles and remain firm in holding them; otherwise I do not know whether any art exists that could accommodate the proofs to our capricious inconstancy.

For the method of pleasing is incomparably more difficult: it is more subtle, more useful, and more admirable, and if I do not discuss it, this is because I am not capable of doing so. And so strongly do I feel that such a task is beyond my capacity, that I believe the thing to be absolutely impossible.

Not that I do not believe that there may be rules for pleasing which are as reliable as those for demonstrating; and that anyone who had a perfect knowledge of both arts, and could practice them both, would as surely make himself beloved by kings and by all manner of folk, as he would by demonstrating the elements of geometry to anybody who had enough imagination to understand the hypotheses of that science.

But I am of the opinion (and perhaps it is my weakness that makes me think so), that it is impossible to formulate and practice the rules for pleasing. At any rate I know that if indeed there be anyone capable of doing so, they are certain persons known to myself, and nobody else has such clear and enlightened ideas on the subject.

The reason for the extraordinary difficulty of the thing is this; that the principles that determine the being pleased are not fixed and stable. They differ for every man, and they vary for each individual with such diversity that there is scarcely a greater difference between one man and another than there is in the same person at different times. A man's pleasures are not those of a woman; the rich and the poor amuse themselves in different ways; a prince, a soldier, a merchant, a citizen, a peasant, the aged and the young, the whole and the sick, all of these have their differing opinions of what constitutes pleasure; and the slightest accident will change their point of view.

Now there is one art, and it is this that I propose to discuss, for making clear the connection of truths with their principles, whether in relation to what is true or to what is pleasing; always provided that the principles, once accepted, remain unchanged and stable, and are never put out of mind.

But there are very few principles of this kind. Apart from the principles of geometry, which apply only to very simple figures, there are scarcely any truths which men would accept as applying at all times and to all people; and there are still fewer pleasures in this class, for concerning pleasure our notions change from one hour to the next. I cannot say whether there is any way of formulating strict rules for adapting discussion to the inconstancy of human caprice.

This art, which I call "the art of persuading" is nothing more, strictly speaking, than the methodical carrying through to their conclusion of a complete set of satisfactory proofs. It comprises three essential parts: the clear definition of all the terms employed; to propose only self-evident principles (axioms) to prove the matter in hand; always to substitute mentally in the demonstration, the definitions for the things defined.

The reasons for the method are obvious: for it would be useless to advance a proposition and offer to prove it, unless all such terms as are not intelligible are first clearly defined. It is also necessary that any demonstration be preceded by supplying the self-evident principles that are implied, for if we cannot guarantee the foundation it is scarcely possible to guarantee the building. Finally, the mental substitution of the definition for the thing defined avoids ambiguity in the use of terms, which may have different meanings according to the context. It is easy to see that if we use such a method we are certain to convince our opponent, since when we have defined our terms they are understood, and entirely free from equivocation; and if all the principles are agreed, we have only to apply our third rule, consistently making a mental substitution of the definition for the thing defined, and the invincible force of the conclusion cannot but have its full effect.

An argument conducted according to these rules can never be subject to the slightest doubt; whereas one in which they are either wanting or misapplied can never carry any weight.

It is very important therefore to understand the reasons for the rules and to have a good grasp of how to apply them. I will therefore summarize the three sets of rules, so as to cover all that is necessary in a perfect definition, a perfect axiom, a perfect demonstration; and consequently in a perfect complete procedure using geometrical proofs in the art of persuading.

The rules for definition: 1. Never undertake to define a thing which is in itself so well known that no unambiguous terms are available in which to explain it. 2. Never admit any term in the slightest degree obscure or ambiguous, without providing a definition. 3. Never employ in any definition any but well-known words, or words already explained.

The rules for framing axioms: 1. Never admit any of the requisite principles, without first securing general agreement, however clear and self-evident the principles may be. 2. Never lay down as an axiom anything that is not immediately self-evident.

The rules for demonstration: 1. Never undertake to demonstrate a thing self-evident, and requiring no elucidation by way of proof. 2. Prove every proposition that is in the least obscure, and use for such proof only very obvious axioms, or propositions already agreed upon or demonstrated. 3. Always substitute mentally the definition for the thing defined, so as not to deceive by equivocation in the use of terms having a restricted meaning.

These eight rules contain the precepts for arriving at well-founded and unshakeable proofs. Of these rules there are three which are not absolutely necessary, and we may neglect them without fear of error; since it is difficult, even at times impossible, to observe them strictly, though it would be better to observe them wherever possible. The three which may be neglected are the first in each group: For definitions, 1. Never to define a term the meaning of which is well known; For exioms, 1. Never to use an axiom without prior agreement; For demonstrations, 1. Never proceed to demonstrate any thing self-evident.

For clearly there is no grave fault in defining and explaining anything, even though it is already familiar; nor in securing prior agreement to the use of axioms which nobody would think of rejecting; nor in proving propositions which would be accepted without proof.

But the five rules remaining are absolutely necessary, and they may not be dispensed with, or the result will be an argument defective in an essential point, and frequently there will be actual error. For this reason I now return to the remaining rules, and will discuss them in detail.

The necessary rules for definition. Never to admit any term in the slightest degree ambiguous or obscure, without a definition. Never to employ in any definition, any but well-known words, or words already explained.

The necessary rule for axioms. Never to employ in an axiom any term not self-evident.

The necessary rules for demonstration. Prove every proposition, and prove it by very obvious axioms, or by propositions already agreed upon and demonstrated. Never attempt to deceive by equivocation, by omitting the mental substitution of the definition for the thing defined, since such definitions are explanatory or limiting.

These five rules provide all that is necessary to render proofs convincing, unshakeable and, in a word, geometrical. And if all eight rules are applied, the method will indeed be perfect.

I now pass to the question of the order in which propositions should be arranged if they are to be in the best, that is, the geometrical, order. . . .

This then is the method in the art of persuading, and we may summarize it in two rules: Define every term that is to be used; and, prove every proposition, making mental substitution of the definition for the thing defined.

At this point it seems but proper to forestall three major objections that might be made to this method. The first of these is that it contains nothing new.

Another objection: That it is easily learnt, and that there is no need to study the elements of geometry for the purpose of argument, since the proposed method consists of the said two rules, and these are perfectly known at a first reading.

And finally: That the method is in any case of limited value, since its employment is in practice limited to such matters as can be discussed in terms of geometry.

As to which objections we have to show, that scarcely anything is so little known as this method, so difficult to put into practice; and that nothing is more useful, nothing more general in its application.

As to the first objection, that the rules are already common, and well known to everybody; that of course everything has to be defined and proved, and that logicians have themselves accepted these rules into their art. I certainly wish these claims were true, that the rules of this system were indeed well known, and that I need never have gone to so much trouble to trace to its source all the false reasoning that is heard in the world, and which is certainly common enough. But so far is this objection from being true, that with the single exception of geometers—who are so few in numbers that they appear but rarely in any nation, and when they do appear they stand out as giants among their people—we never meet anybody who in fact accepts these rules as common knowledge. It will be a simple matter to make the art understood by all who have perfectly followed my line of reasoning thus far; but if they have not understood it perfectly, I assure you they will learn nothing at all from it.

But if they have entered into the spirit of these rules, and if the rules have made sufficient impression, taken root and begun to grow, they will sense the difference there is between what is said here and the rash statements of which logicians are occasionally guilty in their writings.

Those who possess a discerning mind know how much difference there may be between two similar words, according to the place and the circumstances in which they are used. Will anyone believe, for example, that two persons who have read the same book and learnt it by heart are equally familiar with it, if the one comprehends it in such a way that he understands all its principles, realizes the force of all its consequences, has answers to all the objections that can be brought against it, and is conversant with it as a whole; whereas in the mind of the other it is but dead words, and the seed sown there, although resembling that which has elsewhere produced some very noble trees, has remained dry and infertile in that sterile mind, in which it was sown in vain?

Not all men who say the same things understand them in the same way. This is why the incomparable author of *L'art de conférer* is so careful to stop short of implying that man's understanding is to be assessed on the basis of some quip he has been heard to utter. We may admire readiness of speech, but instead of extending that admiration to the person who displays it, let us (says our author) penetrate into the mind whence that speech comes: let us inquire whether it is something he has memorized, or whether it was a happy accident. Let us receive the speaker with coolness and scorn, and see whether he resents it when we do not give to his saying the esteem that its polish seems to deserve. We shall generally find that he instantly withdraws whatever it was he said; and he will allow himself to be drawn far beyond the range of his thought—which was better than he knew—and will recast it in a form quite vulgar and ridiculous. We must then probe how deep the thought was lodged within its author; how and by what means he came by it; and how far he has made it his own. And if he proves unable to defend it, his precipitate utterance will be pronounced a rash one.

I would like to ask any fair-minded person whether the principles that "Matter is of its nature incapable of thought," and "I think, therefore I am," have in fact precisely the same meaning in the mind of Descartes as they have in that of Saint Augustine, who said the same thing twelve hundred years before his time?

I am indeed very far from saying that Descartes was not the true author of these principles, even though he only grasped their meaning through his reading of that great Saint. For I know what a world of difference there is between the casual writing of a word without bestowing upon it any prolonged or analytical thought; and the perception in that word of a marvelous sequence of consequences demonstrating that the physical world and the world of spiritual things are distinct; and then deriving from his demonstration a well-grounded and reliable principle as a firm basis for a complete system of physical knowledge, as Descartes claims to have done. I need not inquire whether he did in fact succeed in his enterprise, but will assume that he did so; and I say that this expression, as used by him, is as different in meaning to that which it bears in other authors who have chanced to mention it, as is a living man in good health and full of vigor, to a dead man.

One such man will repeat a thing mechanically, paying no attention to the nobility of the thought; while the other will discern the wonderful succession of consequences following from it. So that we might be pardoned for boldly saying that it was no longer the same word that was being used, that he did not owe it to the author whom he cites as his source, that a splendid tree is not the handiwork of the woodman who, without much thought and no knowledge of forestry, planted it in a good, deep soil, where the tree simply grew as it did because it had a good, healthy root.

The same thoughts will at times reproduce themselves quite differently in a mind that is not their author's: though sterile on their native soil, they flourish abundantly when transplanted.

But it happens much more often that a man with a well-ordered mind can develop from his own thoughts all the fruit of which those thoughts are capable; and that then other people, having heard him commended, borrow those thoughts and adopt them for their own without acknowledging their worth; and it is then, when the same expression is expounded by different minds, that the differences in the power of comprehension are most clearly seen.

Perhaps this has been the method of logicians who have borrowed the rules of geometry without an understanding of the rigorous method of that art. It by no means follows that when they incorporate the rules of geometry into their own system, they have acquired a knowledge of geometrical method. And I am very much mistaken if they have not added somewhat to the rules of geometry, though without indicating that they have done so, to show that they know how to apply this science, which teaches the true method of guiding the intelligence.

My own wish, however, would be to exclude such people from our discussion once and for all. For to make a statement casually, without consideration of all that is involved in it; failure to discern the principle and follow it to its conclusion, getting side-tracked and lost in futile investigations, and mistaking the illusory results of their efforts for finding the truth, which such inquiries cannot yield—these considerations show plainly enough that such people are lacking in insight, and (still more plainly) that they failed to follow the argument to its conclusion because they did not understand it.

The whole world is in search of a method of reasoning that does not go astray. Logicians claim that they have such a method: but only geometers have in fact perfected it, and outside of their art (and others based upon it), there is no such thing as an infallible demonstration. The whole of the art is summarized in the few rules that I have given: they are sufficient, they are all that is required, and they alone provide infallible proof. All other rules are either superfluous or liable to error.

This is something I know from a long experience of books and people of every description.

This experience has given me a similar opinion of those who say that these rules of the geometers tell us nothing that is new, since in effect (say they) we have always known them, but they have been obscured by a multitude of other rules, useless or erroneous, from which it was impossible to distinguish them. They are like men looking for a real diamond in a heap of synthetic ones, all of which are good imitations. They cannot pick out the genuine stone, and so they console themselves with boasting that they virtually possess it—it is here somewhere, here in this heap of artificial stones. But their challenger can laugh at them, for he holds in the hollow of his hand the stone they are looking for—and they refuse to throw away the trash, although if they did so, they might discover the true stone.

The defects in a chain of false reasoning are due to disorder, and the condition may be remedied by our two rules. Other cures for it have been devised, but the mixture is always compounded of quantities of noxious herbs which smother the healing ones, and the harmful elements in the mixture neutralize the effects of the good ones.

Logicians have endeavored to meet sophistry and ambiguity in reasoning by inventing a terminology full of barbarous names which cause dismay in all who hear them; and instead of making it easy to unravel the twists in this perplexing web of knots, by simply pulling on one of the ends marked for them by the geometers, they have attached their own labels to a surprising number of other ends as well as the geometrical ones, and now they cannot tell how to identify the good end which provides the answer.

Thus they point out to us a number of different roads, any of which, say they, will lead us to the place we want to reach. But only two roads will in fact take us there, and we must know how to identify these two in particular. Geometry indicates them with great precision: they allege that it only teaches what it learned from others, who taught precisely the same thing, and other things besides; not observing that the old method was self-defeating through its very prolixity, and that the Ancients lost their hold when they complicated their method.

Nothing is so commonplace as what is good: the difficulty lies in discerning it. It is equally certain that all the good things are part of the order of Nature, and therefore within our reach; it may even be true that they are already known to everybody, but we are still unable to discern them. This is the case with us all. It is not in things exceptional and freakish, whatever the order, that excellence is found. We may lift ourselves up in our quest of what is good—and we find that it recedes ever further beyond our grasp: it would as a rule be better to bow down. The best books are those which the reader believes he could have written himself; and Nature, who alone is good, is altogether common and familiar.

I have not the slightest doubt therefore that these rules are the true ones, and are for that very reason simple, limpid, natural. A chain of reasoning does not depend on *barbara* and *baralipton*. There is no need to inflate the mind, which is only filled with a foolish presumption by strenuous and difficult methods. If it accepts such methods it is filled with a vain and ridiculous bombast, which swells it with wind instead of filling it with good and strengthening food.

One of the principal forces tending to discourage a man, once he has begun to acquire this knowledge of the way of truth, the road he ought to follow, is that of the imagination, which persuades him that the knowledge of the good is for him inaccessible; and he calls it by such names as great, high, elevated, and sublime. Such a belief will ruin everything. Let me rather call them basic and elementary, ordinary, familiar: these descriptions suit them better. I have a hatred of bombast. . . .

A Conversation with Monsieur de Saci

In January of 1655 Pascal decided to make a spiritual retreat of prayer and reflection at Port-Royal des Champs. Lemaistre de Saci, who served as a sort of superior to this little religious group seems to have invited Pascal to give a conference to the community. Since Saci's habit was to discuss with his retreatants on the subjects he deemed closest to their hearts, he turned Pascal's thoughts to philosophy. There ensued the admirable conversation on Epictetus and Montaigne. Pascal, who greatly admired both the Stoic and the skeptic, points out the greatness of each and their defects. The Stoic elevates man, insisting upon ethical values, underscoring the power of the human will, insisting upon submission to the will of God, detachment, and moral vigor. But experience and observation had proved to Pascal that the Stoic's noble demands were simply not possible to man left to his own devices.

Pascal then contrasts this doctrine with the skepticism of his beloved mentor, Montaigne, all too realistic, too aware of man's miseries. But Montaigne does not win his approval either. He depreciates man, with his vanity and weakness, too much for Pascal. His pessimism fails to take into account the glory of Christ's grace, as Epictetus failed to realize man's weakness without grace.

[About that time, M. Pascal also came to stay at Port-Royal des Champs. I shall not pause here to give an account of this man, who was the admiration not only of France but all of Europe. His mind was always sprightly [1] and active, of a range, a nobility, a boldness, a penetration, and precision, far exceeding that of ordinary men. There was no man learned in mathematics, who did not acknowledge him to be a master of that subject: witness his

[1] A necessary asset in any person admitted to the fashionable salons, as was Pascal at this time.

famous solution of the problem of the cycloid,[2] which was at that time the talk of mathematicians everywhere. It was common knowledge that he seemed able to animate copper, and to give to brass the power of thought.[3] Little unthinking wheels, each rimmed with the ten digits, were so arranged by him that they could render an account[4] of themselves, even to persons of considerable skill with figures; and he could in a sense make dumb machines speak, for those wheels as they revolved worked out the solutions of problems about figures which had baffled even the wisest. I have seen this machine myself, and it is the admiration of the world. Its design and development, however, cost him so much in concentration and mental effort,[5] that his own brain was as good as turned by it for more than three years.] This remarkable man was in the end touched by the hand of God, and brought under the easy yoke of Jesus Christ: that great and noble heart embraced with humility a life of penance. He came to Paris, and threw himself into the arms of M. Singlin, resolved to do whatever might be commanded.

When M. Singlin had seen this man of genius, he thought it might be a good thing to send him to Port-Royal des Champs, where M. Arnauld would be a match for him as far as the pure sciences were concerned; and where M. de Saci would teach him to despise them. He came, then, to stay at Port Royal. M. de Saci could not, without a breach of good manners, excuse himself from seeing him, especially as it was M. Singlin who had asked him to do so; but the sanctified insight which he had gained from the study of the Scriptures and the fathers, led him to hope that he would not be at all dazzled by those brilliant qualities in M. Pascal which so charmed and captivated everybody he met.

In the result, M. de Saci found that he could approve of all that was said by M. Pascal. He acknowledged with

[2] The name given to the curve described by a nail in a cartwheel in one complete revolution of the wheel. This solution makes Pascal the actual creator of integral calculus.

[3] The reference is to the brass and copper components of Pascal's celebrated arithmetical machine, which was the first computer.

[4] *Rendre raison:* to cast accounts. Pascal designed his machine to simplify his father's work as a tax collector.

[5] The assembly of the components of the machine was a matter of great difficulty for the workmen employed by Pascal, and this was another factor which brought about his illness.

pleasure the vigor of his mind and the forcefulness of his conversation. But in what he said there was nothing new: all the fine things that M. Pascal brought out, M. de Saci had already come across in Saint Augustine. Being willing therefore to do justice to all, he said: "M. Pascal is much to be commended because, although he had never read the Fathers of the Church, he had, by the penetrating power of his own mind, discovered for himself the same truths as they had found. M. Pascal said that the Fathers came to him as a surprise, for he had never seen them anywhere else; whereas we are accustomed to them, and can meet them at any time in our books." That sagacious priest had learned that the old Fathers were possessed of as much light as modern writers, and therefore he followed them; and he thought very highly of M. Pascal, because his ideas corresponded at all points with those of Saint Augustine.

When M. de Saci was talking to people, his custom was to accommodate his conversation to the tastes and pursuits of those to whom he spoke. If, for example, his visitor was M. de Champaigne, he would talk to him about painting; if he was with M. Hamon, he would turn the conversation to medicine; if he was seeing the surgeon of the place, he would ask him about points of surgery. Vine-dressers, husbandmen, those who followed the plow, would find themselves telling him the rules of their calling. All these things did but serve him as stepping-stones to God, by which he might also bring other men to Him. He therefore thought it but natural to set M. Pascal at ease by asking him about his reading in philosophy, and the authors he preferred. M. de Saci brought him round to the subject in the first conversations they had together. M. Pascal said that his favorite writers had been Epictetus and Montaigne, and he expressed a high opinion of them both. Now M. de Saci had always held that these particular authors ought to be avoided, or read but little; and he invited M. Pascal to discuss them in detail with him.

"Epictetus," said Pascal, "is a philosopher who understands better than any other, what are the duties of man. Above all, he teaches that man should regard God as his chief end; that he should firmly believe that God orders all things with justice; that he should submit to the will of God with all his heart; and that he should in all things conform himself to the divine order, because all that God does is done in wisdom. Such a disposition would put a stop to all complaint and murmuring, and would prepare the mind of man to suffer with patience all that befalls him, however unfortunate. 'Never say,' says Epictetus, 'I have lost such a thing,' but say rather, 'I have given it back: My son is dead, I have given him back. My wife is dead, I have given her back.' Similarly with possessions and all other things. 'But,' you say, 'whoever takes from me my possessions is a villain.' Now, why are you distressed as to the agent, through whom He that lent you the thing requires it of you again? For as long a time as He allows you the use of it, take care of the thing, as of something of value that belongs to another, as a traveler does in a wayside inn. You ought not, says Epictetus, to desire that the things that happen should be such as you yourself would wish: you should rather desire them to be as they are. As he says somewhere else: Bear in mind that you are here as an actor on a stage, playing a part in a comedy—any part that the producer may choose to give you. If He gives you a short part, play it short; if He gives you a long part, play it long; if He wants you to play the part of a beggar, you should do it with all the simplicity you can muster; and so on. It is your part to play well the character you have been given: to select it is the business of another. Have daily before your eyes the spectacle of death and of evils unendurable: your thinking will never then be mean, and you will desire nothing to excess.

"Epictetus has also shown me in a thousand ways what is the duty of man. He teaches that man should practice humility, that he should conceal his good resolutions, especially when he is beginning, and that he should carry them out in secret. Nothing spoils them more than display. He is never weary of repeating that all the study, all the desire of man should be to recognize the will of God, and do it.

"Here, then," said M. Pascal to M. de Saci, "we have evidence of the enlightened eminence of that great mind, which understood so well the duty of man. I venture to say that he would merit veneration, if he had been as well aware of the powerlessness of humanity: for a man would need to be divine before he could teach both truths to men. We can also see how—since Epictetus was a man, and since man is dust and ashes—the philosopher falls into presumption, despite his clear understanding of moral duty. He does so, for example, when he teaches that man is able to raise himself up to God by an act of the will; that God has endowed man with all the strength he requires to fulfill all his obligations; that the means of doing so are within man's power; that he must seek his happiness in the things that are within his reach—since God has bestowed those things on man precisely that he might be happy in the possession of them; that man must investigate for himself the limits of his own freedom; that property, life, and reputation are not within man's power, and therefore do not lead him to God; that the mind, on the other hand, can never be compelled to believe what it knows to be false, nor the will to love anything which it knows can render it unhappy; that therefore the mind and the will are free, and a man may by the right use of them attain to his own perfection as well as to a perfect knowledge of God: may love, obey, and please Him, heal himself of all his vices, acquire all the virtues, and thereby attain holiness and the divine friendship. These are the elements of satanic pride, and they lead man into yet other errors, such as, that the human soul is a part of the divine substance; that sorrow and death are not misfortunes; that a man may end his own life if persecution should become so severe that he seems justified in regarding that fact as an indication of the will of God, 'hears the voice of God calling him'; and so on.

"Coming now to Montaigne, of whom also, Sir, you wished me to say something. He was born into Christianity, and he professed the Catholic religion: thus far, he possesses no special characteristics. But he was concerned to discover what kind of morality might be dictated by a reason not enlightened by faith. He laid down certain principles, such as might be proposed by a mind knowing nothing of the doctrine of Original Sin; and assuming man to lack the light of revelation, he proceeded as follows. He reduced all things to a condition of universal doubt, a doubt so general that it is self-defeating: if he doubts, and if he doubts that he doubts, a man's incertitude necessarily turns full circle, and he will never find a state of rest. He will be at variance, not only with those for whom nothing is certain, but also with those who maintain that not everything is uncertain: for he himself is unwilling to affirm anything. This condition, of a doubt which even doubts itself, the state of ignorance which does not even know itself for what it is, and which those who profess it call their 'guiding principle,' is the essence of

Montaigne's opinion, and he was unable to express it in any more positive terms. For if he doubts that he doubts, he is himself the loser, he is false to his own principle: his doubting is the one thing of which he is certain. But since this state of affairs is contrary to his formal intention, he can only explain himself by posing a question. He does not wish to say, 'I do not know,' and so he asks, 'What do I know?' and he makes those words his device to set below his arms: a pair of scales for weighing contradictories, which are seen to balance perfectly. Montaigne, you see, is a pure skeptic, a thorough-going Pyrrhonian. All his discourses, all his *Essais,* turn upon the skeptic position, the only philosophical attitude he claims to be able to justify—although his own skepticism is not always explicitly declared. His preferred method is to erode by a gradual process all that men normally accept as certain. Nor does he do this in order to establish the certitude of the opposed position, for he is the enemy of all certitude. He does it only to show that where the arguments are of equivalent weight on either side, we cannot know what we are to believe.

"In this spirit, Montaigne mocks at all certainty. He is, for example, opposed to those who would like to see in France the application of some remedy for our interminable lawsuits, which are due to an excess of legislation, and to the claims that are made for the equity of our legal system. As though [says he] it were possible to cut out those roots of distrust in which lawsuits are born, or to erect a sort of dike to dam the floodwaters of uncertainty, or to keep the conflict of laws a prisoner! This is his reason for saying that he would as soon submit his quarrel to the first passer-by, as to judges so heavily armed with sanctions, orders, and regulations. He makes no claim that the structure of the state should be changed, his ambitions do not reach so far; nor that his own verdict would be found a better one, for he has no high opinion of it himself. He seeks only to demonstrate the vanity of received opinions, and to show that the abandonment of all law would do more to reduce the number of disputes than does our plethora of enactments, which serve only to increase litigation: for the more carefully they are weighed in the scales of justice, the heavier do our differences become. The obscurities multiply as the commentary increases; and the surest way to understand the meaning of a speech is to take it as it comes, without examination, for if it be studied but a little, all its lucidity disappears. Thus does Montaigne arrive at his own random judgment of all the actions of men, all the great events of history. He proceeds now by one method, now by another, but always following up his first impression, reserving his freedom to go where it leads him. He will not harness his thought by the rules of reasoning, which are always misleading; he is delighted when he can quote examples of self-contradiction from some philosopher. To this entirely emancipated genius it is a matter of indifference whether or not he wins an argument, for he is always able to quote some instance of the worthlessness of opinions; having gained thus much from his universal doubt, that he is as securely fortified by defeat as by victory.

"It was from such an entrenchment as this, though waterlogged and insecure, that Montaigne did battle, and with invincible resolution, against the heretics of his own time, and especially against their claim that they alone understood the true sense of the Scriptures; and, further, that he scourged with such vigor the horrid irreligion which dared to deny the existence of God. To these latter he issued a direct challenge in his *Apologie de Raymond de Sabonde*. Finding that they had voluntarily deprived themselves of the support of revelation, and were entirely dependent upon 'the light of nature,' faith being ruled out altogether, Montaigne demanded by what authority they presumed to judge the Supreme Being (Who is by definition infinite), when they themselves had no reliable understanding of anything in Nature. He asked them upon what principles they took their stand, and urged them to produce demonstrations. He examined such as they were able to bring forward, and he analyzed them with such care—an art in which he excelled—that he exposed the vanity even of those notions which pass for the most common and the best established. He inquired whether the soul is able to know anything? Whether she knows herself? Whether the soul is substance or accident, matter or spirit? What each of these expressions means, and whether there can exist anything whatsoever which does not belong to one or other of these four orders of things? Whether the soul knows the body to which she belongs? Whether she knows the nature of matter? Whether she is able to discriminate between the infinite numbers of bodies, once these begin to come into existence? How is it that, if the soul is mere matter, she is able to follow an argument? And how it is that if the soul is spirit, she can be united to one body, and to that one body only, feeling the sufferings of that body? When did the soul begin to be? With the origin of the body, or before it? Whether or no she dies when the body dies? Whether the soul can be deceived? Whether she recognizes error—seeing that the essence of error is the failure to recognize error for what it is? Whether, in the midst of all these perplexities, the soul does not tend to believe just as firmly that three and two add up to six, as she later securely knows that they make five? Whether animals can reason, think, or speak? And who has power to decide the nature of time, space, extension, movement, unity —all those familiar things which nobody can explain? And what are health and sickness, life and death, good and evil, justice and sin—ideas of which we are talking all day long? Whether we have within ourselves any of the principles of truth? And if so, whether those we accept—which are known as axioms or first principles or common notions, and are held by all men—are in conformity with essential truth? And since it is by faith alone that we believe in a Being altogether good, who has bestowed upon us those common notions, and who by a creative act has brought us into existence that we might know those things to be true, how can we know with certainty, apart from the light of truth, whether those common notions are not due to some accident, and are therefore uncertain? Or whether they are not rather the artifice of some treacherous and wicked being, who has instilled these false notions into us in order to deceive us and lead us into error? By means of this chain of arguments, Montaigne demonstrates that God and truth are inseparable, and that if one of these is or is not, if one of them is certain or uncertain, then it follows of necessity that the other is so. Who then can know whether common sense, which we take to be the judge of what is true, partakes of the being of Him who created it? Moreover, does anybody know what truth is— and how, if we are unable to recognize it, may we know that we possess it? Who indeed knows what it is 'to be,' since 'being' itself cannot be defined? For there is no term more universal, and whoever attempts a definition must begin with the word itself: 'Being is . . .' And since we do not know what the soul is, nor the body nor time, space, movement, truth, nor even being; and since we cannot explain the notion we form of it in our own minds, how can we be certain that the notion of it is the same in every mind? Seeing that we have no other criterion than the uniformity of the consequences—which does not by any means indicate identity of the principles. For the 'principles' might well be different [for different minds], and yet lead to the same conclusion. For everybody knows that it is often possible to draw a true conclusion from false premisses.

"And finally: Montaigne deals so shrewdly with the sciences, and especially with geometry, when he shows that certain of her axioms are by no means self-evident, and terms such as 'extension' and 'movement' are not defined. He shows also that physics is without certitude in many of its branches, medicine in an infinite number of subjects; he makes the same point in relation to history, political theory, moral theology, jurisprudence, and the rest. All this he does so effectively as to leave us convinced that our thinking nowadays is no better than a dream, from which we shall only awake at death. While we are thus dreaming, moreover, we have as little grasp of the principles of truth as we have in ordinary sleep. Thus, with the touch of a master and the most ruthless savagery, he devours the claims of any reasoning which is devoid of faith: for when this unassisted reason causes man to doubt reason, to doubt whether animals also may not be reasonable beings, or at any rate are not possessed of reason in some measure, Montaigne perceives that he must accord to reason less of nobility than she claims for herself, and he compels her to descend from her throne, scarcely ranking her even with the instinct of animals. He is reluctant to allow her any higher dignity than that of the brute creation, until she shall have been instructed by her Creator Himself concerning her true nobility, of which she at present knows nothing whatever.[6] And in case she should complain, he holds in reserve the threat of reducing her lower than all other things—and this may be as easily done as the contrary work of ennobling her. The only activity he would allow to such a mind meanwhile, is

[6] Cf. Montaigne's attack: "Oh, what a vile and abject thing is man, unless he raise himself above humanity! . . . He may elevate himself by forsaking and renouncing his own instruments, and suffering himself to be elevated and raised by mere heavenly instruments. It is for our Christian faith, not for his Stoic virtue, to pretend or aspire to this divine metamorphosis or miraculous transmutation."

that of acknowledging with a sincere humility her own weakness, instead of lifting herself up in foolish and insolent pride."

M. de Saci thought he must be living in a new country and hearing a new language. The words of Saint Augustine passed through his mind: "O God of truth, are those that know these subtle ways of argument any more pleasing to Thee?" He was full of sorrow for a philosopher who could goad himself, tearing his own flesh to pieces with barbs which he had made for himself—as Saint Augustine says of his own behavior when he was in the same condition. After a notable pause, he said to M. Pascal:

"I am obliged to you, Sir. I am sure that, even if I had been reading Montaigne for a long time, I should not have understood him half as well as I do now, after the exposition you have just given me. A man like that might well wish to be known only by the account that you give of his writings. He could certainly say with Saint Augustine: 'Such as you see me, so I was: therefore pay attention.' I fully believe that Montaigne had a penetrating mind; but I am not sure that your very careful statement of his ideas does not credit him with a better mind than in fact he had. You may well imagine that, my way of life being what it is, I have not often been advised to read this author. None of his books contain anything that we particularly need to study, for (the precept that guides us is, again, Saint Augustine's) his words do not appear to spring from any great depth of humility and goodness. We may pardon those ancient philosophers whom we know as the Peripatetics, for putting all things in doubt: but what need had Montaigne to allow his own mind to go astray, and to revive a doctrine which to modern Christians is mere foolishness? That would be the verdict of Saint Augustine himself upon such people: for we may say of Montaigne in Saint Augustine's words, that 'From all that he says, faith is excluded; therefore we, who have faith, may exclude all that he says.' I do not in the least condemn the brilliance and wit of this writer, which was obviously a special gift from God; but he could have made better use of it, and he could have chosen to dedicate it to God rather than to the devil. 'What shall become of him?', asked that same holy Doctor, with reference to himself before his conversion. You are fortunate, Sir, in that you have raised yourself above those persons we nowadays call 'Doctors,' who are plunged into a kind of drunkenness [for scientific knowledge], but whose hearts are quite empty of any truth. God has shed into your own heart other sweetnesses, other attractions than those you formerly found for yourself in Montaigne. God has called you away from that dangerous delight—from what Saint Augustine, thanking God for pardon of those sins committed when he was drinking deep of vanity, calls 'that pestilential pleasantness.' Saint Augustine is the more to be believed on this subject, as he had formerly held the same beliefs as Montaigne is seen to hold. You said of Montaigne that he used the weapon of universal doubt to combat the heresies of his time: Saint Augustine made similar use of the doubt of the Peripatetic philosophers, to overthrow the heresy of the Manichees. From the moment that he belonged to God, he renounced those vanities which he described as sacrilege, [and dealt somewhat summarily with certain other delights]. He perceived the wisdom of Saint Paul's warning, that we must not allow ourselves to be led away by teachers of strange doctrines. He acknowledges that there is in such ideas a certain attractive element which might sweep us off our feet: we are sometimes inclined to believe a thing to be true, merely because the speaker has the gift of eloquence. Such notions are dangerous diet, says Saint Paul, and they that proffer them serve them up in dainty dishes. But such meats do not nourish the heart: on the contrary, they make it empty. Then they that have eaten become like men that sleep, and dream they are eating even while they slumber: those imagined foodstuffs leave them as empty as they were before."

M. de Saci said several things of this kind to M. Pascal, who thereupon remarked that, if M. de Saci could compliment him upon a thorough knowledge of Montaigne, he himself could say without flattery that M. de Saci had an even better grasp of Saint Augustine, and a much greater skill in applying what that Father had said—though not to the advantage of poor Montaigne. He declared himself much edified by the credibility of all that M. de Saci had proposed to him. But being still filled with veneration for his own author, he could not restrain himself, and went on to say: "I confess to you, Sir, that I cannot but be pleased to see the pride of reason so completely crushed by this writer—and by its own weapons; and that I approve his violent attack upon that fratricidal strife of men which removes them from the communion with God which they formerly enjoyed, once they had raised themselves thereto by the weak maxims of their own reason; their quarrels reduce them to the level of beasts. I would have loved Montaigne with all my heart as the minister of so salutary a retribution, if only (since he was himself a son of the Church and had the faith) he had adhered to her moral teaching: if he had induced those men, whom he had so effectively humbled, not to offend by new crimes Him who alone is able to save them from sin, and from errors which the unassisted reason is unable to recognize, as He Himself has taught them.

"But instead of doing this, Montaigne behaves like a pagan, thus: he starts from the principle that outside the faith there is no certitude. He then points out how many there are who [have the faith and] are seeking the true and the good, yet who make no progress whatever toward tranquillity. Whence he concludes that the taking of so much trouble of that kind may be left to others; that for his part he will rest quietly, taking his affairs quietly for fear that, if he leans upon them, he may become involved and attached. He will take the true and the good at face value without probing into them: for so far are the true and the good from being solid realities that, however cautiously we hold them, they will slip through our fingers and leave our hands empty. This is why he accepts the opinion that the common notions depend upon sense evidence, since to deny a first principle would require an act of violence to the mind, and since he cannot say whether he would be the gainer if he remained in ignorance of what is true. By the same reasoning he avoids the contemplation of sorrow and death, for this instinct urges him to do so. This instinct he is unwilling to resist, for the reason already given, that he does not know whether experience of these things would be a gain. But in this case he cannot affirm that sorrow and death are in fact misfortunes; for he dare not rely too much upon arguments from the natural reactions of fear—having experienced pleasurable reactions which he was told were wicked, although his nature said the opposite. There is therefore nothing extravagant in his conduct, for he acts as others do; and all that is done by them with the foolish idea that they are following the true good may be done by himself upon a different principle, that since the probabilities on either side are equal, the deciding factors are convenience and example.

"[He therefore follows the mode of behavior in his own country, because this is what is required by custom:] he mounts his horse like any other man—who may not be a philosopher—because the horse allows it, although the horse does not believe that his rider has any rights in the matter. How can the horseman know that the horse has not some idea of making use of *him?* Montaigne also does himself some violence when he avoids certain vices. He will even be faithful to his marriage vows, but only because of the embarrassments that would result from infidelity: if the woman he has married turns out to be a better partner than the mistress he has left, he may rest quietly, for in all his conduct his rule is always his own convenience and quiet. He therefore rejects with vehemence the virtue of the Stoic who is depicted with stern countenance, disapproving eyes, disheveled hair, the furrowed brow beaded with perspiration, the posture strained and uncomfortable, alienated from mankind in a mournful silence upon a pinnacle of rock. Such a phantom of the mind is only fit, he says, to frighten children. The Stoic doctrine seeks a state of rest which it will never find, though it search with the most arduous effort and forevermore. His own idea of virtue is simple and familiar, so pleasant and agreeable that it might be called playful: he follows what suits his humor, trifles heedlessly with chances good or bad, and sleeps softly in the bosom of reposeful idleness. Thus does he demonstrate to all who go to so much trouble to find happiness, that it is only there, in the slothful repose of the place where he himself rests, that happiness is to be found; and that ignorance, and freedom from curiosity, are two of the softest of pillows for a well-ordered mind. So says Montaigne.

"I cannot conceal from you, Sir, that whenever I read Montaigne and compare him with Epictetus, I come to the conclusion that these two men are unquestionably the most redoubtable champions of the two sects best known to the world—the only philosophical systems in conformity with reason. For in our search for truth, one only of these systems can be followed. Either there is a God, and it is in Him that man finds his sovereign good, or the existence of God is uncertain, and so therefore is the existence of any sovereign good, since man is of his own efforts incapable of either creating or finding it.

"When following these arguments I have taken the greatest pleasure in observing the steps by which each philosopher arrives at a certain conformity with that true wisdom which each has sought to know. It is pleasing to observe the design of Nature, and how she depicts God in all His works: for we see in the works of Nature a certain imprint or character which may be said to reflect His attributes. How much more just is it, then, when we consider the productions of the human mind, to observe such effort as that mind may have made to imitate the divine intellect, even when it seeks to escape from its power; and to notice, further, in what respects the human mind attains to an understanding of the divine, and in what respects it goes astray. This I have sought to do in my own studies.

"It is true, Sir, that you have just shown me, and with the greatest acumen, how little profit Christians can derive from these particular philosophical theories. With your permission, however, I will continue to expound my ideas, although I am ready to renounce any that cannot be reconciled with your own. I shall then have the advantage, either of coming upon the truth by a happy coincidence, or of learning it from yourself with certitude. It seems to me that the source of the error in both these philosophies is the failure to realize that the present condition of man is not that in which he was created. The consequence is that Epictetus, observing certain vestiges of man's original dignity, and paying no heed to his obviously tainted nature, deals with humanity as though it were in a state of health and needed no physician—an error which leads him to the very pinnacle of pride. Montaigne, on the other hand, is well acquainted with the present misery of man, but sees no trace of his original dignity. He regards human nature as essentially helpless and beyond healing—an error which causes him to despair of ever arriving at the true good, and which leads before long to extreme laxity. Now, if the whole truth is to be known, these two views of the human condition must be reconciled, they must be understood in relation to one another. Where credence is given to one view only, the consequence in the philosopher will of necessity be one of the two vices, laxity or pride, which mark all men who are not in a state of grace: for if they do not indeed continue in their disorders out of mere laxity, yet they lay aside their faults out of vanity, as you said a moment ago when you mentioned Saint Augustine;[7] a remark which seems to me to have a very wide application. For we do indeed defer to these men in a good many ways.[8]

It is this imperfect enlightenment which leads both writers into error.[9] The first recognizes the duties of man, but he will not acknowledge man's powerlessness, and he shields himself behind a wall of human pride. The second sees only the helplessness of man, and acknowledges no duty; and he debases himself by falling into laxity.[10] Whence it might appear that, since one view is true, and the other false, we have but to unite the [elements of truth in] the two doctrines, and we shall obtain a moral system free from error. But such a combination can never yield peace: it can lead only to strife, and in effect to the destruction of each party by the other. For one system establishes a certainty, the other a doubt; one affirms the dignity of man, the other, his weakness. Thus each system destroys the opposed truth, as well as the opposed error.[11] Neither can stand alone, for each contains a defect; and they cannot unite, because they

7 This is disingenuous: De Saci's remark quoted the words of Saint Augustine, who said that from the moment he belonged to God, he renounced the sacrilegious vanities of his youth.

8 If we accept the late date proposed by Chevalier for the *Entretien,* we may see in this remark a touch of the old Adam surviving in the author of the *Provincial Letters,* with his rooted hatred of the "laxity" of the moral theology of his time.

9 By a single flash of insight, Pascal is able to demolish the position of each philosopher. The formal statement in this paragraph may be the work of his editor, Fontaine.

10 Epictetus hides, but Montaigne debases himself. The distinction indicates the veneration which Pascal retained for the robust teaching of the pagan philosopher.

11 The argument of this paragraph is strictly logical, and is controlled by the fundamental law of logic, the *principle of identity,* which declares that a thing cannot be and not be at the same instant of time. We may set out our series of propositions thus:

Epictetus:	Man is great,	Truth A
	But man is only great	Error B
	(i.e., his powerlessness is ignored)	
Montaigne:	Man is weak	Truth A one
	And man is only weak	Error B one

Compare the opposed thesis, thus:

contain contradictories. Thus they shatter one another, and both come to nothing, so as to make room for the truth of the Gospel. It is *this* truth which reconciles contradictories, by an art entirely divine: uniting what is true, rejecting all that is false, until we see that it is only the truth of the Gospel that can fuse the contradictories into one holy wisdom, in which are reconciled all the conflicting elements in the man-made doctrines. The reason for the human failure is this: Wise though they were as this world estimates wisdom, those men placed their contradictories in one and the same category. One thinker attributed man's greatness to his human nature, and the other derived his weakness from the same human nature. This is not permissible, for the two opposites cannot subsist. But faith teaches us to place the contradictories in different categories; thus, all that pertains to man's weakness is attributable to his human nature, but all that he has of strength is due to grace. Here we have that astounding and unexampled union,[12] the knowledge of which could only be imparted by God Himself, a union which He alone could achieve; and it is no less a thing than an image or reflection of the ineffable union of the two Natures in the one Person of the Son of God.

"I beg pardon, Sir," said M. Pascal to M. de Saci, "that I have been thus carried away in talking to you, and have strayed into your own field of theology, instead of sticking to philosophy—the only subject on which I intended to speak; but I was led into theology before I realized where I was going. It is difficult indeed to avoid the subject, whatever the truth under discussion, because theology lies at the

---

A	A one
Man is great	Man is weak
B	B one
Man is only great	Man is only weak

We observe that: 1. Thesis A destroys the *error* of the opposed thesis B one, and the truth A one destroys the error B. 2. Similarly, each thesis destroys the opposed *truth:* B destroys the truth in A one; B one destroys truth A.

Pascal's argument is therefore valid: the contradictories are incompatible; each negates the other, and truth is destroyed.

[12] Astounding, because the Christian will never in this life fully understand the nature of grace, nor its mode of operation; *unexampled,* because it long postdated the Fall, and was foreshadowed only by the pre-Christian typology of the Old Testament Patriarchs and Prophets.

center of all truth—a fact proved to perfection by our present conversation, since theology obviously contains all the truths that can be discovered in our two philosophers. Moreover, it is difficult to see how either of our thinkers could refuse to submit his doctrines to theological tests. For although they both reason toward a conviction of the greatness of man, what does either of them offer that is not far outweighed by the Gospel promises, which depend upon no less a thing than the ransom paid by the death of God? It was not without a certain satisfaction that our philosophers contemplated the weakness of human nature, yet their notions were by no means adequate to express the actual moral weakness inherent in sin, for which that same death provided the remedy. Thus all men find therein more than they sought, and what is even more remarkable, at that high point they find themselves at one, although at a level infinitely lower, they were irreconcilable and unable to agree."

M. de Saci could not forbear to acknowledge—although with some surprise—that M. Pascal knew very well how to conduct a discussion. He also remarked that not everybody possessed the secret—as M. Pascal evidently did—of reflecting wisely and deeply upon what they read. He said that M. Pascal resembled those skilled physicians who were adept in using the most deadly poisons for curative purposes, for they knew how to employ them in the preparation of healing medicines of wonderful efficacy. He added that he could see very well, from what had been said, that M. Pascal's reading had been of great service to him. And yet he found it hard to believe that such books could do other than harm many people, whose minds lacked the power of concentration: they would not have sufficient detachment to arrive at a mature judgment concerning their authors, and they would not know—as one of the Fathers puts it—how to pull the gold out of the mire. This warning might apply to our two philosophers with special force, for the dunghill of their writings gives off a vapor black and fetid, calculated to dim the wavering faith of any that read them. For this reason he always counseled such persons not to expose themselves thoughtlessly to such reading, for fear that—to use the language of Scripture—they might go astray and be lost, fall a prey to demons, and be food for worms, as had indeed happened to those two philosophers themselves.

"As to the usefulness of such reading," said M. Pascal, "I will tell you quite simply what I think. I find in Epictetus an incomparable gift for troubling the repose of men who seek their rest in external things, and for compelling them to recognize that they are truly slaves, wretched and blind, fleeing in vain from error and sorrow, unless they do so in order to give themselves to God only, and without reserve. Montaigne is beyond compare when he humbles the pride of men who claim that they are able to be truly just without the faith; when he undeceives those who are attached to their own opinions, and who think they can discover unshakeable truths in the sciences. When he demonstrates to the reason how little natural light it has, and how it wanders, he does it so forcibly, that if we apply his principles correctly, it is difficult to be tempted into finding anything repugnant in the mysteries [of the faith]. For the mind is so overwhelmingly convinced about them, that it is far indeed from any desire to investigate whether the Incarnation is possible, or the mystery of the Eucharist either—questions which the vulgar are only too ready to talk to death.

"But if Epictetus rebukes laxity, his teaching certainly leads to pride. He can therefore be very harmful to such men as refuse to believe that even the most careful justice is without merit where the faith is lacking. Montaigne, on the other hand, is entirely pernicious to any reader who has the slightest inclination to irreligion or vice. For these reasons, the reading of these authors ought to be regulated with great care and discretion, with due regard to the age and maturity of the person to whom they may have been commended. I am however of the opinion that it might be no bad thing to advise reading them together, because each destroys the error of the other. Neither has the power to bestow any moral strength; neither can do more than disturb the minds of men who are living bad lives. And once such minds as these find themselves under any strain from opposed stresses of that kind, the one applied to pride, and the other to laxity, they will no longer be able to find clever reasons for continuing in these vices; but neither will they be able of their own strength to lay aside bad habit altogether."

By reasoning the matter thus, these two men, each endowed with a fine intellect, found a way of agreement as to the reading of these philosophers. They found their point of contact, but each arrived at that point by a slightly different method. M. de Saci reached it in a single leap, seeing it by the clear light of his Christian belief. M. Pascal only came to it after much wandering: he went astray because he had started from principles laid down by Epictetus and Montaigne.

[M. de Saci and the community at Port Royal de Champs rejoiced in the news of the conversion of M. Pascal, and listened with interest to the reasoning which had led to it. They marveled at the all-conquering power of grace, and at the mercy which had operated, on a scale almost without precedent to humble that proud mind, so filled with the knowledge of its own achievements.][49]

[49] The family of Pascal and the community of Port Royal worked together for years to demonstrate their veneration for the eminent scientist and notable convert. Mme. Périer in particular contributed largely to the honoring of her brother's memory.

BIBLIOGRAPHY

Baudin, E. *La Philosophie de Pascal.* 4 vols. Neuchâtel: Editions de la Baconniere, 1946–47. This study of Pascal's philosophy is now classic.

Béguin, A. *Pascal par mi-même.* Paris: Editions du Seuil, 1952. Illustrated. Contains an excellent introduction.

Boutroux, E. *Pascal.* Paris: Hachette, 1924. A standard work, with special emphasis on Pascal's philosophy.

Brunschvicg, L. *Le Génie de Pascal.* Paris: Hachette, 1924.

Cailliet, E. *The Clue to Pascal.* Philadelphia: Westminster, 1943.

———. *Pascal, Genius in the Light of Scripture.* Philadelphia: Westminster, 1945.

Chevalier, J. *Pascal.* London: Longmans, Green & Co., 1930. One of the most useful guides to Pascal's thinking as a whole.

Christiani, L. *L'Hérésis de Port Royal.* Paris: Fayard, 1955. A useful, brief description of Jansenism.

Daniel-Rops, H. *Pascal et notre coeur.* Strasbourg: F.-X. Le Roux, 1948.

Eastwood, D. *The Revival of Pascal.* Oxford: Clarendon Press, 1936. Traces the influence of Pascal on modern thought.

Giraud, V. *Pascal, l'homme, l'oeuvre, l'influence.* Paris: Fontemoing, 1900.

Guitton, J. *Génie de Pascal.* Paris: Aubier, 1962.

Guardini, R. *Pascal*. Paris: Editions du Seuil, 1951.

Hubert, Sister M. L. *Pascal's Unfinished Apology*. New Haven, Conn.: Yale University Press, 1952. Important for the history of the *Pensées* and their order.

Jovy, E. *Études Pascaliennes*. 9 vols. Paris: Vrin. 1927–36.

Lafuma, L. *Histoire des Penseés de Pascal*. Paris: Editions du Luxembourg, 1954. Indispensable for the reconstruction of Pascal's plan.

Laporte, J. *La Doctrine de Port Royal*. 2 vols. Paris: P.U.F., 1923.

Mortimer, E. *Blaise Pascal, the Life and Work of a Realist*. London: Methuen & Co., Ltd., 1959. The best book in English for biographical material.

Russier, J. *La Foi selon Pascal*. 2 vols. Paris: P.U.F., 1949. Gives a complete analysis of Pascal's approach to faith, his skepticism and realism.

Sainte-Beuve, C.-A. *Port-Royal*. 7 vols. Paris: Hachette, 1871–78.

Steinmann, J. *Pascal*. Paris: Editions du Cerf, 1964. New York: Harcourt, Brace and World, 1966. The best work on Pascal available in English.

Stewart, H. F. *The Holiness of Pascal*. London: Cambridge University Press, 1915. Everything Stewart has written on Pascal is worthy of study.

———. *The Heart of Pascal*. London: Cambridge University Press, 1945.

Strowski, F. *Pascal et son temps*, 3 vols. Paris: Plon, 1907.

Truc, G. *Pascal, son temps et le notre*. Paris: A. Michel, 1949.

CHRIST AND APOLLO **by William F. Lynch, S.J.**

The role of theology in the works of great writers from Aexchylus to O'Neill. (#MT495—75¢)

DAILY LIFE IN THE TIME OF JESUS
by Henri Daniel-Rops

A comprehensive study of the land and people, political, economic, scientific, and cultural currents, as they existed in Palestine during the time of Jesus. Translated by Patrick O'Brian. (#MQ570—95¢)

LEISURE: THE BASIS OF CULTURE **by Josef Pieper**

In a series of astonishing essays, the author indicts the 20th century cult of "work" and hectic amusements, which can ultimately destroy both our culture and ourselves. Introduction by T. S. Eliot. (#MP550—60¢)

THE LITTLE FLOWERS OF ST. FRANCIS OF ASSISI

Lyric stories about the great medieval saint, composed by his devoted followers. New translation by Serge Hughes. (#MT593—75¢)

THE LOVE OF LEARNING AND THE DESIRE FOR GOD
by Jean Leclerq, O.S.B.

A study of the manuscripts of the medieval monasteries reveals their role in preserving the culture of the past. By a distinguished scholar and Benedictine monk. (#MT432—75¢)

MARIA MONTESSORI: HER LIFE AND WORK
by. E. M. Standing

A friend and colleague of the great educator writes her biography and evaluates her contributions to modern education. With eight pages of photographs. (#MQ425—95¢)

THE PAPAL ENCYCLICALS IN THEIR HISTORICAL CONTEXT **edited by Anne Fremantle**

For the first time in one volume, the teachings of the Catholic Church as expressed by the Popes in their official letters. (#MQ533—95¢)

THE SOCIAL TEACHINGS OF THE CHURCH
edited by Anne Fremantle

A companion volume to *The Papal Encyclicals in Their Historical Context,* this book contains papal encyclicals on social problems from Pope Leo XIII to Pope John XXIII. (#MT549—75¢)